The European left and the f

Manchester University Press

The European left and the financial crisis

Edited by Michael Holmes and Knut Roder

Manchester University Press

Published by Manchester University Press
Oxford Road, Manchester M13 9PL
www.manchesteruniversitypress.co.uk

British Library Cataloguing-in-Publication Data is available

ISBN 978 1 5261 2428 9 hardback
ISBN 978 1 5261 6369 1 paperback

First published by Manchester University Press in hardback 2019

This edition first published 2022

Typeset by Toppan Best-set Premedia Limited

Contents

Figures and tables

Notes on contributors

Ilvija Bruge is an Associated Researcher at the Latvian Institute of International Affairs. She holds a BA in Political Science and an MA in International Relations from Riga Stradins University, and an MSc in Social Anthropology from the University of Edinburgh where she is currently a PhD candidate. She is a co-editor and author of several articles and books and has worked as a research analyst for a UK-based political risk advisory and as a national expert for various international research projects. Her research interests are linked to socio-economic, historic, political and cultural development in the post-Soviet area.

Karlis Bukovskis is the Deputy Director and a researcher at the Latvian Institute of International Affairs (LIIA), the author of numerous articles, and the scientific editor of several books. Bukovskis is also a lecturer on global political economy, international financial system and the EU integration at Riga Graduate School of Law and Riga Stradins University. He has been Associate Fellow of the European Council on Foreign Relations since December 2017. Bukovskis has dealt with the institutional, political and economic future of the EU and the EMU not only as an analyst and frequent media commentator, but also while serving at the Ministry of Foreign Affairs of Latvia, the Secretariat of the Latvian presidency of the Council of the European Union (where he developed the presidency's six-month work programme), and also at the Ministry of Finance of Latvia.

Michael Holmes is Associate Professor of Political Science at ESPOL, Catholic University of Lille. He was also Senior Visiting Research Scholar at ESPOL – the European School of Politics, Université Catholique de Lille in 2017, a position funded by the Conseil Régional Hauts-de-France. His work focuses on the impact of European integration on political parties, with a particular emphasis on left-wing parties, and on Ireland's relationship with the European Union. He is also active in the FEPS Next Left research group.

Yiannos Katsourides holds a PhD in Political Science from the University of Cyprus. He is Assistant Professor of Political Science, Department of Politics and Governance, University of Nicosia, Cyprus. He held visiting fellowships at the Hellenic Observatory of the European Institute of the LSE and the Institute of Commonwealth Studies of the University of London. His research interests include Cyprus and Greek politics, radical left and extreme right political parties, political participation and the Europeanisation of political parties. He is the author of three books: *The history of the Communist Party in Cyprus* (2014); *The radical left in government: the cases of SYRIZA and AKEL* (2016); *The Greek Cypriot nationalist right in the era of British colonialism* (2017). His articles have appeared in *West European Politics*, *South European Society and Politics*, and in the *Journal of European Integration*, among others.

Julien Navarro is Associate Professor of Political Science at the Catholic University of Lille and the Francophone Chair of Political Science at the Vienna School of International Studies. His research interests include European Union politics, parliamentary institutions and political elites. His articles have appeared in *Politiques et Sociétés*, *Revue Française de Science Politique*, *French Politics*, *Revue Internationale de Politique Comparée* and the *Journal of Legislative Studies*. He is the author of *Les députés européens et leur rôle: sociologie interprétative des pratiques parlementaires* (2009) and the co-editor of *Le cumul des mandats: causes et conséquences* (2013).

Nikolaos (Nikos) Nikolakakis is Assistant Professor of Political Science at the British University in Egypt. He obtained his Bachelor's degree in Political Science and History from the Panteion University of Social and Political Sciences of Athens. He then continued his education in the University of Bologna, Italy, where he studied Law. Following that, he received his Master's in International Politics and Security from the University of Dundee, where he commenced his doctoral studies that led to his PhD in European Politics. His research interests relate predominantly to European Party Politics, the process of European Integration, the European Radical Left, as well as Greek, Italian, Spanish and French politics. He is currently working on a monograph comparing the effects of European integration on the stance of the European radical left and has previously published work on the Greek Coalition of the Radical Left, as well as on the Party of the European Left.

Jorge del Palacio Martín is Lecturer of History of Political Thought at Universidad Rey Juan Carlos, Madrid. His main research interests are Contemporary Political Ideologies and Italian Politics. He is co-editor of a recently published book on the 'geography of populism' *Geografía del* *populismo: un viaje por el universo del populismo desde sus orígenes hasta Trump* (2017).

Tapio Raunio is Professor of Political Science at the University of Tampere. His research interests cover legislatures and political parties, the Europeanisation of domestic politics, semi-presidentialism and the Finnish political system. His recent publications include *Connecting with the electorate? Parliamentary communication in EU affairs* (2014), a special issue of the *Journal of Legislative Studies* (2014, co-edited with Katrin Auel); *The changing balance of political power in Finland* (2016, co-edited with Lauri Karvonen and Heikki Paloheimo); and *Challenging executive dominance: legislatures and foreign affairs*, a special issue of *West European Politics* (2017, co-edited with Wolfgang Wagner).

Carlos Rico Motos is Lecturer in Political Science at the Department of International Relations, Universidad Pontificia Comillas ICAI-ICADE (Madrid). His research focuses on the field of theories of democracy, civic education and models of representation and political deliberation. He has recently published the monograph *Deliberación parlamentaria y democracia representative* [*Parliamentary Deliberation and Representative Democracy*] (2016) and co-edited an issue of *Revista Española de Ciencia Política* on *The left in Spain and Italy after the crisis: parties and strategies* (2017, with Jorge del Palacio).

Knut Roder is Head of Politics and Principal Lecturer at Sheffield Hallam University. His interests cover politics and the political economy of the European Union, political parties and policy-making processes with a focus on Germany and the UK, and the field of teaching and learning politics. He is the author of *Social democracy and labour market policy* (2003); *The left and the European constitution* (2012, co-edited with Michael Holmes); *The missing Linke? Restraint and realignment in the German left, 2005–2017* (2017), as well as *Contemporary politics: teaching the 'contested concepts'* (2012); and *Teaching European Studies: field trips to Brussels – an underutilized resource* (2013).

Antonella Seddone is Associate Professor at the Department of Cultures, Politics and Society of the University of Turin. She is also Research Associate at ESPOL – European School of Political and Social Sciences, Université Catholique de Lille. Her research interests are focused on political parties, primary elections and political communication. She is co-convenor of the Candidate and Leader Selection standing group of the Italian Political Science Association, and she is also co-convenor of the Italian Politics Specialist Group of the UK Political Studies Association. She has published several articles in academic journals including *Parliamentary Affairs, Representation,*

European Politics and Society, *Acta Politica*, *Italian Political Science Review*, *Modern Italy* and *Journal of Modern Italian Studies*.

Andy Storey is Assistant Professor at the School of Politics and International Relations, University College Dublin. His research focuses on the political economy and external relations of the European Union. Publications include: a 2017 working paper on 'The Myths of Ordoliberalism' (www.erc-europeanunions.eu/working-papers/); 'Chronicle of a European crisis foretold: Building neoliberalism from above and options for resistance from below' in Fioramonti, L. (ed.) *Civil society and world regions: how citizens are reshaping regional governance in times of crisis* (2013); 'The ambiguity of resistance: Opposition to neoliberalism in Europe' (*Capital and Class*, 2008); and 'Normative power Europe: Economic partnership agreements and Africa' (*Journal of Contemporary African Studies*, 2006). He is a board member of the Irish non-governmental organisation Action from Ireland (www.afri.ie), campaigning on issues of justice, peace and human rights.

Cláudia Toriz Ramos is Associate Professor of Political Science and International Relations in Universidade Fernando Pessoa, Porto. Her research interests cover European integration, democracy and democratisation and global governance. She has published, among others, *Ideas of Europe in national political discourse* (ed., 2011); *A união Europeia: história, insti-tuições e políticas* (co-ed., 2017); *Cidadania(s): discursos e práticas/Citizenship(s): discourses and practices* (co-ed., 2008) and several journal articles and chapters in collective books.

Glossary and abbreviations

Alter-Europeanism	New left perspective on EU/Eurozone created by crisis
DiEM25	Democracy in Europe Movement 2025
ECB	European Central Bank
EFSF	European Financial Stability Facility
EGP	European Green Party
EMU	Economic and Monetary Union
EP	European Parliament
ESM	European Stability Mechanism
EU	European Union
Eurozone	'Euro area' is the monetary union of 19 of 28 EU member states under the monetary authority of the Eurosystem and under political control of Eurogroup
Fiscal Compact	see TSCG
GDP	gross domestic product
Greens-EFA	Greens-European Free Alliance, or G-EFA
GUE-NGL	European United Left-Nordic Green Left
IMF	International Monetary Fund
Lexit	'Left Exit' from the EU and/or the Eurozone
MoU	Memorandum of Understanding
OECD	Organisation for Economic Co-operation and Development
PEL	Party of the European Left
PES	Party of European Socialists
S&D	Progressive Alliance of Socialists and Democrats (European Parliament)
troika	An economic oversight committee consisting of representatives of the European Commission, ECB and IMF established to supervise the economic

	affairs of countries in receipt of emergency 'bailout' loans from those institutions and/or other European governments
TSCG	Treaty on Stability, Coordination and Governance, also often referred to as the Fiscal Stability Treaty, European Fiscal Compact or Fiscal Compact
TTIP	Transatlantic Trade and Investment Partnership
WTO	World Trade Organization

Translations into English from original sources have been carried out by the relevant chapter authors.

1

The European left and the crisis: opportunity or catastrophe?

Michael Holmes and Knut Roder

Introduction

This book examines how the European left reacted to the economic crisis triggered by the banking collapses of 2008. For some, the crisis was an opportunity for a triumphant comeback for left-wing ideas and policies and for the left to regain the political initiative. The German Social Democrats talked about the crisis being 'a new starting point for more democracy and a new common ground' (SPD, 2009: 5), and there were assertions that 'the crisis in Europe can be a chance for social democracy to rediscover itself' (Martell, 2013: 33). The crisis was interpreted as a failure of the neoliberal model. As SPD (Sozialdemokratische Partei Deutschlands, or Social Democratic Party of Germany) leader Sigmar Gabriel put it, 'we, the Social Democrats, are convinced that capitalism needs to be tamed a second time' (2011).

But the record of the ten years since the start of the crisis suggests that instead of creating an opportunity for a comeback, left-wing parties have suffered a series of catastrophic electoral defeats across Europe. In 2017 alone, social democratic parties suffered historic losses in a succession of elections. In the Netherlands, the Dutch PvdA was 'hammered by its supporters' (Graham, 2017) as it endured by far its worst-ever result. In Germany, SPD leader Martin Schulz admitted to 'a difficult and bitter day for social democrats in Germany' (BBC, 2017) as the party recorded its worst post-war result. In France, a commentator could ask 'is France's Socialist Party dead?' after its candidate fell to fifth in the presidential election (Schofield, 2017).

This book examines this crucial period for the left in Europe. It presents a comparative analysis across two dimensions. The first is between ten EU member states during the economic crisis, including bailout countries and what could be termed 'creditor' countries. The second dimension compares the different party families of the left, from social democracy through green left to the radical left. Even allowing for the fact that not every member state has a party system in which all these varieties of the left are present, it still leaves quite some range to consider. Rather than try to prescribe a rigid approach for every chapter, the book presents three loose over-arching questions.

First, it explores how the left-wing political parties in each country responded to the crisis both programmatically and politically. Each of our case study contributions outlines the left in their country, with the focus being primarily on parties that are present in parliament. However, one of the features of the crisis was the important role of extra-parliamentary actors and movements, so the contributors were free to broaden their analysis where appropriate. The chapters evaluate how the left has dealt with the crisis, focusing particularly on similarities and differences between the different families of the left.

Second, the chapters examine what the crisis means for the relationship between the left and European integration. This includes in particular how the parties responded to the headline events of the crisis in the EU, particularly the bailouts (and the Greek crisis has an especially significant role in this regard) and the policy adaptations of the EU such as the Fiscal Stability Treaty. The chapters also consider the parties' wider positions on issues such as economic reform in the EU, the role of the euro and the democratic deficit.

Third, the book explores what the crisis means for socialism as an economic, political and social project. It asks whether the crisis simply reinforced the extent to which a Europeanised and globalised structure limits the left's available choices; or whether it made possible the idea of a return to more traditional interventionist politics and policies; or indeed whether it created the space for new ideas and projects.

The following section introduces the basic features of the economic crisis that hit the global economy in 2008. The chapter will then go on to examine how the crisis had very particular implications for the European Union. Economies in the Eurozone face particular constraints and demands, and this added to the problems they faced when the global crisis struck. The chapter then examines how the crisis created a challenge for left-wing parties in Europe, setting out the political ideas linked to the economic crisis. The chapter proceeds by outlining the left, identifying the three main left-wing party families that are present in Europe today: the social democratic left, the green left and the radical left. Finally, the chapter sets out the countries chosen for the case studies in this book.

Crisis: the Great Recession

The global economic crisis is more accurately thought of as a series of inter-connected crises, stemming from a banking crisis in the autumn of

2008, which tipped the global economy rapidly from growth to recession. This 'financial carnage' (Keeley & Love, 2010: 11) was the start of 'the most serious financial and economic crisis since the Great Depression' (IMF, 2014). The moment that is usually taken to signal the start of the crisis is the bankruptcy of the US investment bank Lehman Brothers in September 2008, and this was followed by a succession of bank collapses. In the United States, several other banks went bust, while others had to be bought out.[1] Indeed, the federal government intervened to put the two largest US mortgage providers, Fannie Mae and Freddie Mac,[2] into 'conservatorship' – essentially a form of nationalisation, and 'one of the most sweeping government interventions in private financial markets in decades' (Goldfarb et al., 2008).

Why did the initial US banking crisis occur? Most analyses point to the development of very high-risk investment strategies, particularly in relation to so-called 'sub-prime' mortgages. This was made possible by a variety of factors. Banks borrowed excessively to fuel their investments, they developed new financial packages that allowed them to pass on some of the bad loans they were being exposed to, and systems of corporate governance and of regulation failed. Overall, it amounted to a 'systemic breakdown in accountability and ethics' (FCIC, 2011: xxii).

The next step was the globalisation of the banking crisis. The problems were by no means confined to the US financial sector, and they quickly spilled over. Indeed, even in 2007 problems with sub-prime loans had started to become evident in Europe, with Northern Rock bank in the UK almost going under before being propped up and temporarily nationalised, while BNP-Paribas suspended trading on several of its funds.[3] When the full crisis hit, Fortis bank in the Benelux countries was partially nationalised in September 2008, while in the UK the government intervened to protect RBS, HBOS and Lloyds-TSB. In Iceland, the three main banks collapsed in October 2008, resulting in an International Monetary Fund (IMF) loan of $2.1 billion in November 2008.

This globalisation of the crisis is easily explained. It is one of the features of the crisis that it exposed the high degree of interdependency of financial institutions around the globe. Global capital markets had been liberalised, regulations had been reduced or removed, and banks had become international enterprises. This is particularly evident in the Icelandic collapse. The country had deregulated its banking sector in 2001, allowing its three big banks, Glitnir, Kaupthing and Landsbanki, to grow rapidly on the basis of trading in short-term international loans. By the time of the collapse, the accumulated loans of the three banks were many times the size of Iceland's gross domestic product (GDP) (see Ingimundarson et al., 2016; Jónsson & Sigurgeirsson, 2016).

The next step in the evolving crisis was the development of a sovereign debt crisis. We have already noted how governments in several countries tried to prop up their failing banking systems. Effectively, they nationalised their financial institutions, both through loans and the direct use of public money and state guarantees. US Secretary of State Hank Paulson took Fannie Mae and Freddie Mac into public ownership 'because he feared a systemic global financial crisis that would prompt the biggest depression since the 1930s' (Elliott, 2008). These nationalisations left the public exchequers seriously weakened in many countries. As will be discussed in greater depth throughout this book, this sovereign debt crisis was felt particularly severely in the EU's Eurozone economies, where the criteria for monetary union greatly restricted the scope for borrowing or investment by the state.

In order to balance the books, governments adopted severe austerity programmes, either of their own volition or as a result of imposition by external funding agencies, which led to a deepening of social and political problems. The World Bank estimated that the total world economy contracted by 2.9% in 2009 (World Bank, 2009: 12), while in the Organisation for Economic Co-operation and Development (OECD) area alone, the contraction was 4.7% (Keeley & Love, 2010: 12). 'The closing months of 2008 and the start of 2009 saw precipitous drops in global production and trade' (WTO, 2009), and the UN recorded a fall in the volume of global trade of 12.2% (Shelburne, 2010: 2). An International Labour Organization report indicated that unemployment rose by 2.5% in developed countries in that year (Jansen & von Uexkull, 2010: 33).

Thus, what was initially a global financial crisis led to a European sovereign debt crisis, and this begat a broader social and political crisis. After several years, countries returned to growth, but there was no dramatic bounce-back. Ten years after the initial shock, growth rates remained generally poor, economic activity remained weak, and employment rates did not recover rapidly.

The European Union and the Eurozone crisis

Jean Pisani-Ferry puts a precise date – 16 October 2009 – on when 'the euro decisively ceased being boring' (Pisani-Ferry, 2014: 8). This was the day when the newly elected Greek Prime Minister, George Papandreou, announced that official Greek debt and deficit figures had been manipulated for many years. This triggered a dramatic divergence of bond spreads (the cost of state borrowing) among Eurozone members, effectively 'differentiating between "good" and "bad" borrowers' (Pisani-Ferry, 2014: 8). These differences exposed the incomplete nature of the Economic and Monetary

Union (EMU) construction, and raised political questions of how to manage the euro crisis.

The member states of the EU had gone down the path of similar policies to those in the US. The financial sector was subject to very light-touch regulation and had jumped on the bandwagon of high-risk financial speculation. Meeusen suggests the crisis did not simply have an impact on Europe's economy, it also had a sharp effect on policy-makers in the EU, 'many of whom lost their bearings, at economics as a scientific discipline and, specifically, at the process of European integration itself' (2011: 1). In similar vein, Dinan argues that the crisis 'proved difficult to understand for political leaders, policy-makers, and professional analysis alike' (Dinan et al., 2017: 55).

The 19 Eurozone economies were particularly vulnerable, for two reasons. First, the 'one size fits all' monetary policy had allowed weaker economies to borrow at very low interest rates that were more a reflection of the strength of other economies such as Germany. Second, when the crisis hit, the rules of the single currency meant that individual Eurozone member states could not avail of some of the devices that might have restored stability for their economies, such as currency devaluation or a loose monetary policy. As their financial sectors came under increased stress, they were obliged to respond within the confines dictated by the EMU criteria and policed by the European Central Bank (ECB).

By 2009, several Eurozone economies were in deep trouble. As Table 1.1 shows, every EU state bar one (Poland) recorded negative growth in 2009, and the Eurozone countries recorded two further years of negative growth, in 2012 and 2013. In some countries, the levels of indebtedness were extremely high, and the banking sector was in real danger of collapse. The prospect of a Eurozone state defaulting on its debts terrified the markets, as it was felt that 'such defaults would probably trigger the collapse of Europe's banking system' as banks held huge quantities of government bonds (Authers, 2012: 4).

In response, the EU decided to intervene. It had already agreed emergency financial assistance programmes with three EU states outside the Eurozone, Latvia and Hungary in 2008 and Romania in 2009. This was followed by a series of programmes with the five Eurozone states facing the greatest difficulties. A series of Economic Adjustment Programmes was agreed between the European Commission, the ECB, the IMF and (though their input into the process was limited) the relevant member states (see Table 1.2). These bailouts provided funding to maintain the financial sector in exchange for commitments to deep structural reforms. Each of the bailout programmes was accompanied by strict adjustment conditions. In addition to these programmes, Italy also undertook a programme of extensive structural adjustments at the behest of the EU, though this was intended to stave off the need for a full bailout.

Table 1.1 Real GDP growth rate, EU 28, 2008–2018 (% change on previous year)

	2008	2009	2010	2011	2012	2013	2014	2015	2016	2017	2018
Austria	1.5	-3.8	1.8	2.9	0.7	0	0.7	1.1	2.0	2.6	2.7
Belgium	0.8	-2.3	2.7	1.8	0.2	0.2	1.3	1.7	1.5	1.7	1.4
Cyprus	3.6	-2.0	1.3	0.4	-2.9	-5.8	-1.3	2.0	4.8	4.5ᴾ	3.9ᴾ
Estonia	-5.4	-14.7	2.3	7.6	4.3	1.9	2.9	1.9	3.5	4.9	3.9
Finland	0.7	-8.3	3.0	2.6	-1.4	-0.8	-0.6	0.5	2.8	2.7	2.3
France	0.3	-2.9	1.9	2.2	0.3	0.6	1.0	1.1	1.1	2.3ᴾ	1.7ᴾ
Germany	1.1	-5.6	4.1	3.7	0.5	0.5	2.2	1.7	2.2	2.2	1.4
Greece	-0.3	-4.3	-5.5	-9.1ᴾ	-7.3ᴾ	-3.2ᴾ	0.7ᴾ	-0.4ᴾ	-0.2ᴾ	1.5ᴾ	1.9ᴾ
Ireland	-4.4	-5.0	1.9	3.7	0.2	1.3	8.8	25.1	5.0	7.2	6.7
Italy	-1.1	-5.5	1.7	0.6	-2.8	-1.7	0.1	0.9	1.1	1.7	0.9
Latvia	-3.5	-14.4	-3.9	6.4	4.0	2.4	1.9	3.0	2.1	4.6	4.8
Lithuania	2.6	-14.8	1.6	6.0	3.8	3.5	3.5	2.0	2.4	4.1	3.5
Luxembourg	-1.3	-4.4	4.9	2.5	-0.4	3.7	4.3	3.9	2.4	1.5	2.6
Malta	3.3	-2.5	3.5	1.3	2.8	4.6	8.7	10.8	5.6	6.8	6.7
Netherlands	2.2	-3.7	1.3	1.6	-1.0	-0.1	1.4	2.0	2.2	2.9	2.7ᴾ
Portugal	0.2	-3.0	1.9	-1.8	-4.0	-1.1	0.9	1.8	1.9	2.8ᴾ	2.1ᴾ
Slovakia	5.6	-5.4	5.0	2.8	1.7	1.5	2.8	4.2	3.1	3.2	4.1
Slovenia	3.3	-7.8	1.2	0.6	-2.7	-1.1	3.0	2.3	3.1	4.9	4.5
Spain	1.1	-3.6	0	-1.0	-2.9	-1.7	1.4	3.6	3.2ᴾ	3.0ᴾ	2.6ᴾ
Euro 19ᵃ	*0.5*	*-4.5*	*2.1*	*1.6*	*-0.9*	*-0.2*	*1.4*	*2.1*	*1.9*	*2.4*	*1.9*
Czech Rep.	2.7	-4.8	2.3	1.8	-0.8	-0.5	2.7	5.3	2.5	4.4	2.9
Denmark	-0.5	-4.9	1.9	1.3	0.2	0.9	1.6	2.3	2.4	2.3	1.4
Bulgaria	6.0	-3.6	1.3	1.9	0	0.5	1.8	3.5	3.9	3.8	3.1ᴾ
Croatia	2.0	-7.3	-1.5	-0.3	-2.3	-0.5	-0.1	2.4	3.5	2.9	2.6
Hungary	0.9	-6.6	0.7	1.7	-1.6	2.1	4.2	3.5	2.3	4.1	4.9
Poland	4.2	2.8	3.6	5.0	1.6	1.4	3.3	3.8	3.1	4.8	5.1
Romania	9.3	-5.5	-3.9	2.0	2.1	3.5	3.4	3.9	4.8	7.0ᴾ	4.1ᴾ
Sweden	-0.6	-5.2	6.0	2.7	-0.3	1.2	2.6	4.5	2.7	2.1	2.4
UK	-0.3	-4.2	1.7	1.6	1.4	2.0	2.9	2.3	1.8	1.8	1.4
EU 28	*0.5*	*-4.3*	*2.1*	*1.8*	*-0.4*	*0.3*	*1.8*	*2.3*	*2.0*	*2.5*	*2.0*

Source: Eurostat, 2019

Notes: ᵃ the current 19 Eurozone members – note that Cyprus joined in 2008,
    Slovakia in 2009, Estonia in 2011, Latvia in 2014 and Lithuania in 2015
    ᴾ provisional figures
    Case study countries are highlighted in light grey

Table 1.2 EU-ECB-IMF bailouts

2 May 2010	Greece (1)	€110 billion	Ended March 2012[a]
16 December 2010	Ireland	€85 billion	Exited December 2013
16 May 2011	Portugal	€78 billion	Exited June 2014
1 March 2012	Greece (2)	€130 billion	Expired June 2015
9 June 2012	Spain	€100 billion	Exited January 2014
16 March 2013	Cyprus	€10 billion	Exited March 2016
12 July 2015	Greece (3)	€86 billion	Expired August 2018

Source: European Commission, n.d.
Notes: [a] superseded by the second bailout

The EU adopted a number of new policies to deal with the unprecedented crisis. In May 2009, a European Financial Stability Facility (EFSF) was set up to issue bonds and other forms of debt instruments. In January 2011, this was joined by the European Financial Stabilisation Mechanism (EFSM), which provided for emergency funding programmes that could be guaranteed by the EU. These two were superseded in September 2012 by the European Stability Mechanism (ESM), which put the various bailout mechanisms onto a permanent footing. Alongside this, in March 2012 the Treaty on Stability, Coordination and Governance in the Economic and Monetary Union (TSCG, also referred to just as the Fiscal Stability Treaty or the European Fiscal Compact) was agreed. This established strict limits on government spending and borrowing for Eurozone members, and also introduced clear penalties for any state breaching those limits. It was signed by 22 EU states – all 19 Eurozone members, plus Bulgaria, Denmark and Romania, who had chosen to opt in to the treaty.

All of this took place against a backdrop of social crisis. This played out differently in various member states. Table 1.3 indicates the differences in severity and sequencing of the EU-wide unemployment crisis. Substantial variations document the diverging experience of the impact of the crisis over time. While unemployment peaked or stabilised by 2010 in Latvia, France, Finland and Germany (and even declined afterwards), it continued to rise steeply in Ireland until 2012 and in Greece, Cyprus, Spain, Portugal and Italy until 2013. In all cases (except Germany), the levels of unemployment were a relevant indicator of the degree to which the crisis was experienced and continued to remain far higher than they were at the pre-2008 crisis level.

This highlights the social consequences of the economic crisis, and also indicates the extent to which the crisis contributed to political life. It took place in a period framed by electoral cycles, competition for votes, strategic

Table 1.3 Unemployment rates in EU member states, 2008–2018 (%)

	2008	2009	2010	2011	2012	2013	2014	2015	2016	2017	2018
Austria	4.1	5.3	4.8	4.6	4.9	5.4	5.6	5.7	6.0	5.5	4.9
Belgium	7.0	7.9	8.3	7.2	7.6	8.4	8.5	8.5	7.8	7.1	6.0
Cyprus	3.7	5.4	6.3	7.9	11.9	15.9	16.1	15.0	13.0	11.1	8.4
Estonia	5.5	13.5	16.7	12.3	10.0	8.6	7.4	6.2	6.8	5.8	5.4
Finland	6.4	8.2	8.4	7.8	7.7	8.2	8.7	9.4	8.8	8.6	7.4
France	7.4	8.7	8.9	8.8	9.4	9.9	10.3	10.4	10.1	9.4	9.1
Germany	7.4	7.8	7.0	5.8	5.4	5.2	5.0	4.6	4.1	3.8	3.4
Greece	7.8	9.6	12.7	17.9	24.5	27.5	26.5	24.9	23.6	21.5	19.3
Ireland	6.8	12.6	14.6	15.4	15.5	13.8	11.9	10.0	8.4	6.7	5.8
Italy	6.7	7.8	8.4	8.4	10.7	12.2	12.7	11.9	11.7	11.2	10.6
Latvia	7.7	17.5	19.5	16.2	15.0	11.9	10.8	9.9	9.6	8.7	7.4
Lithuania	5.8	13.8	17.8	15.4	13.4	11.8	10.7	9.1	7.9	7.1	6.2
Luxembourg	4.9	5.1	4.4	4.9	5.1	5.9	5.9	6.7	6.3	5.5	5.6
Malta	6.0	6.9	6.9	6.4	6.2	6.1	5.7	5.4	4.7	4.0	3.7
Netherlands	3.7	4.4	5.0	5.0	5.8	7.3	7.4	6.9	6.0	4.9	3.8
Portugal	8.8	9.6	11.0	12.9	15.8	16.4	14.1	12.6	11.2	9.0	7.1
Slovakia	9.6	12.0	14.4	13.6	14.0	14.2	13.2	11.5	9.7	8.1	6.5
Slovenia	4.4	5.9	7.3	8.2	8.9	10.1	9.7	9.0	8.0	6.6	5.1
Spain	11.3	17.9	19.9	21.4	24.8	26.1	24.5	22.1	19.6	17.2	15.3
Euro 19[a]	*6.6*	*9.6*	*10.1*	*10.2*	*11.3*	*12.0*	*11.6*	*10.9*	*10.0*	*9.1*	*8.2*
Bulgaria	5.6	6.8	10.3	11.3	12.3	13.0	11.4	9.2	7.6	6.2	5.2
Croatia	5.3	9.2	11.7	13.7	16.0	17.3	17.3	16.2	13.1	11.2	8.5
Czech Rep.	4.4	6.7	7.3	6.7	7.0	7.0	6.1	5.1	4.0	2.9	2.2
Denmark	3.4	6.0	7.5	7.6	7.5	7.0	6.6	6.2	6.2	5.7	5.0
Hungary	7.8	10.0	11.2	11.0	11.0	10.2	7.7	6.8	5.1	4.2	3.7
Poland	7.1	8.2	9.7	9.7	10.1	10.3	9.0	7.5	6.2	4.9	3.9
Romania	5.6	6.9	7.0	7.2	6.8	7.1	6.8	6.8	5.9	4.9	4.2
Sweden	6.2	8.4	8.6	7.8	8.0	8.1	8.0	7.4	7.0	6.7	6.3
UK	5.6	7.6	7.8	8.1	7.9	7.5	6.1	5.3	4.8	4.3	4.0
EU 28	*6.4*	*8.9*	*9.6*	*9.6*	*10.4*	*10.8*	*10.2*	*9.4*	*8.6*	*7.6*	*6.8*

Source: Eurostat, 2019

Notes: [a] the current 19 Eurozone members – note that Cyprus joined in 2008,
   Slovakia in 2009, Estonia in 2011, Latvia in 2014 and Lithuania in 2015
   Case study countries are highlighted in light grey

considerations, party political behaviour, and in some cases even coalition building and government office, while proposing policy narratives and ideas that would be credible as well as appeal to the wider electorate. We turn next to this political dimension, and particularly to the left-wing response to the crisis.

What is the left?

The first things that needs to be done is to define the left. Although the left can be segregated into several distinct party families, and the relationships among these parties are often very fractious, nonetheless there is something that binds them together. Left-wing politics is characterised by a number of features. It is based on a belief in social cooperation, which historically was often especially focused on one particular social group, the working class. There is a strong commitment to the principle of equality in social, political and economic terms, although the extent of that equality in practice has varied. Above all, the left is based on the principle of socialism. While socialism 'contains a bewildering variety of divisions and rival traditions', it is 'an ideology defined by its opposition to capitalism and its attempt to provide a more humane and socially worthwhile alternative' (Heywood, 2017: 95). Within those broad boundaries, two broad approaches exist: reformist and radical.

Reformists work within the confines of capitalism to bring about improvement. Indeed, they have increasingly come to see the role of the left not as outright opposition to capitalism, but as engineering a capitalism that can guarantee socially just policies. This has been the focus of social democratic parties, which grew to be the dominant force on the European left in the post-Second World War era. Whether a humane capitalism is possible is open to question, with Marlière arguing that 'capitalism has been more successful at transforming social democracy than vice versa' (Ladrech & Marlière, 1999: 1). This seemed particularly true in the later twentieth century, when many social democratic parties accepted the 'embrace of neo-liberalism' (Lavelle, 2009: 9). Their commitment to the principle of equality and society remained the same, but was reinterpreted to focus on equality of opportunity, not equality of outcome. For some, this resulted in an 'eviscerated version of social democracy' (Unger, 2005: 7).

By contrast, for radicals the opposition to capitalism is absolute, and the project of left-wing parties must be to replace capitalism by some form of socialist economy. What exactly that socialist alternative might look like remains a hazy concept, and indeed radical left parties are often defined simply as being 'to the left of social democracy' (Dunphy, 2004: 2; Hudson, 2012: 2; March & Keith, 2016: 1). Over time, the insistence on revolutionary overthrow of capitalism has waned, and instead there is acceptance of the need for evolution. This has brought the radical left closer to the reformists – or at least, closer to the positions held by reformists before their neoliberal drift. The radical left parties include a wide range, from former communists to student radicals to a new generation of alter-globalisation protesters.

One variant worth adding to this list is the green left, which combines left-wing policies in many areas with a strong environmental dimension. Initially, the green left was closer to the radical left side of the spectrum, but over time – and as green parties have been drawn ever closer to the orbit of government – their positions have moderated and a more reformist position has emerged.

This rather disparate set can be organised and simplified by reference to party groupings at the EU level. There are two types of European grouping worth considering. First, there are broad pan-European federations of like-minded parties. Second, there are European Parliament (EP) groups. With both of these types, we can clearly see a three-fold division of the European left. First, and by far the largest, there is a social democratic family, consisting of a federation (the Party of European Socialists, or PES) and an EP grouping (the Socialists and Democrats group[4]). Next, there is a radical left family, again made up of a federation (the Party of the European Left, or PEL) and an EP group (European United Left-Nordic Green Left, or GUE-NGL). Finally, there is a green federation (the European Green Party, or EGP), which cooperates with another federation to form an EP grouping (Greens-European Free Alliance, or G-EFA).

These three party families of the European left form the basic frame of reference for this book. The membership of these family federations and groupings does not correspond exactly. First, the federations usually stretch their membership to include parties from non-EU states.[5] Second, not every party from an EU state ends up winning an EP seat, leaving a discrepancy between federation membership and participation in the EP grouping. Third, some parties have chosen membership in one group but not the other – for example, several GUE-NGL member parties remain outside PEL.

The focus of this book is on the political consequences of the crisis in the European Union, and particularly on Eurozone states. We have included ten countries, including all those that received bailouts and a number of creditor countries. The book begins with analyses of the political impact of the crisis in the five countries that received bailouts and one – Italy – where the imposition of a severe austerity programme was the price of avoiding a full bailout. It then looks at Latvia, one of the few eastern European states in the Eurozone, before analysing three 'creditor' states, Finland, France and Germany.

Greece may be the country that has been most deeply affected by the crisis. It suffered from a particularly intense economic crisis and from the 'extreme austerity' (Karyotis & Gerodimos, 2015: 4) imposed on the country. The chapter here by Nikos Nikolakakis explains the collapse of the traditional bipartisan system in Greece and examines the rise to power of the radical left SYRIZA. The chapter illustrates how SYRIZA have tried to balance – not by any means always successfully – a very critical stance towards aspects of the EU with a strong commitment to the principle of integration. Nikolakakis argues that the crisis was a catalyst that transformed not just the Greek political system but also the balance of political power on the left.

In Spain, there is a similar narrative of transformation of the party system and of the left in particular. The chapter by Carlos Rico Motos examines the crisis of Spain's political order. Established parties such as the social democratic PSOE have declined precipitously while new ones such as the radical left Podemos have experienced rapid growth. Spain has also witnessed a transformation of the political agenda. On Europe, Podemos evolved from an initially quite Eurosceptic position towards a more ambiguous stance that focused on a discourse of national sovereignty against a 'Brussels technocracy'.

The next chapter looks at Portugal. It is a slightly different case, a bailout country where the traditional social democratic party has survived relatively unscathed but the radical left has also become stronger. Cláudia Toriz Ramos describes how the country witnessed an intensive public debate on EMU as bailout conditions meant the implementation of severe austerity measures. Similar to Spain, ordinary citizens were drawn to widespread protest. The public perception of European integration shifted from positive associations with modernisation and funding to being increasingly linked with more negative concepts such as austerity and poverty. Although the left-of-centre Socialist Party (PS) lost power when the crisis began, the crisis eventually led to a historically significant and unprecedented cooperation between the country's centre left and radical left parties in 2015.

Ireland was the first EU country to go into recession at the start of the crisis. To begin with, the social democratic Labour Party profited from the crisis, gaining a historic result in the 2011 election. But it then went into a coalition government that continued to implement austerity measures, and subsequently suffered an equally historic defeat in 2016. Meanwhile, various radical left groups gained ground steadily. The radical left used the EU's handling of the crisis and questions over how to respond to austerity measures as a means of separating themselves from the Irish centre left. There were fundamental disagreements between the parties over the issue of European integration.

A different story emerges in Cyprus, which is distinctive as the only EU state with a radical left government prior to the crisis. The chapter by Yiannos Katsourides examines how that AKEL party coped with the bailout. AKEL held government office at the height of the crisis, and the public largely blamed them for the harsh austerity measures that were implemented. AKEL's inability to attempt any alternative policies was not consistent with the party's radical left identity, and eventually voters punished them when the party lost power in 2013. AKEL offers a good example of how, while the crisis appeared tailor-made for the left to offer a critical alternative to neoliberalism, in practice left-wing parties were unable to make a difference when in government.

Although Italy did not receive a bailout, it underwent a severe structural adjustment programme that once again triggered political upheaval. Jorge del Palacio Martin shows how the crisis triggered more general political, social and institutional upheaval that led to major changes in Italy's party political system. The social democratic left under Matteo Renzi concentrated on constitutional reform rather than any challenge to austerity, but faced a major new opponent in the Five Star Movement. The Five Star Movement espoused anti-establishment discourse and a populist programme which drew in voters from left and right. They succeeded in ending the previous left–right bipolarism of Italian politics, and the centre left suffered a disastrous defeat in 2018.

The next chapter, by Karlis Bukovskis and Ilvija Bruge, examines Latvia. Here, the narratives around the left and the crisis were very different from those elsewhere. Even though the crisis resulted in high unemployment, increasing inequality and austerity in Latvia, this did not amplify any doubts about integration. Indeed, Latvia actually joined the euro in the midst of the Eurozone crisis, in 2014. The Latvian case also shows a continuing stigmatisation of the left, which is seen as a derogatory term in Latvia. While Bukovskis and Bruge argue that centre left social democratic policy ideas are visible and are embraced by most parties, this has not led to a resurrection of a social democratic or socialist left party.

In neighbouring Finland, Tapio Raunio explores the unusual situation of a multi-party government that included the social democrats, the green and the radical left, but also parties to their right. The crisis revealed the fragility of Finland's domestic consensus over European integration, with the anti-integration Finns Party being very successful in turning public discourse on the EU in a far more cautious and critical direction. While it is not an outright Eurosceptic stance, it is certainly one that aims for an EU characterised more by free trade than by social solidarity. Parties on the left in Finland have struggled to find an effective response to this.

Julien Navarro and Antonella Seddone look at France, where once again the story is of the decline of the social democrats during the crisis. The crisis had a major impact on French citizens' satisfaction with domestic and EU politics, with austerity measures being widely perceived as an outside imposition. Austerity fuelled feelings of Euroscepticism and anti-politics, and opened up electoral opportunities for radical parties both from the left and right. The economic crisis also highlighted the deep divisions between the different sections of the left. Although the Socialists had regained power in 2012, they rapidly ran into problems. By 2017, the Socialist Party was unable to find any electoral space between the pro-European centrism of Emmanuel Macron, a more EU-critical stance on the radical left and the outright hostility to the EU of the far right Front National.

Knut Roder's chapter looks at Germany, where the SPD has been partly in government but also in decline, while the radical left has been overtaken by the radical right. Germany is often viewed as having come quite well through the crisis. But there was a very deeply rooted narrative that the crisis was the fault of other countries in the Eurozone, which were to blame for their own troubles and should not be bailed out at the expense of German tax payers. The SPD was a junior partner in grand coalition governments during this period, which meant that the party shared responsibility for the German government's approach towards the crisis. It made it virtually impossible for the left to find common ground and challenge the handling of the crisis by the Merkel governments.

Finally, Andy Storey examines the complex relationship between left-wing parties and EU governance. His analysis looks at voters' attitudes to integration and nationalism, and argues that there is a distinct left-wing form of Euroscepticism. This feeds into the concluding chapter, where we argue that the crisis reveals a left that is neither entirely pro-European nor Eurosceptic. We raise the idea of alter-Europeanism, a distinct left-wing approach to integration that seeks a different path to European cooperation, but we also identify the constraints inhibiting the development of a real project for alter-Europeanism.

The left and the crisis

At first, the crisis seemed to present an opportunity for the left in Europe. It was easy for the left in Europe to blame the crisis on a neoliberal, Anglo-American model of financial capitalism. The crisis was widely viewed as proof that aspects of the dominant economic wisdom, and particularly ideas of deregulation and neoliberalism, were at best inadequate and at worst dangerous. In addition, the response to the crisis adopted by centre right governments should have given further ammunition to the left. A crisis largely created by free market financial speculation and private debt led paradoxically to public austerity and restrictions on public deficits and debt.

The puzzle therefore is why the left has struggled to be effective, given a political terrain seemingly so propitious for them. The left began to put forward alternative narratives, with Ryner imagining that the crisis could signal 'the obituary of the Third Way' (2010). On the social democratic side, the narrative emphasised a return to strong regulation and advocated the revival of Keynesian demand management policies. Similar policies emerged from the green left, while on the radical left there were arguments for a fundamental re-think of the economic system.

However, it can be argued that economic depressions generally tend to favour the right rather than the left (Gamble, 2009: 109–110). Diamond stated that 'despite the worst global economic crisis for over 80 years, it is Christian democracy which is ascendant in today's Europe' (2012: 1), and March noted wryly that 'rumours of the death of neo-liberalism have been exaggerated' (2012: 1). Rather than being a return to the left, social inequality has widened, and 'the financial crisis since 2008 has been handled at the almost exclusive expenses of tax payers and public finances' (Hillebrand & Maas, 2011: 6), to the extent that the crisis has been interpreted cynically as a kind of 'socialism for the rich' (Jones, 2014).

The left proved unable to control the narratives. Particularly when the banking crisis shifted to become the EU sovereign debt crisis, the perception of the problems and of appropriate solutions shifted rapidly. When the bailout programmes were imposed, the debate shifted away from a flawed financial system. Instead, the arguments focused on re-starting the European economy. For many countries, the discussion became one of 'irresponsible' management of national economies, with an attendant refusal to countenance any form of social or economic solidarity among EU countries.

Social democratic parties were especially ill-placed to respond to the crisis. Most of these parties had only relatively recently embraced neoliberalism, and had done so on the grounds that there was no alternative – exactly the position that was now being challenged. Their 'decade-long strategy of full accommodation to neo-liberalism in order to skim off the surplus for ameliorative social spending has collapsed with the end of the growth upon which it depended' (Guinan, 2012). In addition, many social democratic parties found themselves in government during the crisis, but they were being required to implement austerity programmes and had no space in which to engineer any alternative models.

This focuses attention on the relationship between the left and the European Union. Embedded within all of this was a big question: if you are going to try to re-design the European economy, whether in a social democratic or radical direction, how does that fit with the existing treaties of the EU? The crisis was thus a challenge to the economic policies of the left, but also to their understanding of the process of European integration. The crisis and the party responses to it pose questions about the very essence of EU integration. The crisis has significantly impacted on the programmatic alignment and strategic responses undertaken by political parties, and as is the focus of this book, on political parties on the European left. As we write in 2019, the crisis is in the daily headlines less than before. But it is very far from being resolved or from having played itself out. The analysis in this book suggests that for the left, the transformations triggered by the crisis are only just starting to take effect.

Notes

1 Washington Mutual Bank and Wachovia Bank were among those that went bankrupt, while the investment banks Bear Sterns and Merrill Lynch were taken over (by JP Morgan Chase and by Bank of America respectively). JP Morgan Chase and Goldman Sachs also altered their banking status to make themselves subject to more strict regulation and thus to try to reduce their degree of exposure to unknown risks.
2 Properly, the Federal National Mortgage Association and the Federal Home Loan Mortgage Company. Together, these two companies held an estimated $5 trillion in home loans.
3 This was effectively a statement that the bank had no way of accurately gauging the value of the complex assets bundled together in the funds.
4 This name was adopted in 2009; prior to then they had been known as the Socialist Group.
5 For example, Norwegian parties are members of PES and EGP, while Swiss parties are in PEL and EGP.

Bibliography

Authers, J. (2012) *Europe's financial crisis: a short guide to how the euro fell into crisis, and the consequences for the world*, New Jersey: Pearson.
BBC (2017) 'German election: Merkel wins fourth term, AfD nationalists rise', BBC, 25 September. www.bbc.co.uk/news/world-europe-41376577 (accessed 15 April 2018).
Diamond, P. (2012) 'From fatalism to fraternity: governing purpose and the good society', in O. Cramme & P. Diamond (eds) *After the Third Way: the future of social democracy in Europe*, London: Policy Network and I.B. Tauris, 1–28.
Dinan, D., Nugent, N. & Paterson, W. E. (2017), *The European Union in crisis*, London: Palgrave.
Dunphy, R. (2004) *Contesting capitalism? Left parties and European integration*, Manchester: Manchester University Press.
Elliott, L. (2008) 'Saving Fannie Mae and Freddie Mac was nationalisation pure and simple', *Guardian*, 9 September. www.theguardian.com/commentisfree/2008/sep/09/freddiemacandfanniemae.subprimecrisis (accessed 20 May 2018).
European Commission (n.d.) 'EU financial assistance'. https://ec.europa.eu/info/business-economy-euro/economic-and-fiscal-policy-coordination/eu-financial-assistance_en (accessed 20 May 2018).
Eurostat (2019) 'Real GDP growth rate, 2008–2018'. https://ec.europa.eu/eurostat/tgm/table.do?tab=table&init=1&language=en&pcode=tec00115&plugin=1 (accessed 11 June 2019).

Eurostat (2019) 'Unemployment rates in EU member states, 2008–2018'. http://
     appsso.eurostat.ec.europa.eu/nui/show.do?dataset=lfsa_urgan&lang=en (accessed
     11 June 2019).
FCIC (2011) *The Financial Crisis Inquiry report: final report of the National
     Commission on the causes of the financial and economic crisis in the United
     States*, Washington: Financial Crisis Inquiry Commission. www.gpo.gov/fdsys/
     pkg/GPO-FCIC/pdf/GPO-FCIC.pdf (accessed 20 May 2018).
Gabriel, S. (2011) 'Commercial banking should be split from investment banking',
     interview in *Spiegel Online*. www.spiegel.de/international/germany/interview-with-
     german-opposition-leader-commercial-banking-should-be-split-from-investment-
     banking-a-792223.html (accessed 12 May 2017).
Gamble, A. (2009) *The spectre at the feast: capitalist crisis and the politics of
     recession*, Basingstoke: Palgrave Macmillan.
Goldfarb, Z. A., Cho, D. & Binyamin Appelbaum (2008) 'Treasury to rescue Fannie
     and Freddie', *Washington Post*, 7 September. www.washingtonpost.com/wp-dyn/
     content/article/2008/09/06/AR2008090602540.html?hpid=topnews (accessed 20
     April 2017).
Graham, C. (2017) 'Who won the Dutch election and what does it mean for Geert
     Wilders and the far right in the Netherlands and Europe?' *The Telegraph*, 16
     March. www.telegraph.co.uk/news/2017/03/16/won-dutch-election-does-mean-
     geert-wilders-far-right-netherlands/ (accessed 15 April 2018).
Guinan, J. (2012) 'Social democracy in the age of austerity: the radical potential
     of democratising capital', *Renewal: A Journal of Social Democracy*, 20 (4).
     www.renewal.org.uk/articles/the-radical-potential-of-democratising-capital
     (accessed 14 March 2019).
Heywood, A. (2017) *Political ideologies: an introduction* (5th edn), Basingstoke:
     Palgrave Macmillan.
Hillebrand, E. & Maas, G. (2011) *In search of a new political narrative for a
     solidarity-based society in Europe: ten key questions about the future of social
     democracy in Europe*, Berlin: Friedrich-Ebert-Stiftung.
Hudson, K. (2012) *The new European left: a socialism for the twenty-first century?*,
     Basingstoke: Palgrave Macmillan.
IMF (2014) *IMF response to the financial and economic crisis: evaluation report*,
     Washington: International Monetary Fund/Independent Evaluation Office.
Ingimundarson, V., Urfalino, P. & Erlingsdóttir, I. (eds) (2016) *Iceland's financial
     crisis: the politics of blame, protest and reconstruction*, London: Routledge.
Jansen, M. & von Uexkull, E. (2010) *Trade and employment in the global crisis*,
     Geneva: International Labour Organisation.
Jones, O. (2014) 'It's socialism for the rich and capitalism for the rest of us in
     Britain', *The Guardian*, 29 August. www.theguardian.com/books/2014/aug/29/
     socialism-for-the-rich (accessed 15 May 2017).
Jónsson, Á. & Sigurgeirsson, H. (2016) *The Icelandic financial crisis: a study into
     the world's smallest currency area and its recovery from total banking collapse*,
     Basingstoke: Palgrave Macmillan.
Karyotis, G. & Gerodimos, R. (2015) *The politics of extreme austerity: Greece
     in the Eurozone crisis*, Basingstoke: Palgrave Macmillan.

Keeley, B. & Love, P. (2010) *From crisis to recovery: the causes, course and consequences of the Great Recession*, Paris: OECD.

Ladrech, R. & Marlière, P. (eds) (1999) *Social democratic parties in the European Union: history, organization, policies*, Basingstoke: Palgrave Macmillan.

Lavelle, A. (2009) 'Explanations for the neo-liberal direction of social democracy: Germany, Sweden and Australia compared', in J. Callaghan, N. Fishman, B. Jackson & M. McIvor (eds) *In search of social democracy: responses to crisis and modernisation*, Manchester: Manchester University Press, 9–28.

March, L. (2012) *Radical left parties in Europe*, London & New York: Routledge.

March, L. and Keith, D. (eds) (2016) *Europe's radical left: from marginality to the mainstream?* London: Rowman & Littlefield.

Martell, L. (2013) 'Social democracy after the crisis in Europe and the crisis of social democracy', *Renewal: A Journal of Social Democracy*, 21 (4): 31–38.

Meeusen, W. (ed.) (2011) *The economic crisis and European integration*, Cheltenham: Edward Elgar.

Pisani-Ferry, J. (2014) *The euro crisis and its aftermath*, Oxford: Oxford University Press.

Ryner, M. (2010) 'An obituary for the Third Way: the financial crisis and social democracy in Europe', *Political Quarterly*, 81 (4): 554–563.

Schofield, H. (2017) 'Is France's Socialist Party dead?', BBC News, online. www.bbc.co.uk/news/world-europe-39900003 (accessed 15 April 2018).

Shelburne, R. C. (2010) 'The global financial crisis and its impact on trade: the world and the European emerging economies', *UNECE Discussion paper 2010.2*, Geneva: United Nations Economic Commission for Europe.

SPD (2009) *Sozial und Demokratisch: Anpacken. Für Deutschland – Das Regierungsprogramm der SPD*, Berlin: Sozialdemokratische Partei Deutschlands.

Unger, R. M. (2005) *What should the left propose?*, London & New York: Verso.

World Bank (2009) *Annual report 2009: the year in review*, Washington: World Bank.

WTO (2009) *World trade report 2009: trade policy commitments and contingency measures*, Geneva: World Trade Organization.

2

The Greek left and the crisis: the demise of PASOK and the rise of SYRIZA

Nikolaos Nikolakakis

Introduction

This chapter examines the Greek left through the deep financial crisis from 2008. The crisis in Greece was one of the deepest in the EU and led to arguably the strongest political earthquake in Greek history. The outcome of this political, economic and social crisis brought a radical left party, SYRIZA, from the margins of the political system to government, while consigning the social democrats of PASOK (Panhellenic Socialist Movement) to a catastrophic defeat. The chapter begins with a brief historical overview of the Greek left, before focusing on the eventful period of 2009–2015, during which the Greek political system underwent a series of radical transformations. The historical overview will be followed by an analysis of SYRIZA's responses to the crisis, both from a programmatic and electoral point of view, as well as its stance towards European integration. Finally, the chapter will discuss the relationship between the parties of the left in the Greek political system.

Prior to the crisis, the Greek political system was strongly bipartisan, with alternating single-party governments of the centre right ND (Nea Dimokratia) and the social democratic PASOK. The Greek left was different from other EU countries, with two significant groups to the left of PASOK; the Greek Communist Party (KKE) and the Coalition of Left and Progress (Synaspismos). Synaspismos laid the foundations for the Coalition of the Radical Left (SYRIZA) in 2004.[1] Throughout the 1990s and the 2000s, the electoral performance of the KKE and Synaspismos was rather stable, around 8% and 4% respectively. The bipartisanship of the Greek political system appeared well institutionalised. Electoral laws promoted strong single party governments rather than coalition governments, and this limited the scope of the radical left. The crisis led to the most significant changes to the Greek political system in the country's modern history.

The emergence of SYRIZA and the end of the Greek bipartisan political system, 2009–2012

The period of the complete dominance of ND and PASOK lasted to the general elections of 2009, when PASOK won a landslide triumph under George Papandreou[2] (Ministry Interior, 2009). But the government's decision to sign a Memorandum of Understanding (MoU)[3] with the EC-ECB-IMF troika in 2010 initiated huge socio-economic-political turmoil. The MoU was meant to tackle the grave financial issues that were affecting the country and consisted of a series of draconian austerity measures, such as a significant reduction of public sector pensions and salaries, an additional tax on properties, and an increase in existing taxes on basic goods and services. These measures generated massive societal outcry and led to growing social tension between public and private sector employees.[4] The government's decision to pursue these policies created realignment inside the Greek left and more specifically inside Synaspismos, at the time the strongest political formation inside the coalition of SYRIZA. The party's 'renewers', led by Fotis Kouvelis, decided to break away and form a new political group to the left of PASOK, which took the name Democratic Left (DIMAR, 2010).

The societal opposition to the austerity measures imposed by PASOK grew and paved the way for SYRIZA's surprising emergence as the country's most popular party. In the May 2012 general elections, PASOK and the ND lost more than half of their combined vote share,[5] while SYRIZA quadrupled its vote, which rose to 16.8% and made them the second most popular party (Ministry Interior, 2012a). The elections of May 2012 created a very fragmented parliament, which resulted in the inability of the parties' leaders to form a government. As a result, new snap elections took place in June 2012, which saw SYRIZA's vote grow even further, despite losing the election to ND by a mere 3% (Ministry Interior, 2012b).

SYRIZA's impressive electoral performance signified the end of bipolar politics. Following the June elections, SYRIZA was the major opposition force inside the Greek parliament. The party's alternative political narrative that called for a different Europe and an alternative way out of the crisis gained momentum inside Greek society and especially among the lower middle classes that for years had supported the Social Democrats of PASOK (Voulgaris & Nicolakopoulos, 2014: 55–58). The party's success also served as a catalyst for further harmonisation of SYRIZA and led to it becoming a unitary party, with Synaspismos dissolving and merging into SYRIZA a few months before SYRIZA's first Congress in July 2013 (Synaspismos, 2013).

The 2015 elections and the government of the left

Following the 2012 legislative elections, the two long-standing rivals, ND and PASOK, formed a coalition government, while SYRIZA became the major opposition party. During this time, SYRIZA sought to challenge the coalition's austerity measures. They utilised their position in the political spotlight to gain a larger vote share both from the party's right as well as the party's left. The growing instability of the coalition government as well as the critical state of the Greek economy rendered the possibility of early elections a highly likely scenario. In addition to this, the coalition government had to face a presidential election in 2015.[6]

Given that the coalition had no more than a simple majority inside the parliament, and with the coalition polling low,[7] SYRIZA pressed on the austerity issue as early as the autumn of 2014. SYRIZA questioned the democratic legitimacy of the government and criticised the MoU and the attendant austerity measures.[8] The political turmoil and the alleged unwillingness of the troika to sign a new deal with a highly unstable government led Prime Minister Samaras to call for an early presidential election on 17 December 2014 (Enikos, 2014a). The coalition government arguably tried to apply pressure to the increasing number of independent MPs and those from DIMAR to aid the government. Nonetheless, the attempt proved unsuccessful as the Greek parliament failed to elect a new president even after three rounds of voting. As a result, legislative elections were announced immediately for 25 January 2015.

The electoral campaign was short and intense. SYRIZA continued to poll higher than its major opponents of ND and PASOK combined. SYRIZA's core objective was to secure an overall parliamentary majority. SYRIZA's campaign emphasised hope of change in Greece and in the EU, with the main slogan declaring 'Hope is coming, Greece moves forward, Europe is changing' (SYRIZA, 2015). Their campaign was significantly supported by Party of the European Left member parties, which sent delegations to Athens. During the party's central political rally, the President of SYRIZA, Alexis Tsipras, invited Pablo Iglesias of Podemos onto the stage, and his slogan of 'SYRIZA, *Podemos, Venceremos*' swiftly took off among the European left. It was an attempt to trigger a kind of domino effect, where the electoral victory of one European left party in one national political arena could bring about a chain reaction in the EU, spreading the political earthquake throughout Europe.

SYRIZA was successful, winning the elections and electing 150 MPs.[9] Technically, SYRIZA could have formed a government on its own, as the opposition would not have been able to propose a vote of no confidence against them, but in an attempt to avoid any political instability, they quickly came to an understanding with the right-wing populist party of Independent Greeks (ANEL).[10] The decision to form a coalition with ANEL[11] caused some turmoil inside SYRIZA and especially among the members of the more radical Left Platform.[12] The coalition between ANEL and SYRIZA is quite unique, given their considerable ideological differences, but opposition to austerity united the two parties. The move was thus a consequence of the crisis, and the government then sought to renegotiate the terms of the country's bailout agreement with the troika. The MoU had created a line of division in Greek politics, relating to the country's involvement with the EU and the obligations of membership.

The new government sought to initiate negotiations with the country's European partners immediately. The newly appointed Finance Minister, Yanis Varoufakis,[13] met with his most important EU counterparts upon his nomination. Concurrently, Tsipras visited several EU prime ministers as well as the President of the European Commission, Jean-Claude Juncker, and President of the European Parliament, Martin Schulz. But the balance of political power inside the EU was not favourable towards SYRIZA's proposals, and the country's European partners strongly opposed the government's plans for ending austerity. Despite this opposition, the SYRIZA-led government managed to come to an initial understanding with its European partners in late February 2015. This understanding caused once again a chain reaction inside SYRIZA, as some of the Left Platform's prominent members heavily criticised the agreement and suggested that the EU's stance clearly suggested that the end of austerity could not be achieved inside the Eurozone. Major pressure was thus applied to the Greek economy, and several serious dilemmas were posed relating to the country's EU membership. The financial crisis had the effect of reminding the Greek citizenry of the increasing relevance of European issues to their daily lives.

The first negotiations with the troika led to a stalemate in June 2015, when the Commission issued an ultimatum demanding a series of austerity measures as a *conditio sine qua non* for continued support for the Greek banking system (Nikolakakis, 2016: 7). On 28 June 2015 Tsipras called a snap referendum on whether to accept the ultimatum. During the politically heated week that led to the referendum, SYRIZA called for a 'No' vote and gathered thousands of citizens at a rally in Syntagma Square in Athens, with the most important member parties of the European left in attendance (Nikolakakis, 2016: 8). The referendum was held on 5 July, and the 'No' vote secured 61.3% (Ministry Interior, 2015b). This led to a second round

Table 2.1 Electoral results in Greek general elections, 2004–2015 (in % of vote)

Party	National Elections/Year						
	2004	2007	2009	May 2012	June 2012	January 2015	September 2015
ND	45.3	41.8	33.4	18.8	29.6	27.8	28.0
Synaspismos/SYRIZA	3.2	5.0	4.6	16.7	26.8	36.3	35.4
PASOK	40.5	43.9	43.9	13.1	13.1	4.6	6.2
KKE	5.9	8.1	7.5	8.4	4.5	5.4	5.5
DIMAR	-	-	-	6.1	6.2	-	-
LAE	-	-	-	-	-	-	2.8
Enosi Kentroon	0.2	-	-	-	0.2	1.7	3.4
LAOS	2.1	3.8	5.6	2.9	1.5	1.0	-
Golden Dawn	-	-	-	6.9	6.9	6.2	6.9
ANEL	-	-	-	10.6	7.5	4.7	3.6

Source: Ministry of Interior (2009, 2012a, 2012b, 2015a, 2015b, 2015c)

of brief negotiations, and after one of the longest summit meetings in the history of the EU on 11 July 2015, an initial agreement was reached (Nikolakakis, 2016: 8). But the agreement was seen by SYRIZA and the rest of the European left as a financial coup d'état, as the EU had threatened Greece with expulsion from the Eurozone if the government did not accept the austerity measures (Nikolakakis, 2016: 8).

Dissatisfaction was growing among the Greek electorate, and the Left Platform component in SYRIZA criticised Tsipras's decision to accept the agreement, which was seen as a capitulation. The Left Platform's leadership soon opted to withdraw from SYRIZA and form a new party called Popular Unity (Laïkí Enótita, LAE). In the snap election in September 2015, LAE took part independently from SYRIZA. However, despite the negative outcome of the government's negotiations with the troika, the election verified the primacy of SYRIZA. The party maintained its electoral leadership and elected 145 MPs (Ministry Interior, 2015c), forming another coalition government with ANEL. LAE did not manage to reach the threshold for parliamentary representation, as it only managed to secure 2.86% of the vote share (Ministry Interior, 2015c).

SYRIZA's response to the crisis

This part of the chapter presents an overview of SYRIZA's response to the crisis from an ideological and programmatic point of view. The fact that the general elections in Greece were highly Europeanised[14] provides an opportunity to reach significant conclusions regarding SYRIZA's distinct left Europeanism and the effect that the crisis had on it.

By 2010 the effects of the crisis had already reached Greece and resulted in a decisive sharpening of Synaspismos's critique towards the EU. The party criticised the European management of the crisis and argued that the peoples of Europe should fight the neoliberal forces that were seen as an existential threat to the European project. The party put forward a Marxist analysis, arguing that 'we are amid an international capitalist crisis whose root cause is the over-accumulation of capital. In substance it is a structural systemic crisis, which began in 2008 initially in the banking sector and the financial system, and later in investments and the reduction of production and influenced as a natural consequence the working peoples and their incomes' (Synaspismos, 2010: 1). The party argued that the Eurozone sovereign debt crisis was a direct consequence of the neoliberal policies pursued ever since the signing of the Maastricht Treaty, which was interpreted as placing capitalist exploitation in the foundations of the European edifice. This led the party to disown the critical support of the Maastricht Treaty it had expressed during its ratification in 1992 (Synaspismos, 2010: 2).

Despite the negative conclusions that the party reached vis-à-vis the EU, it argued that there could be no real solutions outside the Union. Indeed, the party believed that 'the alternative solution is the struggle of the peoples of Europe for a change in the balance of power in every country as well as the common coordinated struggle for another Europe. A democratic and social Europe, free from monetarism and the compulsion of capital' (Synaspismos, 2010: 3). For Synaspismos there are no national solutions, only pan-European ones. For this reason, the party noted that the European left should intensify its struggle to unite the European peoples under the banner of an alternative exit from the crisis with a socialist outlook. This critical but European stance continued into SYRIZA, for whom austerity was not only posing a threat to Greek citizens but was jeopardising the European project altogether. The worsening of the crisis affecting the EU led SYRIZA to argue that:

> the reason of existence of an EU for the benefit of the peoples is slowly disappearing from the horizon. The euro is mainly seen as the vehicle of German policy, widening the inequalities between countries as well as the inequalities amongst social classes, while Asian patterns are imposed on European societies; patterns which clearly benefit European capital. The future of the EU as well as the Eurozone itself is rendered more and more uncertain. The policies of austerity and recession cause the disintegration of the bonds amongst the European states, strengthen Euroscepticism and anti-Europeanism, and widen the nationalist juxtapositions and render the revival of fascism easier. (Synaspismos, 2013: 1)[15]

Yanis Varoufakis and the American economist James K. Galbraith shared this negative view. Indeed, they found that the only viable solution for Europe's problems was constituted by the left,[16] and argued that the emergence of a real left-wing opposition 'wouldn't be a bad thing for Europe or the United States. The policies currently imposed upon Europe's periphery are worsening the crisis, threatening Europe's integrity, and jeopardising growth. A Greek government that rejects these self-defeating policies will do more help than harm' (Galbraith & Varoufakis, 2013: 1). According to them, a government of the left in Greece could be the European project's last hope for a democratic future. Indeed, they argued that SYRIZA's success could lead to a chain reaction leading to more governments of the left across the European South. This close cooperation among the countries of the South was a basis for the survival of the European project and the successful transition to socialism with freedom and democracy.[17]

Although he should not be characterised as a Marxist economist,[18] Varoufakis's economic thinking is hugely influenced by Marxist political economy. In an earlier work, he presented a proposal for saving the Eurozone (Varoufakis et al., 2013), which argues that European federalism is a fundamental requirement for the correct functioning of the common currency and the common market. In Varoufakis's opinion, the Eurozone cannot exist without a sovereign European legislature that would create the necessary system of checks and balances for a democratic EU. In addition to Varoufakis's election as an MP and nomination as Finance Minister, another well-known radical academic, Costas Lapavitsas, was elected as a SYRIZA MP in 2015. Lapavitsas's economic analysis of the Eurozone crisis is a more orthodox Marxist perspective than that of Varoufakis. Lapavitsas presented the possibility of default and even an exit from the Eurozone as a possible solution to the country's issues (2012). In fact, we could argue that Lapavitsas's ideas are closer to the core of the Left Platform and resulted in his resignation from SYRIZA following the schism of August 2015 and his subsequent move to LAE.

SYRIZA's manifesto for the elections of January 2015 sought to immediately tackle the issue of the country's sovereign debt. SYRIZA proposed the holding of a European Debt Conference, and drew parallels with the write-down of German debt in 1953. According to SYRIZA this conference would cancel the greater part of the nominal public debt, enabling it to become sustainable. SYRIZA also proposed a 'growth clause' regarding the repayment of the remaining part 'so that it is growth-financed and not budget-financed' (SYRIZA, 2014). In addition, the party proposed a moratorium in debt servicing to save funds for growth, as well as the exclusion of public investment from the restrictions of the Stability and Growth Pact. Furthermore, the party called for a European New Deal of public investment by the European Investment Bank, and for quantitative easing by the ECB with direct purchases of sovereign bonds. These measures constituted for SYRIZA the basis for achieving a 'socially viable solution to Greece's debt problem so that our country is able to pay off the remaining debt from the creation of new wealth and not from primary surpluses, which deprive society of income' (SYRIZA, 2014). The proposed solution to the country's sovereign debt was entirely coherent with the party's political decision in 2013.

The 2015 Thessaloniki programme proposed four pillars of policies. The first relates to tackling the humanitarian crisis, proposing free electricity, meal subsidies and a housing guarantee for families living under the poverty line. In addition to this, the restitution of additional pension entitlements for pensioners receiving less than €700, as well as free medical and pharmaceutical care for the uninsured unemployed was proposed. The second pillar involved the restarting of the economy and the promotion of tax justice. Under this, SYRIZA proposed a series of measures to alleviate the increasing tax burden especially for middle-class and working-class households. They proposed a system of personal debt relief by restructuring of non-performing loans, the establishment of a public development bank and the restoration of the minimum wage to €751 per month. The third pillar relates to the national plan to regain employment. Under this pillar, SYRIZA proposed a two-year employment programme to create 300,000 jobs, and also 'the restitution of the institutional framework to protect employment rights, the collective agreements and arbitration, as well as the abolition of all regulations allowing for massive and unjustifiable layoffs as well as for renting employees' (SYRIZA, 2014). The fourth pillar deals with reform of the political system. Here, SYRIZA called for the regional organisation of the state, as well as the enhancement of transparency, economic autonomy and effective operation of municipalities and regions. It also called for the empowerment of citizens' democratic participation through the introduction of new institutions, such as a people's legislative initiative, people's veto and people's initiative to call a referendum.

To evaluate SYRIZA's overall response to the crisis, its programmatic positions are very much consistent with its political decisions. On European integration, SYRIZA's stance remained critical yet constructive. The party has chosen ideological consistency, specifically with regards to the EU and the process of European integration, over pragmatism despite its ascent to office. Regardless of the heated internal debate relating to the future of the country inside the EU and the Eurozone, SYRIZA's Europeanism has been strengthened by the crisis, and this is reflected in the party's programmatic positions.

Party competition in the midst of the crisis

The Greek political arena went through a complete restructuring following the end of the bipolar era of the ND and PASOK. The Greek left, particularly following the disintegration of the USSR, had been divided between Synaspismos and the KKE. While the KKE maintained historically a stable and significant electoral performance that allowed the party to achieve a steady parliamentary representation throughout its history,[19] Synaspismos and SYRIZA had constantly struggled to reach the threshold of 3% that would allow it to be represented in the Greek parliament until the crisis. In order to evaluate the effects of the crisis with regards to the party competition inside the Greek left, an examination of SYRIZA's major political opponents will be carried out.

The KKE position is straightforward as the party carried on its traditional rejection of the EU, completely the opposite of SYRIZA's position. For example, at its 19th Congress the party provided a Marxist-Leninist analysis of the crisis and sharpened its critique of SYRIZA's stance. The KKE argued that SYRIZA sought simply to manage capitalism and its goal was 'a new "Marshall plan" for the European South' (KKE, 2013: 1). Moreover, the party argued that SYRIZA identifies itself 'as a left party which unites people coming from the Social Democrats of the 3rd of September up to the so-called "renewing communists", who defend the "social state". [SYRIZA's] strategy in terms of power and the EU is social democratic and monopoly-friendly' (KKE, 2013: 3).[20] The KKE's analysis distinguishes itself from that of DIMAR and SYRIZA, as it places the country's withdrawal from the EU and the Eurozone as essential for any successful socialist transformation of the Greek economy, polity and society. Indeed, the KKE's political document clearly stated that:

> the struggle for the country's release from the EU is bound with the struggle against the power of the monopolies and the struggle of the working class and of its allies for the workers'-popular power. The positions for the exit from euro and the EU coming from bourgeois parties, without affecting the power of monopolies, their ownership, the affixture of Greece in imperialist centres and countries, disorients the popular struggle for the exit from the EU with popular sovereignty and people's power [...] today when the 'prestige' of the EU unravels while the crisis affects other countries, the alliances of the South or the ones with the Euro-Atlantic axis, the US or the UK, do not constitute solutions in favour of the people. Nowadays the struggle for exiting the EU with the people in a position of power must be intensified in every country, in all 27 Member States. (KKE, 2013: 5)

DIMAR's stance was far more convergent with that of SYRIZA. Indeed, DIMAR's decision to take part in the ND-led government following the elections of June 2012 attests to the party's tactical and ideological flexibility when faced with the scenario of the country's withdrawal from the EU (DIMAR, 2013). DIMAR clearly stated that its core opinion with regards to the European question was that 'the country must remain in the Eurozone. Any discussion regarding the possible exit from the euro [...] equates with disaster. The change of policies, the support of the euro and the economic and political unification of Europe constitute the basic terms for the country's future' (DIMAR, 2011). DIMAR's conceptualisation of the crisis was consistent with that of SYRIZA's pro-European majority. Indeed, DIMAR's political documents constructed a discourse that viewed austerity as something inflicted on the peripheral member states of the south by those of the north. Greece was seen by DIMAR as the most critical case. The critical state of the country was seen partially as a result of the Greek 'inefficient administrative structures, the weak production, the significant competitiveness deficit and mainly because of the unwillingness of the dominant political powers to tackle the well-known pathologies of the country's politico-economic system' (DIMAR, 2012: 1). Despite the Greek pathologies, DIMAR considered that the problem was much broader, as Greece was not the sole country affected by the devastating crisis. According to DIMAR's view, the common denominator between Greece, Italy, Spain, Ireland and Portugal was austerity. Indeed, in DIMAR's opinion, the policies of austerity were leading these member states into a vicious circle of economic stagnation and fiscal deficit. Moreover, DIMAR saw the altering of the balance of powers inside the EU as the only possible solution to the issues affecting Europe. Nevertheless, DIMAR argued that Greece addressed the pathologies that were affecting the country, so as to be able to take advantage of a possible change inside the EU (DIMAR, 2012: 4).

These analyses suggest that SYRIZA had very little space for political manoeuvre, with competitors both to its right (DIMAR) and left (KKE). Indeed, following Left Platform's exit from SYRIZA and the subsequent creation of LAE as discussed earlier in this chapter, SYRIZA faced one more opponent to its left. Nevertheless, as a result of the breaking away of LAE, DIMAR became more inclined to possible cooperation with SYRIZA. This presented SYRIZA with more political room to its right, while the competition to its left became significantly more pressing. The implementation of the austerity measures imposed by the accord between the SYRIZA-led government and the troika meant that the parties to SYRIZA's left attempted to revitalise the wave of public protest that flooded the streets between 2010 and 2012. Despite the fact that SYRIZA never had a strong presence inside the Greek trade unions, while the KKE for instance has a very much felt presence, the SYRIZA-led government managed to implement the measures without facing significant societal opposition in the form of demonstrations and massive general strikes. Nevertheless, the political space to the party's left is, as mentioned above, densely populated, something that might push the party to its right, since the social democrats of PASOK and DIMAR are in a process of reshaping their strategy, leaving a lot of space for political manoeuvre for SYRIZA.

SYRIZA, the crisis and the EU

As a result of SYRIZA's Eurocommunist heritage and its core ideological beliefs, the party's stance towards the EU has been critical yet constructive. The party is heavily critical of the neoliberal leitmotif, which it argues has been ever-present since the Maastricht Treaty. Despite this sharp criticism, SYRIZA has constantly argued in favour of Greek membership of the EU and the Eurozone. Indeed, the party's objective is to re-found the European project from within. SYRIZA's conceptualisation of socialism requires a permanent struggle of the unified European working classes. Thus, the process of European integration is a fundamental aspect of the party's ideology, which envisages the transcendence of national divisions of the working classes. Consequently, SYRIZA, unlike communist parties that remain loyal to traditional communist principles such as the KKE, is able to operate with much more ease inside the EU. SYRIZA's ideological anchorage to the idea of a federalist Europe of the peoples created a crisis for the party. But when SYRIZA had to choose between moderation and ideological consistency, the party remained faithful to its core ideology without having to alter its stance towards the EU, despite the dramatic increase of its electoral influence and the subsequent election to office amid the financial crisis. Indeed, the crisis solidified the party's critique of the European architecture and was arguably among the reasons behind the party's electoral success, as SYRIZA managed to represent the electorate's critical support of the EU. Consequently, SYRIZA remained consistent throughout this period. Indeed, in the aftermath of the schism and the creation of LAE, SYRIZA is more coherent and presents much less internal opposition with regards to the austerity policies that it implements. Nevertheless, the impact of the crisis on SYRIZA and on the Greek left is evident when one examines the schisms inside SYRIZA. Indeed, both DIMAR and LAE would not have been created had it not been for the crisis and the sharpening of the internal debate that related predominantly to the party's stance towards the policies imposed by the country's European partners. On the one hand, DIMAR believed that the measures were harsh and unfair but necessary in order to secure the country's EU membership, while on the other, LAE reached a critical point when they could no longer accept SYRIZA's pro-Europeanism.

SYRIZA's electoral victory in January 2015 and the initiation of the negotiations with the troika served as catalysts for the intensification of the internal struggle. Indeed, following the unity demonstrated on the eve of the July 2015 referendum, the subsequent accord with the European institutions constituted the beginning of the end. SYRIZA had to make several important programmatic concessions, which the Europeanist majority saw as a necessary step in the long process of altering the balance of powers inside the EU. However, up to now the party has not altered its ideological profile and more specifically their core left Europeanist view, despite the Left Platform's withdrawal, the re-election in September 2015 and the added competition both to the party's left and right.

As a result, we could argue that SYRIZA has faced and continues to face dilemmas posed by the process of European integration, which the crisis has intensified significantly. As mentioned previously, the crisis served in a sense as a wake-up call for the Greek citizenry, which came quickly to the realisation that EU related matters are a lot more important for their daily lives than it was thought in the past. Nevertheless, the party's distinct Europeanism rendered the party's response much easier than for Euro-rejectionist parties such as the KKE. The financial crisis and its effects solidified SYRIZA's harsh criticism of the EU and provided a substantiation to the party's constant denunciation of the neoliberal EU. Following the party's electoral triumph in January 2015, SYRIZA faced a series of dilemmas, as the negotiations with the European institutions proved harder than expected and arguably confirmed the rigidity of the European edifice. This led to the intensification of the internal struggle in SYRIZA between the Left Platform and the Europeanist majority around the question of the country's Eurozone, and even EU, membership, which ultimately resulted in the Left Platform's collective exit from the party to create LAE. Overall, the crisis has served as a catalyst for events that altered the balance of political powers inside the Greek left, including the social democratic centre left. One cannot argue that the crisis is the sole reason behind the creation of two novel political formations and the almost complete demise of one of the country's strongest political parties, but without its effect on Greek politics, those events would have taken place in a significantly longer period of time.

Notes

1 SYRIZA remained a loose political coalition until 2013 when it became a unitary party.
2 Son of the party's historic leader and founder, Andreas Papandreou, and grandson of arguably the founder of centrist politics in the country, Georgios Papandreou. This is indicative of the underlying problem of nepotism in the country.

 3 Known in Greek simply as the 'memorandum', or *mnimonio*.
 4 This animosity is arguably the result of years of clientelist practices with regards to public servants followed by both ND and PASOK.
 5 PASOK and ND won just 32% of the vote between them (Ministry Interior, 2012a), compared with 77% in 2009 (Ministry Interior, 2009).
 6 The President is elected by the Greek parliament. At first, a two-thirds majority is required. If that is not achieved, a second vote takes place five days later, again with a two-thirds majority. If the second vote is also unsuccessful, a third one takes place five days later, and the requisite majority is reduced to 180 votes. If this third round of voting still fails to produce a victor, the sitting President is obliged to call for new legislative elections.
 7 A representative sample of the polls during the final months of 2014 can be found at (MRB, 2014).
 8 A detailed account of the austerity measures of the so-called Hardouvelis' email can be found here: Enikos (2014b).
 9 The party gained 10% more votes on the previous elections, reaching 36.3% (Ministry Interior, 2015a). They missed out on a parliamentary majority by only one seat.
10 ANEL was founded by former ND MP and Minister Panos Kamenos, who resigned from his seat following the MoU in late 2010.
11 Tsipras announced a cabinet comprising ten ministers with Kamenos himself occupying the Ministry of Defence, and two more ANEL MPs were nominated as undersecretaries.
12 A faction that has been present inside SYRIZA and previously Synaspismos ever since their respective creations.
13 Following his resignation, Varoufakis wrote a memoir (2017) in which he presented an account of the first SYRIZA government and the negotiations with the EU.
14 Indeed, the crisis led to an intensified Europeanisation of national elections, as the financial crisis led citizens to realise that most of the policies affecting their daily lives had a direct connection with EU-wide policies and political decisions. This arguably constitutes the major division inside Greek politics, as on the one hand there are the political forces that would like the country to regain full national sovereignty and exit the EU and the ones that are firm in their belief that the idea of Europe is one that cannot be simply denied. Inside the Greek left, SYRIZA, PASOK and DIMAR, or what is left of the last two in the current state, firmly place their hopes in the European project, following diverse points of view, while KKE completely rejects the notion of an EU friendly to the interests of the European peoples.
15 This argument was also made by Jürgen Habermas who argued that after the first bailouts, 'the realization hit home to me for the first time that the failure of the European project was a real possibility' (Habermas, 2012: 102).
16 In the American printed version of their article, the title appeared as 'Only the Left Can Save Greece'.
17 In an article published in *El País* in May 2013, Alexis Tsipras presented a similar argument (Tsipras, 2013).

18 This is made clear in Varoufakis (2015).
19 With the exception of the periods that KKE was declared illegal.
20 KKE refers to PASOK's founding date, the 3 September 1974 and subsequently to the growing number of elite members of SYRIZA that have previously been involved with PASOK. For KKE this is a clear indication of SYRIZA's opportunism.

Bibliography

DIMAR (2010) *Ηιδρυτική διακήρυξη* [*Founding declaration*], Athens: DIMAR.

DIMAR (2011) *Ανακοίνωση τηςΔημοκρατικής Αριστεράς για τηνοικονομία, τιςεξελίξειςστηνΕυρώπη και τοευρώ* [*Press release of the Democratic Left for the economy, the events in Europe and the euro*], Athens: DIMAR.

DIMAR (2012) *Ενημερωτικό Σημείωμα για τονΕυρωπαϊκό Νότο* [*Briefing note for the European South*], Athens: DIMAR.

DIMAR (2013) *Ανακοίνωση τηςκοινήςσυνεδρίασηςΕκτελεστικής Επιτροπής και Κοινοβουλευτικής Ομάδας τηςΔημ κρατικής Αριστεράς* [*Press release of the joint meeting of Dimar's executive committee and parliamentary group*], Athens: DIMAR.

Enikos (2014a) *17 Δεκεμβρίου η Προεδρική εκλογή* [*The presidential election will take place in December 17*]. www.enikos.gr/poliitcs/283240,17-Dekemvrioy-h-Proedrikh-eklogh.html (accessed 10 March 2015).

Enikos (2014b) *Τρόικα στον Χαρδούβελη: έχεις mail…* [*Troika to Hardouvelis: you have mail…*]. www.enikos.gr/economy/281721,BINTEO-Troika-ston-Xardoyvelh-exeis-mail.html (accessed 10 March 2015).

Galbraith, J. & Varoufakis, Y. (2013) 'Only SYRIZA can save Greece', *New York Times*, 23 June. www.nytimes.com/2013/06/24/opinion/only-syriza-can-save-greece.html (accessed 14 March 2019).

Habermas, J. (2012) *The crisis of the European Union: a response*, Paris: Presses Universitaires de France.

KKE (2013) *Πολιτική απόφαση του 19ου συνεδρίουτου KKE* [*Political decision of KKE's 19th congress*], Athens: KKE.

Lapavitsas, C. (2012) *Crisis in the Eurozone*, London: Verso.

Ministry of Interior (2009) *ΒουλευτικέςΕκλογές 2009* [*General elections 2009*]. http://ekloges-prev.singularlogic.eu/e2009/pages/index.html (accessed 15 July 2013).

Ministry of Interior (2012a) *ΒουλευτικέςΕκλογές 2012* [*General elections 2012*]. http://ekloges-prev.singularlogic.eu/v2012a/public/index.html (accessed 15 July 2013).

Ministry of Interior (2012b) *ΒουλευτικέςΕκλογές 2012* [*General elections 2012*]. http://ekloges.ypes.gr/v2012b/public/index.html (accessed 15 July 2013).

Ministry of Interior (2015a) *ΕθνικέςΕκλογές Ιανουάριος 2015* [*General elections of January 2015*]. www.ekloges.ypes.gr/current/v/public/["cls":"main","params":]} (accessed 15 March 2015).

Ministry of Interior (2015b) *Δημοψήφισμα Ιούλιος 2015* [*Referendum July 2015*]. http://ekloges-prev.singularlogic.eu/r2015/e/public/index.html (accessed 18 September 2015).

Ministry of Interior (2015c) *Εθνικέ ςΕκλογέ ςΣεπτέμβριος 2015* [*General elections of September 2015*]. http://ekloges.ypes.gr/current/v/public/index.html#{"cls": "main","params":{}}. (accessed 18 December 2015).

MRB (2014) *MRB Hellas S.A.* www.mrb.gr/Mrb/media/AGORA-17-19-11-2014. pdf (accessed 10 March 2015).

Nikolakakis, N. (2016) 'SYRIZA's stance vis-à-vis the European Union following the financial crisis: the persistence of left Europeanism and the role of the European Left Party', *European Politics and Society*, 18 (2): 1–20.

Synaspismos (2010) *Πολιτική απόφαση 6ου (έκτακτου) συνεδρίουτουΣυνασπισμού τηςΑριστεράς τωνΚινημάτων και τηςΟικολογίας* [*Political decision of the 6th (extraordinary) congress of the Coalition of the Left of Movements and Ecology*], Athens: Synapsismos.

Synaspismos (2013) *Απόφαση τουδιαρκούς συνεδρίουτουΣυνασπισμού τηςΑριστεράς, τωνΚινημάτων και τηςΟικολογίας* [*Decision of the standing congress of the Coalition of the Left, of Movements and Ecology*], Athens: Synapsismos.

SYRIZA (2014) *SYRIZA.* www.syriza.gr/article/SYRIZA—THE-THESSALONIKI-PROGRAMME.html.VV35umCpo5Q (accessed 16 March 2015).

SYRIZA (2015) *SYRIZA.* www.syriza.net.gr/index.php/el/campaign/mm/2015-01-02-12-00-39 (accessed 10 March 2015).

Tsipras, A. (2013), 'La alianza del sur europeo', *El País*, 22 May. https://elpais.com/elpais/2013/05/21/opinion/1369133148_741526.html (accessed 14 March 2019).

Varoufakis, Y. (2015) 'How I became an erratic Marxist', *The Guardian*, 18 February. www.theguardian.com/news/2015/feb/18/yanis-varoufakis-how-i-became-an-erratic-marxist (accessed 18 February 2015).

Varoufakis, Y. (2017) *Adults in the room*. New York: Farrar, Straus and Giroux.

Varoufakis, Y., Holland, S. & Galbraith, J. (2013) *A modest proposal for resolving the Eurozone crisis*. https://varoufakis.files.wordpress.com/2013/07/a-modest-proposal-for-resolving-the-eurozone-crisis-version-4-0-final1.pdf (accessed 20 February 2015).

Voulgaris, Y. & Nicolakopoulos, E. (eds) (2014) *2012: Ο Διπλός ΕκλογικόςΣεισμός* [*2012: the double electoral earthquake*], Athens, Themelio.

3

The changing nature of the Spanish left: an uncertain balance

Carlos Rico Motos

After decades without significant changes, in the short period from the May 2014 European elections to the June 2016 general elections, Spanish politics experienced the emergence of new political actors, new electoral dynamics and new issues on the agenda. This intense transformation has its roots in the economic crisis that started in 2008, which turned into a profound institutional crisis after 2010 that especially altered the patterns of competition between the social democratic and radical left. In this new scenario, the Spanish left has developed new discourses on the crisis in parallel with a mounting debate on Europe's response to its challenges.

When analysing Spain's politics, we must highlight its evolving nature, which means that the party system's ongoing transformation is likely to require more time and elections before becoming fully consolidated. Acknowledging this limitation, this chapter aims to synthesise the main changes in Spain's political system during the crisis, with a special focus on the leftist parties. Thus, the first section will summarise the evolution of the Spanish left since 2008. The second section will address the country's new party system after the 2015 and 2016 general elections and the patterns of interaction among its main actors. The third section will analyse the discourse, tactics and ideology of the leftist parties to shed light on the controversial nature of the newcomers. Finally, the analysis will focus on the Spanish left's attitude towards European integration.

The evolution of the Spanish left since 2008

The PSOE (Partido Socialista Obrero Español – Spanish Workers' Socialist Party) won the 2008 general election, its second consecutive victory and the sixth in the 13 general elections held since the democratic restoration. PSOE's record vote haul – almost 11.3 million – confirmed its hegemony in Spain's centre left and heralded eight uninterrupted years of Prime Minister Rodríguez Zapatero's social democratic government in a European context in which conservatism prevailed. IU (Izquierda Unida – United Left), Spain's main representative of the radical left, earned a meagre 3.7% of the votes and two parliamentary seats, becoming a weak rival for PSOE's supremacy on the left.

This scenario faded soon after the elections. The European recession that had started by mid-2008 had a dramatic impact on Spain in both economic and social terms, revealing the weaknesses of an economy based on low productivity and unskilled labour, especially in the construction industry. The burst of the housing bubble led to an escalation of unemployment from 11.2% in 2008 to 24.8% in 2012 (INE, 2017). In early 2010, the Greek debt crisis signalled the mutation of the financial crisis into a problem of sovereign debt in the Eurozone's peripheral economies (Bosco & Verney, 2012). Under European pressure to reduce the budget deficit, in May 2010 Rodríguez Zapatero decided on a U-turn over the neo-Keynesian social policies attempted since 2009.[1] In June, the government approved a reform of labour laws that introduced greater flexibility in working conditions, which was contested by the major trade unions with a general strike. Despite the social contestation, in 2011 the speculative pressures on Spain's sovereign debt led Rodríguez Zapatero to negotiate a reform of article 135 of the Spanish Constitution with the conservative PP (Partido Popular – Popular Party) in order to introduce a cap on future deficits and secure the payment of the debts acquired in the financial markets (Tremlett, 2011).

Rodríguez Zapatero's U-turn in May 2010 signalled a turning point in Spain's politics. Most of PSOE's cadres and voters were orphaned from a discourse that promised a social management of the crisis in contrast to the EU's austerity under the conservative leadership of Angela Merkel, the German chancellor. Many citizens viewed this radical change in PSOE's economic policies as a betrayal of its social democratic principles, which prompted an erosion of its popular support. Thus, after a devastating defeat in the May 2011 regional and local elections, PSOE suffered a 'collapse' in the November 2011 general election (Martín & Urquizu-Sancho, 2012), when it ended up with its worst showing since 1977, losing more than four million voters compared to 2008. In contrast, the right-wing PP secured an absolute majority, receiving 44.6% of votes, and Mariano Rajoy took control of the government to implement an even harsher programme of austerity and social cuts aimed at avoiding the need to apply for a European rescue package.

The change in Spain's bipartisan dynamics has its roots in the street protest in Madrid organised by youth groups and social movements on 15 May 2011, under the motto 'real democracy now'. After the march, the protesters decided to set up camp in Puerta del Sol square on the days leading up to the local elections, which gave them a massive presence in the media and social networks. The '15-M movement', also known as the *'indignados* movement', became a decentralised phenomenon with diffuse demands ranging from universalistic goals – participatory democracy and the end of corruption and austerity measures – to more specific issues such as electoral reform, the democratisation of political parties and an end to bank bailouts (Flesher Fominaya, 2014a). These demands never crystallised in a specific document because the *indignados'* main goal was to spread a contra-hegemonic discourse against Spain's political and economic elites. In doing so, they avoided the traditional language of leftist radical parties (Colon, 2015).

The 15-M movement revealed a serious decline in citizens' trust in the political and institutional system while also introducing a debate on partisan politics as a persistent problem.[2] Beyond the economic situation, this phenomenon was a manifestation of the crisis of the consensual culture of the Spanish political transition and the institutional map designed by the elites who drove it (Sampedro & Lobera, 2014). Although most public opinion originally sympathised with 15-M, the movement's ideology was clearly tilted to the left (Likki, 2012: 6). Despite this, the *indignados* were sensitive about protecting the movement's autonomy and imbuing it with assembly-based methods, direct democracy and citizen participation (Flesher Fominaya, 2014a, 2014b). Thus, they rejected formal links with established parties or unions and avoided personal leaderships or transforming the 15-M into a party.

The lack of institutionalisation became a reason for 15-M's decline after the end of the street camps in June 2011 (Colon, 2015), but its impact had revitalised citizens' political interest and set the conditions for a subsequent transformation in Spain's politics. However, during the following months, neither the increase in political awareness nor the spread of a critical discourse against the status quo was manifested in the electoral polls. The early discrediting of Rajoy's government due to its austerity agenda, broken promises and corruption scandals did not benefit PSOE, nor was there a substantive increase in support for the other two nationwide parties, IU and the centrist UPyD (Unión Progreso y Democracia – Union, Progress and Democracy). Instead of strengthening IU as the radical leftist party closest to the 15-M movement, the main beneficiaries of the discontent with the mainstream parties were blank votes, abstentions and indecision (Orriols & Cordero, 2016: 7).

The rupture of the *status quo* came with the breakthrough of Podemos (We Can) in the May 2014 European elections. A new left-wing party created a few months before the elections with no formal structures, running an informal election campaign on social networks and with a leader – Pablo Iglesias – who was barely known except by a small part of the electorate, became the fourth Spanish political force with 1.2 million voters and five seats in the European Parliament (Gómez & Kadner, 2014). Together with a group of academics from the Complutense University of Madrid as party leaders and anti-capitalist organisations close to IU,[3] Podemos capitalised on 15-M's legacy to replace the traditional 'left vs. right' dichotomy with an ideological framework that pitted the people who were suffering from the crisis against a political and financial elite. By March 2015, this party had successfully set the political agenda, leading the polls with a discourse that criticised the Spanish Transition as an elitist agreement (Rodríguez-Teruel et al., 2016).

Hence, after the May 2015 regional and local elections, both Podemos and Ciudadanos (Citizens), a new centrist party operating country-wide and focused on liberal reforms both in the economy and the political system, became decisive actors in the formation of local and regional governments (Rodon & Hierro, 2016). The newcomers' successful breakthrough forced the traditional parties to deal with a generational boundary in which Podemos and Ciudadanos were considered representatives of the 'new politics', a modern political style associated with democratic regeneration and the opening of innovative channels for political participation and communication, as opposed to PP and PSOE, which were viewed as representatives of the 'old politics' linked to corruption and partisan arrangements (Galindo & León, 2015).

A new party system

During the last few decades, Spain's political system has been viewed as an *imperfect bipartisanship*, that is, a two-party system with PP and PSOE respectively covering the centre right and centre left spectrum, reaching parliamentary agreements with minor non-statewide parties when needed, especially the Catalan and Basque nationalists (Linz & Montero, 1999: 77). On the other hand, IU, the third nationwide party, has traditionally won between 3.7% and 10.5% of the vote, keeping an electoral base of nearly one million voters, which reached 2.6 million at its peak (Ramiro & Verge, 2013). However, both PSOE's calls for a strategic vote and the majoritarian effects of the electoral system have consistently weakened IU's parliamentary representation and ability to influence national politics. Thus, more than 80% of parliamentary seats have been traditionally held by PP and PSOE.

The elections held between the May 2014 European elections and the June 2016 general election profoundly transformed the two-party system. Although the 2015 regional and local elections showed the first signs of

Table 3.1 Combined European and Spanish general election results (in % of vote)

Election Year	PSOE	IU	Podemos*	PP	Ciudadanos	National Government or European Parl.
GE March 2008	43.8	3.7	–	39.9	–	PSOE
GE November 2011	28.7	6.9	–	44.6	–	PP
EP May 2014	23.0	10.0	7.9	26.0	3.1	EP
GE December 2015	22.0	3.6	20.6	28.7	13.9	No investiture
GE June 2016	22.6	–	21.1	33.0	13.0	PP
GE April 2019	25.7	–	14.3	16.7	15.9	–
EP May 2019	32.8	–	10.1	20.1	12.2	EP

Source: author's elaboration
Note: * Since the 2016 elections Podemos engaged in an electoral alliance with IU
(Unidos Podemos)

change (Rodon & Hierro, 2016), it was not until the December 2015 general election that a multi-party system with five nationwide actors emerged: PP, PSOE, Podemos, Ciudadanos and IU. This transformation, with PP and PSOE barely retaining 50% of the total votes, was consolidated in the June 2016 early general election (Ramiro, 2016).[4]

Focusing on the parties' spatial location (Downs, 1957), the appearance of Podemos and Ciudadanos has challenged PSOE's traditional position both in discursive and electoral terms. After monopolising the centre left for decades, PSOE's current dilemma is how to cover two different spaces: if they try a radical discourse to address the competition from Podemos there is a risk of losing their centrist voters to Ciudadanos, and vice versa (Galindo & León, 2015). In this sense, Podemos is a more dangerous competitor than IU because it benefits from the widespread discontent with traditional parties and has a powerful populist appeal. Hence, Podemos and PSOE are engaged in a competitive dynamic, since the electoral growth of the former largely depends on a weakening of the latter.[5]

In turn, the space of the radical left has changed. The rise of Podemos initially created fierce competition with IU, which suffered from major defections in its cadres, members and voters in favour of the new party. However, this trend changed in the June 2016 general election due to a coalition agreement called UP (Unidos Podemos – United We Can), aimed at maximising both parties' electoral performance as a pole to attract small green, regional and nationalistic leftist parties, as well as other left-wing

Table 3.2 Balance on the Spanish left (in % of vote)

Election Year	Cumulative vote for left-wing parties (PSOE, IU, Podemos)	Social Democracy (PSOE)	Radical Left (IU + Podemos)
GE March 2008	47.5	43.8	3.7
GE November 2011	35.6	28.7	6.9
EP May 2014	40.9	23.0	17.9
GE December 2015	46.2	22.0	24.2
GE June 2016	43.7	22.6	21.1
GE April 2019	43.0	28.7	14.3
EP May 2019	42.9	32.8	10.1

Source: author's elaboration

movements.[6] In this sense, the UP coalition gave rise to a more polarised version of the 'right vs. left' division during the electoral campaign.

Finally, there is an additional territorial cleavage that conditions the political positions within the Spanish left. The presence of nationalist parties in Catalonia and the Basque Country has generated a specific pattern of relations between the country-wide political system and these regional sub-systems. Traditionally, the dominant centre right nationalist parties, CiU (Convergencia i Unió – Convergence and Union) in Catalonia and PNV (Partido Nacionalista Vasco – Basque Nationalist Party) in the Basque Country, played a moderate role at the state level, alternately supporting PP or PSOE's socio-economic initiatives in exchange for transferring state competences to the regional level (Linz & Montero, 1999).

The crisis has substantially altered this balance. Firstly, its harsh economic and social effects in Catalonia have reinforced the calls for independence in this region (Orriols & Cordero, 2016: 8). Thus, the CiU has abandoned its traditional ambivalence and joined the ERC (Esquerra Republicana de Catalunya – Republican Left of Catalonia), a radical leftist nationalist party, in an open demand for independence and to put an end to what they claim to be Spain's unfair economic burden sharing. In addition, the rise of Podemos has substantially altered the Basque and Catalan subsystems with a discourse that recognises these territories' 'right to decide', at the same time that it defends a confederal agreement to keep them in Spain (Rodríguez-Teruel et al., 2016). Therefore, the 'centre vs. periphery' cleavage has evolved into an open debate on Spain's political nature that has divided the leftist parties. While PSOE asserts that Spain's national sovereignty cannot be divided, both Podemos and IU argue that the solution to the territorial conflict entails accepting that the country consists of several nations with a unilateral right to decide on their relationship with the rest of the state.

In addition, the territorial debate has also had effects on the parties' internal organisation. PSOE's special association with the Socialist Party of Catalonia (an autonomous party that represents PSOE in this community while at the same time considering Catalonia as a nation within the Spanish state) is a source of internal conflicts, making it difficult for this party to offer a homogeneous discourse on Spain's territorial problem.[7] In turn, Podemos's complex alliances with other nationalist leftist forces in Catalonia, Galicia and Valencia introduce a centrifugal dynamic into its organisational structure, which may end up leading this party to evolve into a confederal structure (Rodríguez-Teruel et al., 2016).

Will the new party system be based on a moderate or polarised pluralism? (Sartori, 2005). The answer to this question is uncertain due to the electoral volatility and the strife among the leftist parties, both the newcomers and the traditional players. On the one hand, there is a harsh debate within Podemos between those who want to return to its initial populist, cross-cutting strategy and those who argue that the party's natural place is on the radical left (Manetto & García de Blas, 2016). IU, in turn, is grappling with a debate among those who claim that the coalition with Podemos is a *de facto* dilution of the party into a populist experiment, and a majority headed by its current leader, Alberto Garzón, who defends the idea that UP is the best way to mobilise a 'popular front' in Spain (García de Blas, 2016). On the other hand, PSOE suffered from a dramatic crisis at the end of 2016 in relation to the party's position on supporting Rajoy in his bid for a second term as Prime Minister. In October, the party split between those arguing that an abstention was needed as a sign of institutional responsibility to break the political deadlock in Spain, and those followers of the party leader, Pedro Sánchez, who were radically opposed to PSOE allowing the PP another term in government, even if that would have meant an unprecedented third general election in less than a year (*El País*, 2016a).[8]

PSOE's internal crisis shows how the Spanish social democrats have struggled to defend moderate positions in the face of antagonistic discourse within the radical left that demonises any agreement with the PP, which is viewed as corrupt, anti-social and lacking in democratic credentials. In this sense, the parliamentary vote of no confidence that ousted Rajoy and invested Sánchez as President in June 2018 relied on a heterogeneous coalition between the leftist groups and the Catalan and Basque nationalists, whose only common point was to oust the PP from government after a judicial ruling that established the party illegal financing between 1999 and 2005. With just 85 out of 350 deputies, the new PSOE's government gained the weakest parliamentary support since 1977. It faced further uncertainty over the initial support from the Catalan secessionists and radical left groups, raising questions over Sánchez's ability to successfully manage the Catalonian secessionist crisis that had started in October 2017. Sánchez's refusal to form a coalition government with Podemos also shows the ambiguous relationship between the Spanish social democracy and the radical left that, while united over their rejection of the PP, remain deeply separated in many programmatic and strategic positions.

Discourses, tactics and ideologies

Ideologies are a disputed realm in Spanish politics that sprang from the crisis. While it is easy to classify the two traditional leftist parties, PSOE as a social democratic party and IU representing the diverse families – communists, socialists, environmentalists, feminists – within the radical left (Colon, 2015), it becomes more difficult to grasp the strategic approach taken by Podemos. During its short life, this party has shifted from an anti-capitalist manifesto in the European elections to identifying itself with Nordic social democrats in the 2015 general elections, to finally opposing 'old vs. new social democracy' in the 2016 elections (Arias Maldonado, 2016).

Podemos's ambiguous position can be understood by analysing the ideas of Ernesto Laclau and Chantal Mouffe.[9] In accordance with this background, Podemos's initial communicative strategy was clearly populist and focused on cross-cutting labels ('people', 'up vs. down') aimed at gaining a discursive hegemony. Subsequently, the difficulty of maintaining this frame led them to redefine themselves with the help of more moderate labels, such as 'social democrat', in order to continue to appeal to a large sector of society. However, as mentioned above, the strategic dispute within Podemos after the 2016 elections pits those who defend a convergence with the radical left represented by IU and other hard leftist groups, in line with the party's top leader, Pablo Iglesias, against those who argue that Podemos needs to strengthen its cross-cutting appeal to be perceived as a mass party anchored to the centre left in order to weaken PSOE's dominance, supporting the position of the secretary of strategy and campaigns, Íñigo Errejón. This dispute – tilted towards Iglesias's position in Podemos's Second Citizen Assembly (February 2017) – also reflects an ongoing debate on getting closer to the 'street, grassroots movement' versus 'playing a more institutional role' (Jones, 2016a).

Podemos's fight for meaning has subdued the abstraction of ideological labels under the force of discourses and electoral tactics more than ever. However, if we go beyond discourses to analyse the leftist parties' manifestos, we can see a clear separation between PSOE's social democracy and the orthodox socialism represented by IU. In economic terms, PSOE sees the market and private initiative not only as instruments for creating wealth but also as a source of inequality that must be addressed through the welfare state's redistributive policies (PSOE, 2016: 11, 15). However, the party's ideological disorientation becomes clear in its proposal to rectify Rodríguez Zapatero's 2011 constitutional reform in order to make deficit reduction compatible with guaranteeing public investment and the funding of the welfare state (PSOE, 2016).

Contrary to the social democratic model, IU represents a radical left in which the state must rebalance markets in order to 'democratise the economy', which leads this party to defend the state as the 'last resort employer' and introduce 'sustainable planning' in a new productive model (IU, 2015: 122–125). In turn, Podemos's position is more ambiguous. Its initial manifesto proposed a basic universal income, the nationalisation of strategic sectors, and a 'citizen audit' to decide which part of the state's public debt could be considered illegitimate and thus should not be re-paid (Podemos, 2014). However, these proposals were softened in the 2015 and 2016 general elections and evolved towards a social democratic style of neo-Keynesianism (Colon, 2015). Despite this, Podemos's high degree of state interventionism through an aggressive fiscal policy and its defence of a powerful welfare state situates the party close to IU's economic positions.[10]

However, there are differences in strategy and communication that could explain the disappointing electoral results of the UP coalition in 2016, in which they received nearly 1.2 million fewer votes than the 6.1 million that both parties, Podemos and IU, won separately in the elections of December 2015. For example, while IU does not hide its communist, socialist and anti-Francoist roots, and linked to this are policies that reject NATO and call for the establishment of a Third Spanish Republic, Podemos has tried to keep a strategy with cross-cutting appeal that rejects the classical leftist issues and rhetoric. By doing so, it has triumphed where IU has repeatedly failed: instead of using the ideological language of an 'intellectual vanguard', Podemos has presented itself as the representative of ordinary people who are 'not willing to think in terms of anti-capitalism but are open to criticisms of fraudulent bankers and corrupt politicians' (Flesher Fominaya, 2014b).

The main difference between Podemos and its competitors on the left does not lie in materialistic issues but on successfully embodying the 15-M movement's egalitarian aspirations through a political language that goes beyond socio-economic cleavages to inspire citizens with a promise to relaunch democracy on a participatory, anti-elitist basis. Thus, instead of the rigid party membership structures of PSOE and IU, Podemos uses participatory methodologies that allow every interested citizen to participate in the development of the party's electoral manifestos or in the internal election of organic and institutional candidates (Flesher Fominaya, 2014a, 2014b; Podemos, 2014). Podemos's successful appeal to citizen engagement in politics has encouraged further changes in the internal organisation of the other leftist parties. In the case of IU, this means the strengthening of those within the party who advocated loosening the party's internal structures in order to engage more effectively with other leftist groups and social movements (Ramiro & Verge, 2013). In the case of PSOE, in 2014 the party decided to allow the direct election of the party's leader by the grassroots members. At the same time, this election was separated in time from the subsequent selection of the remaining party organs and political guidelines in a federal congress, taken by delegates. Hence, during the internal crisis in October 2016, Sánchez contrasted its 'grass-roots legitimacy' against the 'party elites' who criticised his strategic decisions. In turn, Sánchez's critics argued that he was changing the party's organisational culture to imitate Podemos (Jones, 2016b).[11]

Therefore, the ideological differences within Spain's leftist parties also spread to their democratic models. While PSOE sees citizen participation as a complementation aimed at improving the bond between representatives and their constituents without altering the representative essence of democracy (PSOE, 2016: 89), Podemos and IU embraced more strongly notions of participatory democracy (Held, 2006) at the core of their political model. Coherently, both parties' electoral manifestos in 2015 and 2016 included pledges for allowing a 'recall referendum against the breach of electoral promises', the strengthening of citizens' legal initiatives, and, in broad terms, a reform of Spain's political system to make referendums and citizen participation common procedures in the country's decision-making processes.

The Spanish left and the European project

Hard Euroscepticism has never been a characteristic of Spain's partisan discourse because its parties have traditionally seen the EU as an opportunity to overcome the country's historic isolation and bring economic growth (Ruiz Jiménez & Egea de Haro, 2011: 124). Therefore, the low salience of the political debate on the European issue partially explains the pro-European attitudes among the majority of Spaniards. On the other hand, this implies that a change in the elite's consensual attitude could increase the levels of Euroscepticism (Ruiz Jiménez & Egea de Haro, 2011: 126).

The economic crisis has weakened this consensual attitude (Ramos & Cornago, 2016). While before 2008, IU was the only party that openly criticised the 'democratic deficit' in European integration and the EU's 'neoliberal' orientation, after Rodríguez Zapatero's radical policy change in May 2010 the EMU became a more contested issue (Rodríguez-Teruel et al., 2016: 14). Focusing on the leftist parties, PSOE, IU and Podemos share their criticism of the austerity policy approach that has been advocated by the European institutions under German leadership. The three parties of the left claim that the European right used the economic crisis as an excuse to set up a neoliberal agenda against the welfare state. They also share a generic call to relax deficit reduction measures and call for a review of the Stability and Growth Pact to allow a substantial increase in public investment. Likewise, the three parties agree on reforming the European Central Bank to increase its commitment to economic growth and job creation by using instruments of fiscal solidarity (IU, 2014; PSOE, 2014; Podemos, 2015).

However, there are substantial differences among the three parties regarding the EU. These differences are coherent with their transnational linkages: while PSOE is part of the Socialist & Democrats Group in the European Parliament, both Podemos and IU belong to the European United Left Group (radical left). Hence, PSOE's manifestos during the period 2014–2016 state that Rodríguez Zapatero's submission to the austerity agenda was due to the weaknesses of social democratic positions within the EU. Thus, the party demanded a change in the EU's political orientation without rejecting its institutional framework, to which Spanish social democracy decisively contributed during Felipe González's governments. In PSOE's programmatic documents, a response to the European crisis is further integration by creating a federal Europe and a deepening of the EMU to achieve fiscal and banking union (PSOE, 2016: 247–251). Furthermore, the party argued that the so-called 'democratic deficit' should be addressed through a reformist agenda aimed at strengthening the representativeness of the EU's institutional framework and by creating a genuine European *demos*: European media system, European political parties, policies such as the Erasmus programme, etc.

While rejecting PSOE's demands for such reformism, IU offered a more global critique of European integration since the Maastricht Treaty (1992) as a neoliberal project in which the EU is the 'board game for European capital' (IU, 2014: 5, 21). A European democracy, IU argues, is not possible under the current treaties and thus the solution entails 'breaking the Europe of the Euro' by abolishing its main treaties and launching a constitutional process through an assembly elected by universal suffrage (IU, 2014: 22–23). Likewise, IU advocates a 'citizen audit' to question the repayment of 'illegitimate public debt' (IU, 2014: 15; 2015: 107). Finally, its European manifesto also includes the demands for the nationalisation of strategic sectors and large productive enterprises (IU, 2014: 10).

Consistently, Podemos's approach to the European question is ambivalent (Ramos & Cornago, 2016). Throughout 2014, this party visibly allied itself with the Greek SYRIZA party as a political reference point linking itself to the southern European people's struggle to defend the sovereignty of their countries against the financial markets, German conservative hegemony and the institutions represented by the troika (García de Blas, 2015). For the first time in Spain, this approach introduced a nationalist discourse from a leftist party which called for the rescue of national sovereignty, making the criticism that it had moved to supranational institutions that lacked popular legitimacy (Eklundh, 2016: 128–129). With the aim of acting against the Brussels technocracy, Podemos converges with the IU in demanding a participatory democracy through binding referendums at EU level before taking any macroeconomic policy decisions (Podemos, 2014: 32–33).

However, in comparison to other Europhobic parties, Podemos's criticisms were not based on a new and genuine Spanish nationalism but instead a condemnation of what was seen as the EU's elitist nature (Rodríguez-Teruel et al., 2016). In this sense, Podemos's position is closer to what can be labelled 'Eurocriticism' or 'soft Euroscepticism' (Ramiro, 2016; Ramos & Cornago, 2016). In addition, to make its discourse fit the logic of electoral competition, Podemos moved in 2015 from its initial call for non-payment of 'illegitimate public debt' and the revocation of the Lisbon Treaty and all the treaties 'that have built the neoliberal and antidemocratic Europe' (Podemos, 2014: 31) to defending negotiations within the Eurozone to ease debts and deficit goals and undertake a coordinated restructuring of debt in parallel to making headway on efforts for tax harmonisation (Podemos, 2015).

Conclusion

The economic crisis that began in 2008 has deeply transformed the Spanish political system. After decades of bipartisanship, the appearance of 15-M in 2011 and Podemos and Ciudadanos in 2014 can be explained as a consequence of the disaffection with the institutions and elites that first emerged in the Transition. Thus, the new actors have revitalised citizens' political awareness at the expense of increasing the critical discourse towards the previous consensus. In the leftist camp, the new multi-party system has altered the balance between social democracy and the radical left, challenging PSOE's undisputed dominance that has existed since the 1980s. However, beyond a debate on socio-economic issues, what really characterises the new era in Spanish politics is a profound change in the styles of practicing and communicating politics.

Focusing on the EU, after Rodríguez Zapatero's radical turn in 2010, the Spain-wide consensus on the EMU was increasingly replaced by an open debate of the European project. The dominance of austerity policies during the crisis made it more difficult to defend the EMU from a leftist perspective because, for the first time since Spain joined the European club, Spanish citizens started to link the EU to cuts in the welfare state instead of its traditional traits of providing economic growth, modernisation and liberties. Hence, more than ever, debates addressing the economic challenges faced by Spain are critically linked to the European dimension. Whereas PSOE wants to reform the EU while retaining the core of its institutional framework, the radical left represented by IU wants to rebuild it. In turn, Podemos has evolved from an initial Euroscepticism towards a more ambiguous position focused on a discourse of national sovereignty versus the 'Brussels technocracy'.

To conclude, the future evolution of the Spanish left and its response to the European crisis will depend first on PSOE's ability to solve its own contradictions, which are a typical manifestation of the broader identity crisis European social democracy currently faces. Likewise, it will be fascinating to follow Podemos's internal debates regarding its future role, as its direction – either as a radical leftist force or a more moderate actor in the new multi-party system – still needs to be fully determined.

Notes

1 This economic turn led to the Real Decreto-Ley 8/2010, 20 May, which sought to reduce the public deficit by imposing an average cut of 5% on the salaries of public employees, a freeze on all pensions above the minimum level, a freeze on public construction projects, cuts in public investment, and an increase in indirect taxes, among other measures (Tremlett & Moya, 2010).

2 The European Social Survey (2013) for the period 2011–2012 shows that Spanish citizens' trust in their institutions was at its lowest level since these surveys started in 2002. This information was in line with the decline in the citizens' trust in parliament, parties and political elites revealed in the studies conducted by the Center for Sociological Research (CIS), a public research institute.

3 See Colon (2015) for a detailed account of the creation of Podemos and its initial relationship with IU through the group Izquierda Anticapitalista (Anticapitalist Left).

4 The 2016 election was forced by the parliamentary deadlock that followed the 2015 voting. The results for the Congress of Deputies were: PP 33% (137 seats), PSOE 22.6% (85 seats), Unidos Podemos 21.1% (71 seats), Ciudadanos 13% (32 seats). An absolute majority is secured with 176 seats, which means that the re-elected Prime Minister Rajoy had to negotiate with other groups to pass his legislative agenda.

5 This competitive pattern explains the lack of agreement between both parties during the negotiations to elect PSOE's candidate, Pedro Sánchez, as the new Prime Minister after the 2015 general election. The failed negotiations led to

an aggressive dispute between PSOE and Podemos in the 2016 electoral campaign, which ended with PSOE retaining its primacy on the left (Ramiro, 2016).

6 This was successful in the 2015 local elections, when newly formed grassroots leftist coalitions performed well in big cities like Madrid and Barcelona, replacing PSOE as the main leftist force and winning the mayor's office (Rondon & Hierro, 2016: 15).

7 In PSOE's 39th Federal Congress, held in June 2017, the party assumed the controversial idea of 'Spain's plurinationality' while stating that national sovereignty cannot be divided (Rodríguez-Teruel, 2017). Hence, it is not clear if this new concept means a relevant change on PSOE's territorial position or just a rhetorical strategy to converge with other leftist and nationalist forces. In any case, PSOE's support of the temporary suspension of the regional autonomy of Catalonia after the unconstitutional declaration of unilateral independence in October 2017 suggests that the party is prone to put on hold the debate on plurinationality in face of the opposition that this idea generates among a vast majority of Spaniards.

8 The internal battle led to the resignation of Sánchez and the investiture of Rajoy after a division in PSOE's parliamentary group (*El País*, 2016b). An interim board took control of the party in order to organise a federal congress by mid-2017 to renew the leadership and heal the party's profound divisions. Surprisingly, in June of 2017 Sánchez again won the internal election and returned to PSOE's leadership, imposing a 'leftist turn' in the 39th Federal Congress (Rodríguez-Teruel, 2017). The lack of integration of the party's moderate faction and the rhetorical nature of Sanchez's leftist calls makes it difficult to determine PSOE's future position at both ideological and strategic levels.

9 These post-Marxist theorists – a reference point for Podemos's top leaders – argue that social and political identities are constructed through political discourses, which allows for a continuous transformation of the space for political action well beyond the determinism of structural conditions. Thus, a political project becomes hegemonic when it is able to discursively establish the norms and meanings that set a dominant framework that guarantees the support of broad social sectors (Laclau & Mouffe, [1985] 2001).

10 In the June 2016 elections, the two parties agreed on a minimum platform with 50 measures such as the repeal of art. 135 of the Constitution, a guaranteed minimum income, an increase in pension benefits and the minimum wage, the creation of a public bank and strengthening the unions in labour negotiations. Where there was no agreement, each group was free to defend its own proposals. The platform is available at: http://podemos.info/wp-content/uploads/2016/05/acuerdo26J_final.pdf (accessed 6 June, 2017).

11 This dispute intensified during the internal competition for the party's leadership in June 2017. Sánchez triumphed with an anti-elitist discourse that confronted the purity of the grassroots members against the spurious interests of the 'aristocracy' represented by his rival, Susana Díaz. After Sánchez's return, PSOE's 39th Federal Congress introduced changes at an organic level, reinforcing the grassroots members' direct vote as opposed to the territorial leaders and party

intermediate organs, with a more representative nature (Rodríguez-Teruel, 2017).

Bibliography

Arias Maldonado, M. (2016) 'Spain election: Podemos' Ikea-style appeal to young voters', *BBC*, 11 June. www.bbc.com/news/world-europe-36506949 (accessed 25 September 2017).

Bosco, A. & Verney, S. (2012) 'Electoral epidemic: the political cost of economic crisis in southern Europe, 2010–11', *South European Society and Politics*, 17 (2): 129–154.

Colon, S. (2015) 'Podemos, the 15M indignados movement and the radical left in Spain', *New Politics*, 17 December. www.newpol.org/content/podemos-15m-indignados-movement-and-radical-left-spain (accessed 25 September 2017).

Downs, A. (1957) *An economic theory of democracy*, New York: Harper & Row.

Eklundh, E. (2016) 'El soberano fantasmático: las implicaciones políticas de la apropiación de Laclau por parte de Podemos', *Relaciones Internacionales*, 31: 111–136.

El País (2016a) 'Socialists under interim control after party chief resigns', *El País*, 3 October. www.elpais.com/elpais/2016/10/02/inenglish/1475406462_358063.html (accessed 25 September 2017).

El País (2016b) 'Rajoy becomes Spain's new PM after a 10-month stalemate', *El País*, 1 November. www.elpais.com/elpais/2016/10/28/inenglish/1477665648_836385.html?rel=mas (accessed 25 September 2017).

European Social Survey (Rounds 1–6). www.europeansocialsurvey.org/data/ (accessed 25 September 2017).

Flesher Fominaya, C. (2014a) 'Debunking spontaneity: Spain's 15.M/*indignados* as autonomous movement', *Social Movement Studies*, 14 (2): 142–163.

Flesher Fominaya, C. (2014b) 'Spain is different: Podemos and 15-M', *Open Democracy*, 29 May. www.opendemocracy.net/can-europe-make-it/cristina-flesher-fominaya/"spain-is-different"-podemos-and-15m (accessed 25 September 2017).

Galindo, J. & León, S. (2015) 'A crowded left: the reconfiguration of Spain's party system', *Policy Network*, 13 November. www.politikon.es/2015/11/16/a-crowded-left-the-reconfiguration-of-spains-party-system/ (accessed 25 September 2017).

García de Blas, E. (2015) 'Podemos: Greece's new political era will come to Spain', *El País*, 26 January. www.elpais.com/elpais/2015/01/26/inenglish/1422267821_418365.html (accessed 25 September 2017).

García de Blas, E. (2016) 'Alberto Garzón quiere "superar IU en un nuevo espacio político lo antes posible"', *El País*, 21 November. www.politica.elpais.com/politica/2016/11/21/actualidad/1479735241_008572.html (accessed 25 September 2017).

Gómez, L. & Kadner, M. (2014) 'The untamed ambition of Podemos, the surprise victor in Sunday's poll', *El País*, 26 May. www.elpais.com/elpais/2014/05/26/inenglish/1401117195_606542.html (accessed 25 September 2017).

Held, D. (2006) *Models of democracy* (3rd edn), Stanford: Stanford University Press.

INE (Instituto Nacional de Estadística) (2017) 'Encuesta de Población Activa'. www.ine.es/prensa/epa_tabla.htm (accessed 25 September 2017).

IU (Izquierda Unida) (2014) 'European Elections Manifesto'. www.izquierda-unida.es/programa_europeas2014 (accessed 25 September 2017).

IU (Izquierda Unida) (2015) 'General Elections Manifesto'. www.izquierda-unida.es/sites/default/files/doc/Programa_Completo_IU_Elecciones_Generales_20D_2015.pdf (accessed 25 September 2017).

Jones, S. (2016a) 'Battle for the heart and soul of Podemos as Spain's political deadlock continues', *The Guardian*, 17 September. www.theguardian.com/world/2016/sep/17/podemos-under-pressure-spain-political-deadlock-continues (accessed 25 September 2017).

Jones, S. (2016b) '"Spanish Socialists" week of turmoil not just down to Pedro Sánchez', *The Guardian*, 30 September. www.theguardian.com/world/2016/sep/30/spanish-socialists-week-of-turmoil-not-just-down-to-pedro-sanchez (accessed 25 September 2017).

Laclau, E. & Mouffe, C. ([1985] 2001) *Hegemony and socialist strategy* (2nd edn), London: Verso.

Likki, T. (2012) '15M revisited: a diverse movement united for change', *Zoom Politico*, 11: 1–15.

Linz, J. J. & Montero, J. R. (1999) 'The party systems of Spain: old cleavages and new challenges', Working Paper 1999/138, Madrid, Juan March Institute.

Manetto, F. & García de Blas, E. (2016) 'Podemos plays blame game after poor performance at the polls', *El País*, 28 June. www.elpais.com/elpais/2016/06/28/inenglish/1467103286_002685.html (accessed 25 September 2017).

Martín, I. & Urquizu-Sancho, I. (2012) 'The 2011 general election in Spain: the collapse of the Socialist Party', *South European Society and Politics*, 17 (2): 347–363.

Orriols, L. & Cordero, G. (2016) 'The breakdown of the Spanish two-party system: the upsurge of Podemos and Ciudadanos in the 2015 general election', *South European Society and Politics*, 21 (4): 469–492 (DOI: 10.1080/13608746.2016.1198454).

Podemos (2014) 'European Elections Manifesto'. www.es.scribd.com/document/219816012/Programa-Podemos-pdf#download&from_embed (accessed 25 September 2017).

Podemos (2015) 'General Elections Manifesto'. http://lasonrisadeunpais.es/programa/ (accessed 25 September 2017).

PSOE (2014) 'European Elections Manifesto'. www.psoe.es/media-content/2015/09/743826–000000599184.pdf (accessed 25 September 2017).

PSOE (2016) 'General Elections Manifesto'. www.psoe.es/media-content/2016/05/PSOE-Programa-Electoral-2016.pdf (accessed 25 September 2017).

Ramiro, L. (2016) 'The June 2016 Spanish elections: stabilizing party system change?', *EPERN*, 21 July. https://epern.wordpress.com/2016/07/21/the-june-2016-spanish-elections-stabilizing-party-system-change/ (accessed 25 September 2017).

Ramiro, L. & Verge, T. (2013) 'Impulse and decadence of linkage processes: evidence from the Spanish radical left', *South European Society and Politics*, 18 (1): 41–60.

Ramos, M. & Cornago, L. (2016) 'Spanish disaffection with the EU: is Podemos Eurosceptic?', *Politikon*, 29 December. http://politikon.es/2016/12/29/spanish-disaffection-with-the-eu-is-podemos-eurosceptic/ (accessed 25 September 2017).

Rodríguez-Teruel, J. (2017) '¿Qué significara el 39° Congreso Federal para el PSOE? Concentración de poder y plurinacionalidad', *Agenda Pública*, 19 June. http://agendapublica.elperiodico.com/significara-39o-congreso-federal-psoe-concentracion-poder-plurinacionalidad/ (accessed 25 September 2017).

Rodríguez-Teruel, J., Barrio, A. & Barberà, O. (2016) 'Fast and furious: Podemos' quest for power in multi-level Spain', *South European Society and Politics*, 21 (4): 561–585 (DOI: 10.1080/13608746.2016.1250397).

Rodon, T. & Hierro, M. J. (2016) 'Podemos and Ciudadanos shake up the Spanish party system: the 2015 local and regional elections', *South European Society and Politics*, 21 (3): 339–357.

Ruiz Jiménez, A. & Egea de Haro, A. (2011) 'Spain: Euroscepticism in a pro-European country?', *South European Society and Politics*, 16 (1): 105–131.

Sampedro, V. & Lobera, J. (2014) 'The Spanish 15-M movement: a consensual dissent?', *Journal of Spanish Cultural Studies*, 15 (1–2): 61–80.

Sartori, G. (2005) *Parties and party systems*, Colchester: European Consortium for Political Research.

Tremlett, G. (2011) 'Spain changes constitution to cap budget deficit', *The Guardian*, 26 August. www.theguardian.com/business/2011/aug/26/spain-constitutional-cap-deficit (accessed 25 September 2017).

Tremlett, G. & Moya, E. (2010) 'Spanish PM makes debt crisis U-turn with emergency cuts', *The Guardian*, 12 May. www.theguardian.com/business/2010/may/12/spanish-pm-debt-crisis-emergency-cuts (accessed 25 September 2017).

4

Geringonça: the Portuguese left approach to the crisis

Cláudia Toriz Ramos

Introduction

Portugal was seriously affected by the financial, economic and sovereign debt crisis. The crisis pushed the debate on European integration, notably on the European Monetary Union, into the public space. The bailout of the Portuguese state by the European institutions and the IMF in 2011 made austerity measures unavoidable and showed the other face of European integration – keywords in the public discourse switched from 'modernisation' and 'funding' to 'austerity' and 'poverty'.

Political impacts were twofold. Initially the left of centre Socialist Party (PS), which was in government at the time, was blamed for the crisis and lost public support, in favour of a centre right pro-austerity coalition. Yet, four years later, discontent had grown and the electoral results in October 2015 enabled a convergence between centre left and radical left parties for the first time in the recent history of Portuguese democracy. This enabled the PS to govern – a government often named *geringonça*, or 'contraption', initially an ironic designation that was to become an emblem of the political solution.[1] Underlying this process there was some reshaping of political attitudes and alignments, resulting from the strong socio-economic impacts of austerity, which may be changing the role of the left in southern Europe.

The structure of the left in Portugal

To understand the present-day Portuguese left, it is necessary to go back to the 1974 revolution. On 25 April 1974 Portugal exited a right-wing authoritarian dictatorship.[2] Political parties either re-emerged from clandestinity or were then created. As a reaction to the dictatorship, the majority of the parties showed a tendency towards *sinistrismo* (Tavares, 2015: 84), in other words leaning to the left. In the first general election in 1975, many of the parties adopted a left-wing stance (CNE, 2016). The establishment of the Portuguese party system thus took place within this setting. The Constitution of 1976 also adopted some socialist standpoints, though these were lessened in subsequent amendments and notably in the framework of accession to the European Communities (Assembleia da República, n.d.a; CRP, n.d.).

The Portuguese party system[3] has been characterised by its stability, and the four main parties are the same as in 1975: the CDS-PP (Centro Democrático Social-Partido Popular – Democratic and Social Centre-Popular Party), the PSD (Partido Social Democrata – Social Democratic Party), the PS (Partido Socialista – Socialist Party) and the PCP (Partido Comunista Português – Portuguese Communist Party). From 1983 onwards under a pre-electoral coalition with the PCP, the PEV (Partido Ecologista 'Os Verdes' – Ecologist Party, the Greens) has also been regularly represented in parliament. In 1999, the BE (Bloco de Esquerda – Left Bloc) entered the Portuguese parliament for the first time and has managed to win seats ever since.

Although this chapter addresses the left in Portugal, the overall political spectrum requires some explanation. Indeed, the names (and the initial party programmes) of the parties to the right provide evidence of *sinistrismo*. Back in 1975 the space of social democracy had yet to be delineated (Lobo & Magalhães, 2004: 83–101). The CDS was born as a 'centre' party, close to Christian democrat stances. The founding fathers of the PSD[4] sought to merge three tendencies (social, liberal and Christian democrat) and created an effective 'catch-all' party (Jalali, 2007: 140–149), though later on it reinforced its liberal and centre right characteristics to the detriment of the social democratic ones. The centre right picture becomes even more evident if the parties' insertion in EP groups is considered. For several years now, the CDS and the PSD have been members of the EPP (Group of the European People's Party).[5] These two parties and the PS have mostly shared a broad pro-integration position (Lobo, 2007: 77–96; Ramos & Vila Maior, 2011: 178–183).[6]

The PS was founded in 1973. After democratisation, it initially combined an openly socialist discourse with centre left policies. The former was to mobilise working-class voters and to define a space against the PCP, the latter was to win the left of centre political space in an elbow-to-elbow game with the PSD (Jalali, 2007: 150–156; Lisi, 2009, 2011: 35–71, 2015: 43–66). The PS has rotated in government with the centre right. That fact, combined with the pro-European stance, has made PS a fairly mainstream socialist party, even including 'third way' elements in its governmental practice (Lobo & Magalhães, 2004: 83–101). The PS was in government when the Portuguese application to the European Communities was put forward, the party having made this one of its flags. Ever since it has been openly pro-integration and even federalist. It became a member of the Party of European Socialists and its standpoints on European affairs are normally in line with mainstream social democratic policies. It is a member of PES and the Progressive Alliance of Socialists and Democrats (S&D) group in the European Parliament.

The PCP dates back to 1921, and throughout the dictatorship it operated clandestinely. Unlike other European communist parties, it never made major programmatic adaptations, and was a fairly orthodox communist party with a Marxist-Leninist programme supporting the USSR. This continued even after the fall of the Berlin Wall, although it faced some internal dissent and defections in the 1990s. But an outstanding characteristic of the PCP is its resilience. Electoral results have declined, but it has managed to hold on to its representation in parliament (Lisi, 2011: 115). The PCP has conducted a long-term policy of Euroscepticism and has voted against ratification of all European treaties in parliament. Except for the initial period in the aftermath of the revolution, the party has been out of government. It has therefore developed a strong opposition role, often coupled with anti-system standpoints, especially from the point of view of the system's affiliation with capitalism (Jalali, 2007: 157–164; Lisi, 2011: 35–71; March & Freire, 2012: 107–243; Lisi, 2015: 43–66).

The PEV was founded in 1982 and soon entered a pre-electoral coalition with the PCP.[7] This accounts for a lack of political autonomy and public visibility of the green left in Portugal, which is often perceived as merged with the Communist Party. Still, in parliament, the party has its own group and often stands for core green ideology causes (Lisi, 2011: 35–71; March & Freire, 2012: 107–243; Lisi, 2015: 43–66). No one exactly knows how many votes the Verdes would gather if they ran alone for the legislative elections, nor if they would win any seats. For EP elections they also run together with PCP, but no member of the party has yet been elected. The party is a member of the EGP.

The BE is a different case. It is the result of a merger in 1999 of several smaller left-wing parties and tendencies, which enabled otherwise scattered votes to come together. Electoral results proved the strategy was good and it has been represented in parliament since 1999. It has developed a strong anti-system discourse; it is often mimetic with social movements and thus adopts causes that will mobilise a lot of protest politics. The party therefore became very popular among parts of the young urban population (Lisi, 2011: 35–71; March & Freire, 2012: 107–243; Tsakatika & Lisi, 2014; Lisi, 2015: 43–66). It has also regularly elected representatives to the European Parliament, although its standpoints are opposed to mainstream European integration, the leitmotif 'another Europe is possible' often being put forward in political discourses. Both the PCP/PEV and the BE are in GUE-NGL, though only the BE is a member of PEL.

Long-term left–right[8] party competition in Portugal shows that at times, the left has won the majority of votes, if all the parties on the left are summed, but the Socialist Party has only won an absolute majority for government once, in 2005. The PSD, alone or in coalition with the CDS, has done it four times.[9] Other than those cases, governments have been more unstable, sometimes depending on post electoral coalitions, but never to the left. Therefore, there has been a clear dividing line across 'the left': the left of centre PS, often in government, and the radical left, always in the opposition. Hence, it is problematic to define common grounds for the Portuguese left (Freire, 2006; Lisi, 2011; March & Freire, 2012; Lisi, 2015).

At the same time, and although centre coalitions have happened only twice (PS with CDS in 1978, and PS with PSD in 1983) there has been an obvious continuity between the right of centre and the left of centre (Jalali, 2007: 192; Lisi, 2011: 35–71, 2015: 43–66). This is partly the result of some original ideological common grounds, partly the result of the centripetal forces exerted by alternating in government which will as a rule account for some continuity, and partly the result of European integration, where the CDS, PSD and PS have been convergent. This has even generated some amount of juxtaposition of the political programmes, with feasible policies constrained within the increasingly tight framework defined by the European treaties and in particular the EMU (Ramos, 2013: 52–55). Given the substantial neoliberal imprint of EMU, it is also possible to argue that it was the PS that was pushed rightwards.

Therefore, until recently, party competition in Portugal partially followed the inverted U pattern (Ramos & Vila Maior, 2011: 190–192), with a large pro-European convergent centre and opposing radical left-wing forces. However, the far right has been absent in the Portuguese political spectrum – there is only a minor political party (PNR, Partido Nacional Renovador) that has never won seats in parliament and has scarce public support. Episodically it has promoted campaigns that touch xenophobic themes (PNR, 2016), but Portugal, unlike other EU countries, has not been under the pressure of immigration, nor has the topic of rejection of immigrants gained much space in public debates.

What are therefore the driving factors for the Portuguese party system? Portugal has a proportional electoral system which accounts for the number of parties in parliament[10] and potential governmental instability (Pasquino, 2005; Freire et al., 2010). Some governmental coalitions have seen the day but not all of them lasted through the entire mandate. Minority governments have also often been formed, whereas absolute majorities – whether one-party or formed by pre-electoral coalitions – have happened five times. However, the left has always been divided between centre and radical left and had no tradition of governmental coalitions. Discontent with democracy has also grown in Portugal, but its expression seems to be more visible in the decreasing turnouts than in effective renovation of the party system, which remains quite stable (Freire & Magalhães, 2002; Viegas & Faria, 2007: 91–109).

The left and the crisis: the facts

The Socialist Party was in government when the crisis struck Portugal. The immediate sign of it was the state nearing bankruptcy. After years of excessive deficit, the state could no longer meet its financing necessities externally, not least because interest rates were mounting. Furthermore, the private sector was also highly indebted, which made the all economic structures of the country very fragile (Ramos, 2013: 55–56; Alexandre et al., 2016: 127–148). By early 2011 the financial situation of the Portuguese state was critical. A series of attempts to adopt programmes that would correct the financial imbalance were negotiated with the European institutions. When the fourth of these plans (República Portuguesa, 2011) was rejected in parliament, the government finally came to the conclusion that formal external intervention from the European institutions and the IMF was necessary. This was negotiated and signed on 17 May, 2011, by Prime Minister José Sócrates of the Socialist Party, who had by then already announced his resignation, though he stayed in office until the new election in July (Ramos, 2013: 57–58; Alexandre et al., 2016: 149–150). Among others, the national banking sector had exerted pressure on the Prime Minister to seek external aid (Ferreira, 2012). In subsequent years, several Portuguese private banking institutions were to collapse (Alexandre et al., 2016: 199–206).

The 2011 election was won by the PSD, which entered a post-electoral coalition with the CDS in order to make viable a government (Magalhães, 2014a: 180–202; 2014b: 125–133). Both the PSD and PS had campaigned with substantial parts of their electoral programmes actually copying the solutions put forward in the MoU previously signed with the international troika (Governo de Portugal, 2015). The CDS was not quite so obvious in its programme, but awareness of the compulsory nature of the agreement was widespread (Ramos, 2013: 58–61). On the left, voters were once again split. The Socialist Party lost 23 seats; the Communist Party gained one; and the Left Bloc, for reasons having to do with internal divides, shrank from 16 MPs to eight. The programmes of the three parties were substantially different – crucially, while the Socialist Party backed the European approach, the other two had always been against the agreement and criticised it outright (Ramos, 2013: 58).

Hence, from 2011 to 2015 the right-of-centre government led the austerity plan as designed with the external partners. While the plan was sometimes presented as successful, it was nevertheless internally painful and generated a lot of popular discontent (Portugal, 2015; Alexandre et al., 2016: 149–171). Initially, the government could count on substantial support, not least because it had been elected for that specific purpose. Yet, ever increasing taxes, cuts in social expenditure and pensions, the reduction of labour costs, starting with civil servants but spreading to other sectors (cutting down labour costs was presented as a strategy to foster national competitiveness), ever growing unemployment rates, notably among the youth, qualified youth migration, all accounted for internal difficulties and mounting dissatisfaction (Table 4.1). Besides, while the government deficit decreased, the external debt increased, raising doubts as to its sustainability (Table 4.2).

The defeated Socialist Party elected a new leader in 2011, António Seguro, who kept backing the pro-European choices of the party and as a consequence keeping opposition to the government at a relatively low profile. He was defeated in direct elections for the leadership in 2014, when António Costa was elected. Soon after, the former socialist Prime Minister, José Sócrates was arrested for questioning, on allegations of corruption, money laundering and tax evasion.[11] These were therefore troubled times for the socialists and yet they went into the 2015 election with a new leader and a programme

Table 4.1 Portuguese socio-economic indicators, 2011–2015

	2011	2012	2013	2014	2015
Unemployment rate	12.7%	15.5%	16.2%	13.9%	12.4%
Net migration (thousands)	-24.3	-37.3	-36.2	-30.1	-10.5
Growth rate of GDP (constant prices)	-1.83	-4.03	-1.6	0.91	1.46

Source: FFMS, n.d.

Table 4.2 The deficit and the debt in Portugal, 2009–2015 (%)

	2009	2010	2011	2012	2013	2014	2015
General government deficit (% GDP)	10.0	11.0	7.2	5.6	5.2	3.6	4.4
General government gross debt (% GDP)	83.7	96.2	111.4	126.2	129.0	130.0	129.0

Source: Eurostat, 2016; FFMS, n.d.

that was in many ways challenging a strict interpretation of austerity and therefore of the European treaties.

The PS's programme was against austerity and argued for a short-term solution for fostering Portuguese economic growth:

1 by augmenting families' income
2 thereby increasing the number of jobs and fighting precarious work
3 by promoting the efficient financing of Portuguese companies

On European Union governance, the programme affirmed that a 'smart' interpretation of budgetary discipline was to be adopted and advocated the use of 'flexibility' on enforcement of the Stability and Growth Pact.[12] A concern with asymmetric effects of EMU was expressed and so was the necessity to correct them. The social dimension of Europe was highlighted. Internally, the role of the state was emphasised, under the title 'a strong, smart and modern State' (PS, 2015a).

Throughout this period the BE also underwent a leadership change, after the decision of its founding leader Francisco Louçã to quit (BE, 2014). This process showed internal fractures and fuelled the emergence of some splinter groups that ran for the 2015 election. Nevertheless, from the political point of view, the party kept fairly visible in campaigning against the troika agreements and regularly argued against austerity and for public debt renegotiation. All these ideas were included in its electoral programme for 2015 (BE, 2015). The party also showed regular support for its Greek twin, SYRIZA, and affinities with Spain's Podemos. The PCP and the Greens also kept their strong anti-system voice throughout the entire period of the external intervention and rejected the MoU policies. The PCP even argued that leaving the Eurozone is something for which the Portuguese should foresee and prepare, a standpoint they included in the 2015 electoral programme (PCP, 2015a).

Results in other elections from 2011 to 2015 also show the evolution of popular attitudes towards the centre right government (Table 4.3). By 2013, the left, particularly the Socialist Party, was already recovering some of its traditional space. The election of 2015 was therefore surrounded by great expectations, not least because of other international cases where forming governments had required coalition efforts.

Nearing the election, surveys estimated that the PS might win with a tiny margin, but the coalition's resilience was also expected (Popstar, 2016). The CDS and PSD ran together as the PàF alliance (Portugal à Frente – 'Portugal Ahead'). Their governance, although painful, was perceived as reasonably successful, at least from the point of view of the fulfilment of the troika plan. By then, the virtues and hindrances of austerity policies were at the

Table 4.3 Election results for the main parties represented in the Portuguese parliament, 2009–2019 (%)

Election results*	CDS-PP	PSD	Coalition: CDS/PSD	PS	PCP/ PEV	BE	Abstention
2009 European Parliament	8.36	31.71	–	26.53	10.64	10.72	63.22
2009 National Parliament	10.43	29.11	–	36.56	7.86	9.81	40.32
2009 Local	3.18	23.67	10.05	38.87	10.0	3.06	40.97
2011 National Parliament	11.71	38.66	–	28.05	7.90	5.17	41.97
2013 Local	3.04	16.70	7.59	36.26	11.06	2.42	47.40
2014 European Parliament	–	–	27.71	31.46	12.68	4.56	66.20
2015 National Parliament	–	–	38.30	33.60	8.6	10.6	44.10
2017 Local	2.59	16.07	8.79	37.82	9.45	3.29	45.0
2019 European Parliament	6.19	21.94	–	33.38	6.88	9.82	69.27

* For local elections the results of coalitions with smaller parties were not added
Source: CNE, 2019; FFMS, n.d.

core of political debates. The PàF alliance came ahead of the PS by a small margin, but did not win an overall majority. Forming a government would imply some kind of agreement with other parties. The PS, led by António Costa, came second, the PCP slightly improved its result, as did the BE to the surprise of many.

Given their common grounds on European politics, a PSD–PS grand coalition might have looked probable. But the PS refused to enter such a coalition, and instead for the first time ever the Socialist Party negotiated a series of agreements with the PCP, the BE and the Verdes. This made viable a Socialist Party minority government, supported in parliament by the other parties of the left (Ramos, 2015). The agreements (PCP, 2015b; PEV, 2015; PS, 2015b) detailed some policy measures and implied some changes to the Socialist Party programme as it had been presented to the electors. The key question was always austerity and therefore concessions had to be made to garner the support of the radical left. In general, there was a shift favourable to labour, pensioners and social policies. There were also specific measures to undo much of what had been done by the previous government, at the level of state expenditure cuts and exceptional taxes. It may seem a 'squaring the circle' exercise, given that the Socialist Party kept its pro-European integration orientation.

However, Costa has often criticised strict interpretations of the TSCG, for example affirming, 'I am ever more convinced that with the continuity of this European policy and this Pact, Europe will hardly turn its economic trajectory and hardly find a robust path for economic growth' (RTP, 2016). From the political point of view, the agreements, highly unlikely if the history and standpoints of the parties involved are considered, were made possible partly by Costa's capability of negotiating with the left. He had shown this before while Mayor of Lisbon, when he had also reached agreements with the left.

The impact of the crisis on the left

The evolution of the left in Portugal may introduce a nuance to the hypothesised losses of the social democratic left to the advantage of the radical left. In terms of electoral results, especially in 2015, although as a whole there was a reinforcement of the left, transference towards the radical left was not highly pronounced. Centrist voters who voted for the PSD or CDS in previous elections may have shown discontent by voting for the PS or even for other left-wing parties (Table 4.3). This is different from the Greek or Spanish cases (Magalhães, 2015). The Socialist Party may have benefited from the fact that social disruption was not as profound as in Greece, and therefore political radicalisation was minor.

Besides, the collaboration of the pro-European centre was more damaging for the social democratic tradition, which found itself pushed into liberal positions under EMU. Breaking away from this preserved some left-wing ideological space for the Socialist Party. The party leaders reinforced this space by often stating that it had been the right of centre that had moved further to the liberal right, thus leaving the traditional centre, with its 'social' imprint, free for the socialists.

At the same time, the crisis re-introduced a strong socio-economic focus in the political debate, therefore reinforcing the left–right axis of political alignments. Labour issues and poverty were strongly back in the daily debate, in a sort of post-post materialist politics (Ramos & EU-Asia Institute, 2015; Santos, 2016: 67–81). The emphasis on internal devaluation as macroeconomic strategy within the conditionality agreements and its, at least partial, lack of success may be one part of the underlying explanation for the emergence of an agreement on the left. Socio-economic problems came to the fore and the middle-class shrunk under unemployment and shorter income (Estanque, 2011: 85–86). Therefore, some voters changed their voting behaviour, which created a certain amount of dispersion in the electoral results. But the final scenario was not lack of agreement on the left in order to make a government viable, unlike in Spain.

In government, the Socialist Party kept its openly pro-European discourse, but the Prime Minister did not refrain from criticising the austerity policies and narrow budgetary aims, as inscribed in EU's guidelines. Without disagreeing with the aims, it is rather the means and the schedule for convergence in the framework of EMU that are often criticised. However, keeping within the European obligations while satisfying the agreements with the radical left is no easy task. A lot of public attention and media coverage were devoted to moments such as the preparation of the annual budget and its submission to the European Commission and the national parliament; or the debate on the possibility of sanctions being applied to Portugal in the framework of the excessive debt procedure (EC, 2016a). Nevertheless, four annual budgets have already met the European requirements and were passed by the Portuguese parliament.[13]

This is partly because, unlike in the past, the radical left softened its anti-system discourse and cooperated with the government. The success of this new balance is yet to be proven and Portugal's Achilles heel is still there: economic structural imbalances coupled with excessive state expenditure, problems of excessive public and private debt, a fragile productive sector tied to weaknesses in the banking sector (Portugal, 2015; Alexandre et al., 2016: 173–206). As a whole, the problem was not overcome with the measures to face the crisis as defined in the MoU – namely austerity as a pathway to structural reforms. Yet, anti-austerity measures will also have to prove their validity. In 2016, the government deficit met EMU criteria, but public debt was still too high. By the end of 2017, signs of economic recovery were obvious (Eurostat, 2016; INE, 2018).

Two main circumstances favoured the 'new political deal' on the Portuguese left. First, the conditionality agreements were over and therefore there was more room for manoeuvre for whoever would be in government. The second was a change in leadership in the main left-wing parties. The whole approach became more 'political' in nature and less submissive to external dictates. International indicators on democracy signal the loss of democratic quality whenever, under external intervention, a state is limited in its autonomous decision capacity (*Economist*, 2015). Internal public perception of such facts is also damaging for those who are in government under such circumstances (Eurosondagem, 2016; Popstar, 2016).

Unlike the previous government, the new one changed substantially and did not try to perform in the EU as a 'good pupil' or an 'obeying and obliged member', at least not from the rhetorical point of view. The case of possible sanctions in 2015 under the excessive debt procedure was accompanied by extensive dialogue with the Commission. Yet, a letter addressed by the Portuguese Prime Minister resorted far more to political arguments than technical ones, notably arguing that the Portuguese reaction to austerity had so far been moderate rather than radical, and that the Portuguese bailout was often presented in the EU as a successful case.[14] Furthermore, the Portuguese PM made it public that, if sanctions were to be applied, the government would appeal to the European Court of Justice against the decision (Almeida, 2016). Of course, the transnational framework of this debate cannot be ignored – Spain was equally a possible target of sanctions, and an election was to be held there soon after the Commission issued its recommendation (EC, 2016b). The political negotiations were therefore multi-level and complex in nature.

However, a more confrontational strategy with the European institutions could have proved risky (the recent case of Greece is well known) unless it was grounded on a sound capacity of standing alone and away from the EU's support. Eventually, a more consistent strategy of dialogue and networking at the European level was developed and adopted. Ultimately also, the left-wing networks seemed to be aware that the problems the European Union faces have common grounds and thus need common solutions. In June 2016, the President of the Party of European Socialists wrote:

> Media reports of a decline of left wing socialist parties across Europe are well wide of the mark. Purely on a statistical basis, parties from the European Party of Socialists are either in power alone or in coalition in at least half of the governments in the European Union. That is not the sign of a political left in serious decline. Admittedly, right wing governments do hold the balance of power in the EU right now. But this can be an opportunity for the left as they are making a mess of things with a short-sighted obsession with austerity. (PES, 2016)

Unlike the previous Portuguese government, which had made every effort not to identify the national problem with the Greek situation and preferred instead to be associated with Ireland, Costa's government showed solidarity with Greece and a common declaration was issued.[15] Strategically, this may in the long run mean identifying the common roots of the southern European problems and eventually mobilising partners for voting together in the Council (Pinto & Morlino, 2013).

Leadership of the radical left was also a relevant factor for the parliamentary agreement leading to the creation of the *geringonça*. A wall truly fell between the PS and the PCP when the agreement was signed. The two parties have carried a history of mutual estrangement ever since the early years of the 1974 revolution. Jerónimo de Sousa, PCP's leader since 2004, was a historical member of the party, a former worker in a steel factory and a long-term MP for his party (Assembleia da República, n.d.b). In his political life he earned a reputation of being a tractable person, capable of dialoguing with his political opponents. Catarina Martins (Assembleia da República, n.d.c), the spokesperson of the BE and a sharp voice, is a new figure in Portuguese politics. A young female actress is far from being a common profile in Portuguese political leadership, but it seems those differences were also relevant in making way for the good result the party achieved in the 2015 election.

The solution which was thought would not last long has to date produced four annual state budgets and the parties have been able to keep within the terms of the parliamentary agreements without hindering European goals. It would seem that in Portugal common ground for a 'left' identity has emerged for parties as disparate as centre left and radical left. In the 2017 local elections, the results remained good for the PS (Table 4.3). As of January 2018, the Portuguese Finance Minister, Mário Centeno (Council of the European Union, 2018), has become president of the Eurogroup, without it having, so far, created major stress upon the parliamentary left 'coalition'. The results of the European Parliament election in 2019 (see Table 4.3) also show that the electors' assessment of the *geringonça* have been positive for the PS and the Left Bloc, although the PCP lost voters.

Conclusion

One of the core problems the European Union faces at present is indeed how to balance 'social Europe', as crafted in the past by Christian democrats and social democrats, with the tides of globalisation, which are undermining the original consensus upon which the Union had been founded. Furthermore, the Eurozone, with its centripetal effect based upon strict rules of monetary and economic convergence, has made internal economic and political dividing lines more evident. Since these negatively affect the lives of ordinary citizens, they will most probably react by changing their voting choices. Languages of protest and populism may prove very effective in this game. Indeed, dissatisfaction with the left of centre is even more likely than with the right of centre, given the social and redistributive nature of social democracy, particularly endangered in this process.

The choice for the democratic left seems indeed narrow, since abiding by existing rules substantially limits the role of the states, especially those carrying structural imbalances as is the Portuguese case. The pathway the

Socialist Party government chose is one that accepts the aims of further European integration, but also discusses the means and the pace adopted. To be able to do so with success it will need external allies. From this point of view, trans-European party politics is gaining relevance and the question of democratic socialism is also to be answered by the Party of European Socialists and the S&D group in the European Parliament.

From the point of view of the Socialist Party, what happened in Portugal was fairly strategic. Survival, for the PS, means avoiding the undifferentiated pro-European centre and leaning instead towards the left, where it can establish an identity distinct from that of the PSD or the CDS. Continuing to lean towards these two would mean persisting in ignoring that the political centre is undergoing a crisis. At the same time, attempts to push those two opponents to the right broadens the political space at the centre for the PS. Besides, further to the right there is no substantial protest vote, hence no partners for coalitions with the PSD and the CDS. Therefore, covering the socialist-democratic centre while mobilising the support of the radical 'left' against the 'right' is a way of guaranteeing an increased number of supporters.

This also requires the radical left to compromise. The stability of the Portuguese party system and the inherently feeble effect of new parties in changing voting choices also helped in building this strategy. As a whole, it seems that 'politics' is back and that left/right divides matter again. In Portugal, common grounds for a 'left' identity have emerged for parties as disparate as centre left and radical left.

Part of the reason for this emergence of a 'left' identity was human agency – leaders that were able to identify the opportunity and take it. Another part was the circumstances of the crisis, which pushed the politics of redistribution to the forefront. However, in the framework of supranational economic integration, redistribution is a difficult issue, because it requires transnational politics and compromising on convergence. Macroeconomic balance, if achieved, will alleviate the tensions and improve the Portuguese negotiation standpoints. Yet, this is a two chessboard game, played in between the push and pull forces of nationalism and integration (ultimately identity politics). This is the circle the socialist government will have to square. Its success, or lack of it, is likely to dictate the future of the left in Portugal.

Notes

1 The term was first used in parliament in a derogatory fashion, by Paulo Portas, the deputy prime minister of the outgoing government (DAR, 2015: 32).
2 See for example Linz & Stepan (1996: 116–129); Pinto (1995).
3 For an overview on the Portuguese party system see among others Jalali (2007); Lisi (2011, 2015); Ramos & Vila Maior (2011).

4 Initially called PPD, or Partido Popular Democrático, Democratic Popular Party.
5 The PSD was affiliated with the European Liberals until 1996.
6 Note that in the early 1990s the CDS flirted with a Eurosceptic stance.
7 Called Coligação Democrática Unitária (CDU).
8 For the conceptualisation of the left–right divide and its use for the Portuguese case, see Freire, 2006; Ferreira & Rosas, 2013. For divisions inside the broad left see March & Freire, 2012: 107–243.
9 Electoral results available from CNE (2016); FFMS (n.d.).
10 Law n° 14/79 of 16 May.
11 At time of going to press, this judicial process had not yet ended.
12 In line with the Commission's guidance document (COM(2015) 12 final provisional of 13.1.2015).
13 Lei 7-A/2016, 30.03.2016; Lei 42/2016, 28.12.2016; Lei 114/2017, 29.12.2017; Lei 71/2018, 31.12.2018.
14 The core arguments were: 'In this context, we strongly argue against the possibility of the Commission presenting a proposal to impose sanctions for the following reasons: – it would be unfair to punish a Member State that is on the right path to correct its excessive deficit and just when it is about to achieve it; – it would be counterproductive, as it would make it harder for Portugal to ensure fiscal consolidation by increasing our public expenditure and potentially causing us a major reputation damage in the international financial markets, possibly triggering negative rating actions; – it would not be understood by the Portuguese people, who have gone through a harsh economic recession and suffered "austerity" measures, and would thus risk fostering an anti-European mood. In addition to these reasons, the result of the United Kingdom referendum and the systemic implications it has and will continue to have in the European Union deserve an enhanced political consideration of the effects that such a decision could have' (República Portuguesa, 2016: 2).
15 'We, as Prime Ministers of two countries with a similar policy experience in the context of their respective adjustment programs, share the conviction that austerity-only policies are wrong and insufficient to overcome the existing challenges. Six years after the first bailout program in Europe, we can safely confirm that austerity alone is failing in its own terms and has had social and economic impact that has gone far from what was anticipated. These policies should be reviewed. … Europe has to change course. Instead of merely adjusting to self-defeating competitiveness and austerity measures, our two countries take the decision to closely cooperate at all levels, bilateral and European, to put forward a progressive program of democratic Eurozone Governance, economic revival, employment creation, centred on quality jobs, and socially just and environmentally responsible growth in Europe and in our countries. This program should be launched without further delays' (MNE, 2016: 2, 4).

Bibliography

Alexandre, F., Conraria, L. A. & Bação, P. (2016) *Crise e Castigo: Os desequilíbrios e o resgate da economia portuguesa*, Lisboa: FFMS.

Almeida, S. J. (2016) 'Costa admite que Portugal não evitará multa de Bruxelas', *Público*, 26 July. www.publico.pt/politica/noticia/costa-admite-que-portugal-nao-evitara-multa-de-bruxelas-1739480 (accessed 12 January 2017).

Assembleia da República (n.d.a) Constitutional Revisions. www.en.parlamento.pt/ConstitutionalRevisions/index.html (accessed 12 January 2017).

Assembleia da República (n.d.b) Biografias. Jerónimo de Sousa. www.parlamento.pt/DeputadoGP/Paginas/Biografia.aspx?BID=210 (accessed 12 January 2017).

Assembleia da República (n.d.c) Biografias. Catarina Martins. www.parlamento.pt/DeputadoGP/Paginas/Biografia.aspx?BID=4161 (accessed 12 January 2017).

BE (Bloco de Esquerda) (2014) 'Mesa Nacional elege Comissão Política e Comissão Permanente'. www.bloco.org/content/view/3005/40/ (accessed 12 January 2017).

BE (Bloco de Esquerda) (2015) Manifesto Eleitoral. Eleições 2015. www.bloco.org/media/manifestolegislativas2015.pdf (accessed 12 January 2017).

CNE (2016) Resultados Eleitorais. http://eleicoes.cne.pt/sel_eleicoes.cfm?m=raster (accessed 12 January 2017).

Council of the European Union (2018) 'Mário Centeno, President of the Eurogroup'. www.consilium.europa.eu/en/council-eu/eurogroup/president/ (accessed 2 February 2018).

CRP (n.d.) *Constitution of the Portuguese Republic. Seventh Revision [2005]*. www.en.parlamento.pt/Legislation/CRP/Constitution7th.pdf (accessed 12 January 2017).

DAR (2015) *Diário da Assembleia da República*. I Série', n.° 4, 11 November, 32.

EC (European Commission) (2016a) 'Economic and social affairs: policy and surveillance', Portugal. http://ec.europa.eu/economy_finance/economic_governance/sgp/deficit/countries/portugal_e n.htm (accessed 12 January 2017).

EC (European Commission) (2016b) 'Economic and social affairs: policy and surveillance', Spain. http://ec.europa.eu/economy_finance/economic_governance/sgp/deficit/countries/spain_en.htm (accessed 12 January 2017).

Economist (2015) 'Democracy Index 2014'. www.eiu.com/public/topical_report.aspx?campaignid=Democracy0115 (accessed 12 January 2017).

Estanque, E. (2011) *A Classe Média: Ascenção e Declínio*, Lisboa: FFMS and Relógio de Água.

Eurosondagem (2016) 'Barómetro Eurosondagem'. www.eurosondagem.pt/inform/barometro.htm (accessed 12 January 2017).

Eurostat (2016) 'Government Finance and EDP Statistics'. http://ec.europa.eu/eurostat/web/government-finance-statistics/statistics-illustrated (accessed 12 January 2017).

Ferreira, C. (2012) 'O dia em que Sócrates pediu a Cavaco para o salvar da troika', *Público*, 1 April. www.publico.pt/destaque/jornal//o-dia-em-que-socrates-pediu-a-cavaco-para-o-salvar-da-troika-24281909 (accessed 12 January 2017).

Ferreira, R. & Rosas, J. (2013) *Ideologias Políticas Contemporâneas*, Coimbra: Almedina.

FFMS (n.d.) 'PORDATA. Base de dados do Portugal Contemporâneo'. www.pordata.pt/en/Portugal (accessed 12 January 2017).

Freire, A. (2006) *Esquerda e Direita na Política Europeia: Portugal, Espanha e Grécia em perspectiva comparada*, Lisboa: ICS.

Freire, A. & Magalhães, P. (2002) *A abstenção eleitoral em Portugal*, Lisboa: ICS.

Freire, A., Moreira, D. & Meirinho, M. (2010) *Para uma melhoria da representação política: a reforma do sistema eleitoral*, Lisboa: Sextante Ed.

Governo de Portugal (2015) 'Documentos do programa de assistência económica e financeira'. www.portugal.gov.pt/pt/os-temas/memorandos/memorandos.aspx (accessed 12 January 2017).

INE (Instituto Nacional de Estatística) (2018) Contas Nacionais. www. ine.pt/xportal/xmain?xpid=INE&xpgid=ine_cnacionais (accessed 12 January 2017).

Jalali, C. (2007) *Partidos e democracia em Portugal. 1974–2005)*, Lisbon: ICS.

Linz, J. & Stepan, A. (1996) *Problems of democratic transition and consolidation: southern Europe, South America, and post-Communist Europe*. Baltimore: The Johns Hopkins University Press.

Lisi, M. (2009) *A arte de ser indispensável. Líder e organização no Partido socialista português*, Lisboa: ICS.

Lisi, M. (2011) *Os partidos políticos em Portugal: continuidade e transformação*, Coimbra: Almedina.

Lisi, M. (2015) *Party change, recent democracies and Portugal: comparative perspectives*, Lexington: Rowman & Littlefield.

Lobo, M. C. (2007) 'A União Europeia e os partidos políticos portugueses: da consolidação à qualidade democrática', in P. Lains & M. C. Lobo (eds) *Portugal em Mudança: 1986–2006*, Estoril: Principia, 77–96.

Lobo, M. C. & Magalhães, P. (2004) 'The Portuguese socialists and the third way', in G. Bonoli & M. Powell (eds) *Social democratic party politics in contemporary Europe*. London: Routledge, 83–101.

Magalhães, P. (2014a) 'The elections of the Great Recession in Portugal: performance voting under a blurred responsibility for the economy', *Journal of Elections, Public Opinion and Parties*, 24 (2): 180–202.

Magalhães, P. (ed.) (2014b) 'Financial crisis, austerity, and electoral politics: special issue', *Journal of Elections, Public Opinion and Parties*, 24 (2): 125–133.

Magalhães, P. (2015) 'The Portuguese missing link', Blog. www.pedro-magalhaes.org/the-portuguese-missing-link/ (accessed 12 January 2017).

March, L. & Freire, A. (2012) *A Esquerda radical em Portugal e na Europa*, Vila do Conde: Quidnovi.

MNE (Ministério dos Negócios Estrangeiros – Embaixada de Portugal na Grécia) (2016) Joint Statement of the Prime Ministers of Greece and Portugal, 11 April. www.atenas.embaixadaportugal.mne.pt/images/joint_statement.pdf (accessed 12 January 2017).

Pasquino, G. (2005) *Sistemas políticos comparados*. Cascais: Principia.

PCP (Partido Comunista Português) (2015a) Programa Eleitoral do PCP – Legislativas 2015. www.pcp.pt/programa-eleitoral-do-pcp (accessed 12 January 2017).

PCP (Partido Comunista Português) (2015b) 'Posição conjunta do PS e do PCP sobre solução política'. www.pcp.pt/sites/default/files/documentos/posicao_conjunta_pcp_ps_sobre_situacao_politica.pdf (accessed 12 January 2017).

PES (Socialists & Democrats) (2016) 'The left has solutions that can never be offered from the right'. www.pes.eu/the_left_has_solutions_that_can_never_be_offered_from_the_right (accessed 12 January 2017).

PEV (Partido Ecologista Os Verdes) (2015) 'Posição conjunta do PS e do PEV sobre solução política'. www.osverdes.pt/media/Parlamento/PosicaoConjuntaPS_PEV.pdf (accessed 12 January 2017).

Pinto, A. (1995) *The Salazar's dictatorship and European fascism: problems of interpretation*, New York: Columbia University Press.

Pinto, A. & Morlino, L. (eds) (2013) *Dealing with the legacy of authoritarianism: the 'politics of the past' in southern European democracies*, London: Routledge.

PNR (Partido Nacional Renovador) (2016) Nacionalismo Renovador. www.pnr.pt/ideario/nacionalismo-renovador/ (accessed 12 January 2017).

Popstar (2016) Polls. www.popstar.pt/sondagens.php (accessed 12 January 2017).

Portugal, P. (2015) *The Portuguese economic crisis: policies and outcomes.* Gütersloh: Bertelsmann Stiftung. www.social-inclusion-monitor.eu/uploads/tx_itao_download/policy_brief_The_Portuguese_Economic_Crisis_2015.pdf (accessed 12 January 2017).

PS (Partido Socialista) (2015a) 'Posição conjunta do PS e do BE sobre solução política'. www.ps.pt/2015/11/10/posicao-conjunta-do-ps-e-do-be-sobre-solucao-politica/ (accessed 12 January 2017).

PS (Partido Socialista) (2015b) 'Programa eleitoral do Partido Socialista. Eleições legislativas de 2015'. www.ps.pt/2016/06/09/programa-eleitoral/ (accessed 12 January 2017).

Ramos, C. (2013) 'Going further peripheral? Portugal, democracy and the crisis', in L. Rye (ed.), *Distant voices: ideas of democracy and the Eurozone crisis*, Oslo/Trondheim: Akademika Pub, 51–74.

Ramos, C. (2015) 'After (?) the crisis: representative democracy and the party system in Portugal'. Paper presented to UACES: 45th Annual Conference, 7–9 September, Bilbao.

EU-Asia Institute (Ramos, C. & 2015) 'Post-post-materialist politics in Portugal: the left is back!'. http://notepad.ideasoneurope.eu/2015/12/08/post-post-materialist-politics-portugal-left-back/ (accessed 12 January 2017).

Ramos, C. & Vila Maior, P. (2011) 'Ideas of Europe in Portuguese political discourse', in C. Ramos (ed.) *Ideas of Europe in national political discourse*. Bologna: Il Mulino, 167–198.

República Portuguesa (2011) 'Programa de Estabilidade e Crescimento. 2011–2014'. www.parlamento.pt/OrcamentoEstado/Documents/pec/21032011-PEC2011_2014.pdf (accessed 12 January 2017).

República Portuguesa (2016) 'Carta do Primeiro-Ministro ao Presidente da Comissão Europeia e à Presidência do Conselho Da UE sobre a questão das sanções', 4 July. www.portugal.gov.pt/pt/pm/documentos/20160707-pm-carta-pres-comeur-pres-conc-ue.aspx (accessed 12 January 2017).

RTP (Rádio e Televisão de Portugal) (2016) 'António Costa insiste que não há plano B e critica regras europeias'. www.rtp.pt/noticias/politica/antonio-costa-insiste-que-nao-ha-plano-b-e-critica-regras-europeias_n933551 (accessed 12 January 2017).

Santos, B. S. (2016) 'À la gauche d'aujourd'hui et de demain', in J. L. Laville & J. L. Coraggio (eds) *Les gauches du XXIe siècle: un dialogue Nord-Sud*, Lormont: Le Bord de L'Eau, 67–81.

Tavares, R. (2015) *Esquerda e Direita: Guia Histórico para o Século XXI*, Lisboa: Tinta da China.

Tsakatika, M. & Lisi, M. (eds) (2014) *Transformations of the radical left in southern Europe: bringing society back in*, London: Routledge.

Viegas, J. M. & Faria, S. (2007) 'A abstenção eleitoral em Portugal: uma perspectiva comparada', in A. Freire, P. Magalhães & M. Lobo (eds) *Eleições e cultura política*, Lisboa: ICS, 91–109.

5

'Frankfurt's way or Labour's way': the Irish left and the crisis

Michael Holmes

Introduction

The Republic of Ireland was one of the countries worst hit by the global financial crisis and the ensuing Eurozone crisis. It was the first EU country to go into recession and the first to require a bailout, it was effectively under the control of the troika and endured austerity measures for several years. Even though the country officially emerged from bailout conditions at the end of 2013, and recorded the highest rate of growth among EU member states in subsequent years, the social costs still weighed heavily on the population and created a greatly changed political context.

During the Irish election campaign in 2011, the leader of the Labour Party, Éamon Gilmore, declared that Irish people faced a choice between 'Frankfurt's way or Labour's way' (Gilmore, 2011). In the short term, this contributed to Labour having one of the best election results in their history. But five years later, after going into government, Labour plunged to one of its worst ever defeats. Similarly, the small Green Party was almost wiped out in the 2011 election after being in coalition. Meanwhile, the various radical left parties have steadily gained support.

This chapter argues that the left has expanded significantly, but has done so in a fragmented way that will be difficult to sustain. And Europe has become an important line of division between the centre left and the radical left. The chapter begins with an overview of the crisis in Ireland. The focus will then be on the programmatic and political responses of the Irish left. The crisis created an opportunity for the left, but there was no consistent left-wing response, and one of the major sources of disagreement among left parties is European integration. Finally, the chapter will evaluate the Irish left in terms of votes, office and policies.

Table 5.1 summarises Irish left-wing parties and their European alliances during the crisis period. There are three parties that can be considered

Table 5.1 Left-wing parties in the Dáil, 2008–2017

	European federation	EP group	Ideology
Labour Party	PES	S&D	centre-left/social democrat
Social Democrats	none	n/a [a]	centre-left/social democrat
Green Party	EGP	G/EFA	centre-left/green
Socialist Party	none	GUE/NGL	radical left/socialist
People Before Profit Alliance	none	n/a [a]	radical left/socialist
Independents 4 Change	none	n/a [a]	radical left/independent
Sinn Féin	none	GUE/NGL	radical left/nationalist

Source: author's elaboration

Notes: [a] party has not held an EP seat, and so has not had to affiliate to an EP group

centre left. The dominant party for many years was the Labour Party, from the social democratic family. A rival Social Democrats party was founded in 2015, and there is also a Green Party. Further left, four main groups held seats in the Dáil (the Irish parliament) during the crisis. Two have their roots in Trotskyism,[1] the Socialist Party and the People Before Profit Alliance (PBPA). And in 2014, a group of left-wing MPs formed Independents 4 Change.

The fourth and most difficult to define is Sinn Féin. The party began life in the early twentieth century as a nationalist party. After independence in 1922, the party became marginalised and effectively the political front for the paramilitary Irish Republican Army (IRA). Overlooking many splits and turns, from the mid-1980s the movement began to pursue a more political path (see de Bréadún, 2015; Patterson, 2015), and with the peace process in Northern Ireland, the IRA has faded into the background and Sinn Féin has gone from strength to strength – both in Northern Ireland and in the Republic. It retains its nationalist identity, but also advocates left-wing positions.

The crisis in Ireland

Ireland was particularly vulnerable to the crisis that erupted in 2008. From the mid-1990s, the country had experienced the 'Celtic Tiger' boom, and from 1994 to 2000 average annual growth exceeded 9%. This was based on a very neoliberal model of economic development, with strong inward FDI (foreign direct investment) flows and generous tax concessions for corporations. O'Toole described Ireland as the 'state that is perhaps more closely allied than any other democracy with the interests of global trans-national corporations' (2016), and Ireland became arguably 'the most globalised nation in the western world' (Ernst & Young, 2013).

Ireland's economic vulnerability was exacerbated by government policy in the 2000s. To try to sustain high growth rates, a Fianna Fáil–Green coalition introduced new tax concessions for the construction industry. This kept growth rates close to 6%, but it also led to a huge surge in property prices and a building boom. Even before the onset of the crisis there were concerns about an 'increasingly reckless banking culture' (Coulter, 2015: 6) with 'excessive and foolhardy lending to the property development sector' (Ó Riain, 2014: 110). Ireland became 'something of the wild west of European finance' (Lavery & O'Brien, 2005).

When the financial crisis began, it became clear that Irish banks were grossly over-exposed. On 30 September 2008, the government guaranteed deposits in the six largest banks to try to stave off collapse. However, the state lacked sufficient resources to carry this out within Eurozone borrowing constraints. In November 2010, the government had to call for EU assistance, resulting in a bailout of €64 billion, the imposition of a strict austerity regime and the effective suspension of Irish economic sovereignty, with major decisions being subject to the imprimatur of the EU-ECB-IMF troika.

The socio-economic consequences were severe. Unemployment soared to almost 15% (OECD, 2014), with particularly harsh problems of youth and long-term unemployment (CSO, 2013), and these figures would have been worse were it not for the traditional Irish safety valve of emigration (Gilmartin, 2017: 195). Disposable incomes fell by about 10%, and income inequality increased (OECD, 2014). Deep cuts were made in public sector expenditure, with for example a 9% fall in health spending (Nolan et al., 2014: 1), and a range of new taxes was introduced.

The responses of the left

The responses of the left can be considered from two perspectives. First, there is the programmatic issue – did they interpret the crisis as a domestic political failure or as a broader systemic collapse of capitalism? Second, there is the political dimension – how did they respond to the crisis in terms of electoral and governmental strategies?

Initially, the programmatic reactions were quite similar. The left was uniformly critical of Fianna Fáil. Labour stated that the crisis was 'a result of the mismanagement of the economy by Fianna Fáil' (Labour Party, 2011), with Ruairí Quinn accusing them of having 'betrayed the Republic' (Dáil

Debates, 15 December 2010), while Sinn Féin declared 'this crisis was "made in Ireland". It was created by the corrupt culture endemic in our financial system and encouraged by successive Fianna Fáil governments out of their love affair with greedy property developers' (Morgan, 2009a). The left parties also agreed on the 'failure of regulation in this country' (Ruairí Quinn, Dáil Debates, 30 September 2008). Even the Green Party – which had of course been in government at this time – argued that the Irish economy had been 'damaged by reckless financial policies, lax regulation and a failed political system' (Green Party, 2011: 3).

The Socialist Party and PBPA were more explicitly critical of capitalism. The PBPA's Richard Boyd Barrett pointed to 'the failed neoliberal policies which have caused the recent economic crisis' (PBPA, 2009), while the Socialist Party declared 'it was the capitalist profiteering that the EU pushed that caused this unprecedented crisis' (2009). But centre left parties made similar points about the neoliberal economic model, with, for example, Labour's Michael D. Higgins declaring 'a model has failed' (Dáil Debates, 30 September 2008).

Initially, all the left-wing parties were also critical of the austerity pro-gramme. There was talk about renegotiating the bailout to require bondhold-ers to bear some or all of the losses; stronger regulation of the banking sector; and a strategy to promote investment. However, when it came to how alternative policies could be implemented, the consensus dissipated. A key issue was whether or not to work within the confines of the bailout.

This came to a head when the Green Party pulled out of the coalition and precipitated an election in 2011. The radical left parties[2] maintained outright opposition to the bailout programme, and initially Labour seemed to do the same. Its manifesto criticised 'excessive austerity, which will put growth and job creation at risk. Labour is proposing a strategy that will maximise investment and growth' (Labour Party, 2011: 12). Indeed, this was when Gilmore made his 'Frankfurt's way or Labour's way' speech and specifically argued against 'more taxes, more cuts, high unemployment and no recovery' (Gilmore, 2011). He stated 'Labour's view is clear. This is a bad deal for Ireland. Because it is a bad deal for Ireland, we will vote against it here and, in the forthcoming election, we will seek a mandate to renegotiate it' (Dáil Debates, 15 December 2010).

But the key word is renegotiation rather than rejection. As Fianna Fáil and the Greens suffered a serious defeat, Labour surged to its second best result in terms of votes, and best in seats (see Table 5.2). But it was still only second behind Fine Gael, and chose to form a coalition with them, thereby accepting the path set by the troika. Gilmore argued 'we had a duty to put the country first. To address the crisis, to get out of the bailout, to

Table 5.2 Result of the Republic of Ireland general election, 25 February 2011

	Votes (%)	+/– since 2007 (%)	Seats	+/– since 2007
Fine Gael	36.1	+8.8	76	+25
Labour	19.4	+9.3	37	+17
Fianna Fáil	17.4	–24.1	20	–58
Sinn Féin	9.9	+3.0	14	+10
United Left	2.7	+1.6	5	+5
Green Party	1.8	–2.8	0	–6
Independents	12.3	+7.1	14	+9

Source: Gallagher, 2011: 145

reverse the loss of employment, to get the economy to recover, and to do so in as fair and just a manner as humanly possible' (Labour Party, 2014a). The FG–Labour coalition did manage some limited alterations – a reduction in the interest rate on the bailout loans and the extension of some loan maturities. But 'talk of the "burning" of bondholders and a renegotiation of the bailout deal quickly went nowhere' (Murphy, 2016: 7). In the words of Ajay Chopra, the IMF member of the troika, 'the fundamental structures remained' (Oireachtas, 2016: 351).

This exposed Labour to criticism from the radical left, which had also done well in the election. Sinn Féin won ten additional seats, and United Left won five. Support for Labour soon declined dramatically, and the 2014 European elections were a disaster for the party (see Table 5.3).[3] Their vote fell to just over 5%, and the party lost all three of its seats. Indeed, one of the three MEPs elected for Labour in 2009, Nessa Childers, had resigned from the party in 2013, stating, 'I no longer want to support a government that is actually hurting people' (RTE, 2013). To rub salt into Labour's wounds, Childers stood again in 2014 as an independent candidate, retained her seat, and ended up sitting with the Socialists and Democrats group (Holmes, 2016). Sinn Féin were the big winners in the election, gaining over 8% and winning three seats.[4]

An immediate consequence for Labour was the resignation of Gilmore as party leader, with Joan Burton succeeding him. But the party did not recover, and crashed to its third worst result in the 2016 election (see Table 5.4). While Burton might have claimed that 'Ireland is firmly in recovery mode, the economy is growing again, and people are returning to work' (Labour Party, 2014b), nonetheless the party found itself implementing deeply unpopular policies. Part of Labour's support stayed in the social democratic camp. A new party, the Social Democrats, launched in 2015, took three seats in the election.[5] The Greens also returned to the parliamentary scene,

Table 5.3 Result of the Republic of Ireland European election, 23 May 2014

	Votes (%)	+/− since 2009 (%)	Seats	+/− since 2009[a]
Fine Gael	22.3	−6.8	4	no change
Fianna Fáil	22.3	−1.8	1	−2
Sinn Féin	19.5	+8.3	3	+3
Labour	5.3	−8.6	0	−3
Green Party	4.9	+3.0	0	no change
Socialist Party	1.8	−0.9	0	−1
PBPA	1.4	+1.4	0	no change
Independents	19.9	+8.4	3	+2

Source: Government of Ireland, 2014
Note: [a] Total number of seats reduced from 12 to 11

Table 5.4 Result of the Republic of Ireland general election, 26 February 2016

	Votes (%)	+/− since 2011 (%)	Seats	+/− since 2011
Fine Gael	25.5	−10.6	49	−27
Fianna Fáil	24.3	+6.9	44	+25
Sinn Féin	13.8	+3.9	23	+9
Labour	6.6	−12.8	7	−30
AAA/PBPA	3.9	+1.2	6	+2
Social Democrats	3.0	+3.0	3	+3
Green Party	2.7	+0.9	2	+2
Independent Alliance	4.2	+4.2	6	+6
Independents 4 Change	1.5	+1.5	4	+4
Other independents	11.5	−1.3	13	−1

Source: Barrett, 2016: 294–299

winning two seats. But there was also further significant growth in the radical left. Sinn Féin won an additional nine seats, while both the Socialists and PBPA[6] picked up extra seats. A further radical left grouping, Independents 4 Change,[7] won four seats.

The varying electoral performances reveal a fundamental challenge for the left during the crisis. Staying in opposition and criticising the bailout and austerity proved a vote-winning strategy. But the radical left remained a very long way from power, and were largely unable to influence policy outcomes. The Labour Party capitalised on opposition in 2011 by going into government, but then had to accept the austerity programme.

Strategies of the left

The crisis threw up challenges for parties' political strategies. A clear cleavage emerged between the radical left and the centre left, particularly the Labour Party. This reached a peak in the protest movement that developed around the issue of water charges. But there were also significant differences between the various radical left parties. Notably, the left-wing nationalism of Sinn Féin is very different from the Marxist perspectives that underpin the Socialist Party and PBPA.

Despite some initial hints from Sinn Féin about 'a combined opposition lobby' (Morgan, 2008), ideas of any broad form of left-wing cooperation were ditched once Labour went into government. The relationship between Labour and the radical left deteriorated dramatically, with Gilmore describing Sinn Féin as having 'fantasy economics' and using 'bullying tactics' (Labour Party, 2014a), while his party colleague Brendan Howlin depicted Sinn Féin leader Gerry Adams as 'the Enver Hoxha of Irish political life' (Dáil Debates, 9 December 2014). In return, Adams declared, 'for God's sake, what is the point of Labour if it does not uphold equality? In cut after cut, the Labour Party, in particular, has attacked the very people it has always claimed to protect' (Dáil Debates, 9 December 2014). They accused Labour of protecting the so-called 'golden circle' of the very wealthy in Ireland (Sinn Féin, 2015).

Labour's relations with the Socialist Party and the PBPA were even more hostile.[8] Labour suggested the radical left represented 'anarchy' and 'chaos' (Howlin, Dáil Debates, 9 December 2014) and talked of taking on 'anti-democratic forces to our left' (Gilmore, in Labour Party, 2014a). The campaign against water charges exacerbated an already very bad relationship. Reform of public water provision had been on the agenda for many years, but the austerity programme brought it to a head. The Fianna Fáil–Green government initially proposed a plan to introduce water charges and water metering, and Fine Gael and Labour continued with the scheme, under strong pressure from the troika.

There were some potential positives to the scheme, not least on the grounds of environmental conservation. However, these were quickly drowned out by criticisms, particularly that the charge represented yet another new tax and that the introduction of metering was an inevitable prelude to privatisation of water services. The Right2Water campaign was established in 2014, and organised several marches and a campaign of civil disobedience.[9] Both the Socialist Party and PBPA were very influential in this campaign from the outset, as were members of the Independents 4 Change group, and Sinn Féin also became heavily involved after an initial period of hesitation.

The Labour Party became closely associated with the water charges, as it was a Labour minister, Alan Kelly, who took over responsibility for the sector in 2014.[10] Labour leader Joan Burton was also caught up in one of the most high-profile incidents associated with the campaign. When attending a constituency function, she was targeted by protesters, who blockaded her car for two hours. This led to the controversial decision to charge some of the protesters – including Paul Murphy, a Socialist Party MP – with 'false imprisonment'.[11] There is thus a very clear cleavage dividing Labour from the radical left, with the former feeling closer to its centre right rivals than it does to those on its left flank. That centrist leaning reinforces a radical left narrative that Labour is indistinguishable from the centre right.

Of course, that does not mean that the rest of the left got on happily together. There was plenty of talk about cooperation, with, for example, a PBPA commitment to 'work closely with other left and progressive organisations' (PBPA, 2009). But there was also plenty of disagreement, epitomised by the failure of the United Left Alliance to last more than a couple of years. Even though the Socialist Party and PBPA continued to work together, they were unable to form a more cohesive group. That might not have been an insurmountable problem. After all, SYRIZA and Podemos emerged from far broader groupings, so perhaps part of the art of a modern political movement is an ability to accommodate divergent strands. But there is always a problem of leadership in a loose grouping.

The big problem was Sinn Féin. During the crisis, it was clearly the biggest radical left party in Ireland. It had a wide appeal throughout the country, not just confined to urban areas. This was in part because of its strong nationalist identity, but that also created an awkward association with the IRA. That legacy continued to cause problems in terms of relations with other parties of all persuasions, not just those on the left. But certainly, other radical left parties were wary of Sinn Féin's socialist credentials. There was also a much more basic political reality. While the Irish electoral system allows a certain amount of 'friendly competition', the various left-wing parties are essentially rivals for votes and seats. A tit-for-tat example can be seen in 2014, when Sinn Féin won a European seat at the expense of the incumbent Socialist Party MEP, Paul Murphy, only for Murphy to win a Dáil by-election in which Sinn Féin were considered the strong favourites.

One analysis of the 2016 election concluded that 'the left may still be weak and divided, but it is no longer the Cinderella figure of Irish politics' (Farrell & Suiter, 2016: 288). There are still personality clashes, ideological differences and disagreements about leadership. But the combined vote for the three radical left parties grew from 8.4% in 2007 to 12.1% in 2011 and 17.9% in 2016. If the vote for Independents 4 Change is included in the latter tally, it grows to 19.4%. In terms of seats, where in 2007 the radical left could at best claim five out of the 166 seats,[12] in 2016 it won 36[13] out

Table 5.5 Votes for left-wing parties in Republic of Ireland general elections, 1981–2016 (%)

	Centre left				Radical left				Left
	Labour	Greens	Other[a]	Total	SF	SP/PBP	Other[b]	Total	Total
1981	9.9			9.9			2.1	2.1	12.0
1982a	9.1			9.1	1.0		2.3	3.3	12.4
1982b	9.4	0.2	0.4	10.0	-		3.3	3.3	13.3
1987	6.4	0.4	0.4	7.2	1.9		3.8	5.7	12.9
1989	9.5	1.5	0.6	11.6	1.2		5.0	6.2	17.8
1992	19.3	1.4		20.7	1.6		3.5	5.1	25.8
1997	10.4	2.8		13.2	2.5	0.8	2.9	6.2	19.4
2002	10.8	3.8		14.6	6.5	1.0	0.2	7.7	22.3
2007	10.1	4.7		14.8	6.9	1.1	0.1	8.1	22.9
2011	19.5	1.8		21.3	9.9	2.2	0.1	12.2	33.5
2016	6.6	2.7	3.0	12.3	13.8	3.9	1.7	19.4	31.7

Source: Coakley, 2018: 374–382
Notes: [a] Democratic Socialist Party (1982–89); Social Democrats (2016)
       [b] Workers' Party (throughout); Democratic Left (1992–97); Independents 4 Change (2016)

of 158 seats – not far from a quarter of the total, and by far the strongest radical left presence ever in the Dáil.

Indeed, in overall terms the crisis period led to the two strongest collective electoral performances by the left in Ireland. Until the 1990s, there had only been one occasion when the combined left vote had exceeded 20%.[14] But from the 1989 election onwards, the left in Ireland has been characterised by growth. Throughout the 1990s and 2000s, the combined left vote averaged around 22%, breaching the 25% mark for the first time ever in 1992, and then exceeding 30% in the two elections in the 2010s. It has also been characterised by fragmentation. In the late 1960s and the 1970s, Labour was the only left-wing party in the Dáil, but since the 1980s, various new left-wing parties have appeared. As Figure 5.1 shows, the 2016 election was the first time that the combined radical left vote exceeded that of the centre left.

But while there was clear growth in the left-wing vote, the left still faced significant obstacles. Ireland was still dominated by the centre right, and the left were distant from government. When they did go into coalitions, they were highly vulnerable to being submerged by centre right partners and then suffering an electoral backlash, as happened to the Greens in 2011 and Labour in 2016. But the strategy of trying to build support in opposition over the long term was equally hazardous, since there is something of a pattern in Ireland of new parties emerging briefly but quickly disappearing.

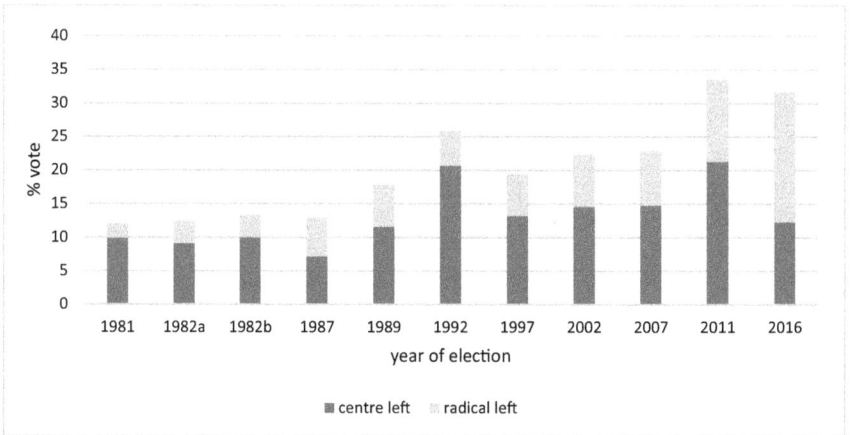

Figure 5.1 Cumulative vote for left-wing parties in the Republic of Ireland, 1981–2016
Source: author's derivation from Coakley, 2018

From that perspective, the 2016 election was interesting because of two competing narratives: a government version, where the crisis was over and Ireland was on the road back, and an opposition version, where the effects of the years of austerity were still being felt. Although the troika had said farewell, full bailout conditions had ended and the Irish economy had returned to growth, the two government parties suffered badly in the election. It was clear that even if Ireland had recovered, many people simply did not feel any effects of that recovery, and there are suggestions that it is simply repeating the policies that caused Ireland's problems in the first instance (Ó Riain, 2017).

The left and European integration

This section evaluates how the crisis affected the attitudes of the Irish left to integration, looking particularly at the 2009 Lisbon Treaty referendum,[15] the 2012 referendum on the Fiscal Compact Treaty and the 2014 European Parliament elections. Attitudes to the EU have become a major source of disagreement between parties of the left. The centre left has remained strongly pro-European, even to the extent of supporting the EU virtually as a point of principle. The radical left has a far more critical perspective, and this represents a significant obstacle to any form of wider left cooperation.

The Irish left has moved from criticism of integration towards increasing acceptance and even enthusiasm (Holmes, 2006; 2015). Most notably, while

the Labour Party led the campaign against membership in the 1972 referendum, by the time of the Treaty on European Union it had become a
supporter of the EU project. Although other left-wing parties have not
travelled as far or as fast down the same road, they show similar trajectories.
However, while the crisis period provides further evidence of some parties
gradually shifting to a more pro-European position, it also reveals cases of
renewed distrust of the EU.

The centre left is more pro-European, and this was largely unchanged
by the crisis. Labour identified itself as 'a resolutely pro-EU party committed
to the vision of a strong, social Europe' (Labour Party, 2016), and stated
that 'the Labour Party is fully committed to the European Union and to
ratification of the Lisbon Treaty' (Costello, 2009). The Green Party had
long been critical of the EU (see Bolleyer & Panke, 2015), but advocated a
Yes vote in the Lisbon II referendum – the first time they had supported an
EU referendum.[16]

However, such support dissipates on the radical left. While 'Sinn Féin
believes that Ireland's place is firmly in Europe' (Sinn Féin, 2008), the party
also insisted that the EU needed to change, stating, 'the European Union
is in crisis – an economic crisis, a social crisis and a political crisis. Poor
design, bad policies and incompetent leadership are to blame … It is time
to call a halt to the failed policies of the Brussels consensus' (Sinn Féin,
2014: 5). They criticised the Union for 'moving in an overly centralised,
privatised and militarised direction' (Adams, 2008). In similar vein, the
PBPA insisted 'People Before Profit are not "anti-Europe" – quite the contrary.
It is the way the EU is run that we object to' (PBPA, 2014), while the Socialist
Party pictured the EU as 'a Europe for the markets and corporations' which
reveals 'contempt for democracy' (Socialist Party, 2015).

All three parties called for No votes in the Lisbon II and Fiscal Treaty
referendums. They branded the Fiscal Treaty 'the Austerity Treaty' (PBPA,
2012; Sinn Féin, 2012), while in the Lisbon re-run, the Socialist Party declared,
'Lisbon is not about a better future. It's about militarism and undermining
workers' rights, public services and democratic rights' (Socialist Party, 2009).
Richard Boyd Barrett stated, 'The people should not be fooled. This is
exactly the same treaty that was rejected last year. Nothing has changed.
This Treaty will lead to the privatisation of public services and increased
militarisation of the EU' (PBPA, 2009). For Sinn Féin, Mary Lou McDonald
asserted that 'the Lisbon Treaty was a bad deal for Ireland and the EU in
2008. The government has not secured a single change to the Treaty since
then. It remains a bad deal for Ireland and the EU' (Sinn Féin, 2009).

However, there was one significant difference. There is a strong nationalist
tinge to many Sinn Féin pronouncements. The title of the party's 2014

European manifesto is revealing: *Putting Ireland first* (Sinn Féin, 2014). They talk of the 'the price of Irish sovereignty' and of how 'this hard-won sovereignty has been diluted by a number of EU referenda' (Peadar Tóibín, Dáil Debates, 5 April 2011). They criticise the accumulation of power at a supranational level and call for 'a new EU convention with an explicit mandate to identify competencies to be returned to member states' (Sinn Féin, 2014: 13).

In overall terms, the crisis has contributed to a deepening division between the centre left and radical left over the issue of Europe. Whereas Labour and the Greens were both prepared to accept the impositions of the troika and to work within the parameters laid down by the EU, the radical left explicitly rejected the EU conditions. While they still talked in terms of being pro-European, it is hard to see how their alternative models could work in the existing EU climate.

The left, the crisis and Europe

The crisis represented a huge challenge for the Irish left, both programmatically and politically. Their responses can be evaluated using Müller and Strøm's framework (1999). Their work suggested that parties face three overlapping objectives. They are vote-seekers, office-seekers and policy-seekers, and these demands can pull them in countervailing directions.

In terms of votes, the crisis has seen an unparalleled growth in support for the left in Ireland. As Kavanagh notes, 'left-leaning parties and groupings – most notably Sinn Féin –have been the main beneficiaries of the dramatic changes sweeping across the Irish political landscape since 2008' (2015: 13).

However, that success in terms of votes led to very different approaches and consequences. Labour chose political office, but having accepted the poisoned chalice of government they suffered the consequences. Labour argued that 'the often difficult but correct choices that Labour has made in government over the past three years have helped put Ireland on the road to recovery' (Costello, 2014), and that 'in the end we helped to change Frankfurt's way' (Gilmore, 2016: 295). But they lost votes, many seats and office. The reason comes back to policies. 'Labour in government implemented policies not so very different from those against which it had inveighed while in opposition' (Gallagher, 2016: 136).

Sinn Féin, the Socialist Party and the PBPA saw their vote increase, but responded with a different strategy. Rather than aim for office, they remained in opposition. The Socialists and PBPA rejected any government supporting the EU austerity agenda, insisting they 'will not give any support' to any government that includes conservative parties (United Left Alliance, 2011). Instead, they advocated extra-parliamentary protest in 'an anti-austerity, anti-coalition approach based on struggle' (United Left Alliance, 2011).

Sinn Féin were different: they clearly aspired to be in government.[17] In the 2016 election, they ruled out supporting either a Fine Gael or Fianna Fáil government, insisting, 'we are not going to go in and prop up a regressive and negative old conservative government' (Gerry Adams, quoted in *The Irish News*, 29 February 2016). Instead, they sought to portray themselves as potential leaders of an alternative government. However, Sinn Féin's former association with paramilitary groups meant that most other parties refused to consider them as suitable coalition partners (O'Malley, 2016: 257–258).

It is worth examining the European aspect in more detail. Ladrech's analysis of the Europeanisation of parties includes consideration of changes in party programmes and in patterns of party competition (Ladrech, 2012). In Ireland, the centre left remained pro-European. Labour called for stronger social policies, but also declared, 'we believe that Ireland will be strong and our interests are best served when there is a strong European Union' (Labour Party, 2016: 118). The Greens recognised 'that Ireland has benefited enormously from our membership of the European Union. Our aim is to create an ecologically sustainable, socially just and peaceful Union' (Green Party, 2016: 49). The radical left parties remained far more critical. Sinn Féin's position repeatedly stressed the need to return powers to member states and reduce the powers of supranational institutions (Sinn Féin, 2016: 30), while others talked of 'a fundamental showdown with capitalism in Europe' (AAA, 2016).

The radical left used the EU as a means of separating themselves from the centre left. They pictured the EU as an institution based on a neoliberal consensus, and branded Labour part of that consensus. They talked of an 'austerity dogma', a 'policy consensus that binds Fianna Fáil, Fine Gael and Labour to the European Commission, the European Council and the European Central Bank' (Sinn Féin, 2014: 5), and suggested 'Fianna Fáil, Fine Gael and Labour are the yes men of Europe. Whatever Brussels and Frankfurt propose they support' (Sinn Féin, 2014: 10).

So was it the left's way or Frankfurt's way? There was no significant left-wing influence on policy in Ireland, nor any evidence of a common left-wing approach to Europe. In fact, it is difficult to assert that any Irish parties really advocated a strong and coherent position on the issue of how to respond to the crisis. The Irish left had some notable electoral advances, but their policy impact was negligible. And as Ireland climbs out of the crisis, the danger for the left is that they will lose the opportunity presented to them by the crisis. Essentially, the outcome was Frankfurt's way.

Notes

1 The Socialist Party is part of the Committee for a Workers' International, while People Before Profit stems partly from the Socialist Workers' Party, affiliated to the International Socialist Tendency.

2 The Socialist Party, PBPA and the Workers' Unemployed Action Group contested the election as the United Left Alliance, which was formed in November 2010. The Alliance became defunct in 2013 after the withdrawal of WUAG in October 2012 and the Socialist Party in January 2013.

3 Labour also lost heavily in the simultaneous local elections (Murphy, 2016: 15).

4 A fourth Sinn Féin MEP was elected in Northern Ireland. The independent MEP, Luke 'Ming' Flanagan, also joined the GUE/NGL group.

5 Both Catherine Murphy and Roisín Shortall had previously been in the Labour Party – indeed, Shortall had been a junior minister in the Fine Gael–Labour coalition.

6 Standing together as the Anti-Austerity Alliance/People Before Profit Alliance.

7 The group is formally registered as a political party.

8 The Socialist Party started from members of Militant Tendency who were expelled from Labour in 1989.

9 The core principle of the campaign was that 'water is a public good, not a commodity' and it aimed to 'change the mind-set in the European Commission from a market-based approach with the focus on competition to a rights-based approach with the focus on public service' (Right2water, n.d.).

10 Initially, the minister responsible for the scheme was Fine Gael's Phil Hogan, but in 2014 he was appointed as European Commissioner.

11 In June 2017, the Circuit Court found Murphy and the others not guilty of the charges.

12 Sinn Féin four seats and one left independent, Tony Gregory.

13 Sinn Féin 23 seats, AAA-PBP 6 seats, Independents 4 Change 4 seats, left independents 3 seats (these three – Catherine Connolly, Maureen O'Sullivan and Thomas Pringle – joined a Dáil technical group with Independents 4 Change).

14 In 1948, Labour won 8.7%, the National Labour Party took 2.6% and Clann na Poblachta 13.3%. The latter were an amalgamation of socialists and republicans, not unlike today's Sinn Féin.

15 The first Treaty of Lisbon referendum was on 12 June 2008, and was defeated by 53.4% to 46.6%. After the negotiation of some guarantees relating to Irish sovereignty, the second poll on 2 October 2009 was passed by 67.1% to 32.9%.

16 Party rules required a two-thirds majority at a party conference to do so. They failed by an extremely narrow margin to secure that level of support for a Yes vote in the first Lisbon referendum, and the re-run was even closer – the 214–107 result was exactly the two-thirds required. In 2012, they again failed to reach the two-thirds figure, and so did not adopt an official position in the Fiscal Treaty referendum.

17 Indeed, since 2007 they have been in a power-sharing executive in Northern Ireland.

Bibliography

AAA (Anti-Austerity Alliance) (2016) 'What we stand for'. http://antiausterityalliance.ie/category/what-we-stand-for/ (accessed 28 February 2016).

Adams, G. (2008) 'Sinn Féin – Ireland's voice in Europe', press statement, 18 October. www.sinnfein.ie/contents/13933 (accessed 20 October 2016).

Barrett, D. (2016) 'Appendices', in M. Gallagher & M. Marsh (eds) *How Ireland voted 2016: the election that nobody won*, Basingstoke: Palgrave Macmillan, 293–312.

Bolleyer, N. & Panke, D. (2015) 'The Irish Green Party and Europe: an unhappy marriage?', in K. Hayward & M. C. Murphy (eds) *The Europeanization of party politics in Ireland, North and South*, Abingdon: Routledge, 127–142.

Coakley, J. (2018) 'Electoral data', in J. Coakley & M. Gallagher (eds) *Politics in the Republic of Ireland* (6th edn), Abingdon: Routledge, 374–382.

Costello, E. (2014) 'Emer Costello launches Dublin European election campaign', speech on 4 May. www.labour.ie/news/press/2014/05/04/emer-costello-launches-dublin-european-election-c/ (accessed 20 October 2016).

Costello, J. (2009) 'Ireland must stay fully engaged with Europe', press release, 2 September. www.labour.ie/news/press/2009/09/02/ireland-must-stay-fully-engaged-with-europe-1/ (accessed 30 October 2016).

Coulter, C. (2015) 'Ireland under austerity', in C. Coulter & A. Nagle (eds) *Ireland under austerity: neoliberal crisis, neoliberal solutions*, Manchester: Manchester University Press, 1–43.

CSO (2013) *Quarterly national household survey (Q1 2013)*, Dublin: Central Statistics Office.

De Bréadún, D. (2015) *Power play: the rise of modern Sinn Féin*, Dublin: Merrion Press.

Ernst & Young (2013) 'EY's latest globalization index released at Davos'. www.ey.com/IE/en/Newsroom/News-releases/Press-release-2013—Globalisation-report (accessed 30 August 2016).

Farrell, D. M. & Suiter, J. (2016) 'The election in context', in M. Gallagher & M. Marsh (eds) *How Ireland voted 2016: the election that nobody won*, Basingstoke: Palgrave Macmillan, 277–292.

Gallagher, M. (2011) 'Ireland's earthquake election: analysis of the results', in M. Gallagher & M. Marsh (eds) *How Ireland voted 2011: the full story of Ireland's earthquake election*, Basingstoke: Palgrave Macmillan, 139–171.

Gallagher, M. (2016) 'The results analysed: the aftershocks continue', in M. Gallagher & M. Marsh (eds) *How Ireland voted 2016: the election that nobody won*. Basingstoke: Palgrave Macmillan, 125–158.

Gilmartin, M. (2017) 'Migration patterns, experiences and consequences in an age of austerity', in E. Heffernan, J. McHale & N. Moore-Cherry (eds) *Debating austerity in Ireland: crisis, experience and recovery*, Dublin: Royal Irish Academy, 191–203.

Gilmore, É. (2011) Press conference, 3 February. www.youtube.com/watch?v=Kpr2zaXvb4M (accessed 24 February 2019).

Gilmore, É. (2016) *Inside the room: the untold story of Ireland's crisis government*, Dublin: Merrion Press.

Government of Ireland (2014) *European Parliament election results 2014*, Department of the Environment, Community and Local Government. www.housing.gov.ie/sites/default/files/migrated-files/en/Publications/LocalGovernment/Voting/FileDownLoad%2C38450%2Cen.pdf (accessed 30 October 2016).

Green Party (2011) *Renewing Ireland*, General election manifesto. http://vote.greenparty.ie/manifesto (accessed 30 October 2016).

Green Party (2016) *Think ahead, act now: progressive, practical and sustainable politics for the 32nd Dáil*. General election manifesto. https://greenparty.ie/wp-content/uploads/2016/02/Manifesto-small-online-filesize.pdf (accessed 17 March 2016).

Holmes, M. (2006) *The development of the Irish Labour Party's European policy: from opposition to support*, Lampeter: Edwin Mellen.

Holmes, M. (2015) 'The Irish Labour Party: the advantages, disadvantages and irrelevance of Europeanisation?', in Katy Hayward & Mary C. Murphy (eds) *The Europeanization of party politics in Ireland, North and South*, Abingdon: Routledge, 111–126.

Holmes, M. (2016) 'Deficits and dilemmas: the Irish Labour Party in government and policy on the EU', in E. Stetter, K. Duffek & A. Skrzypek (eds) *Delivering empowered welfare societies*, Poland: FEPS, 310–323.

Kavanagh, A. P. (2015) 'The May 2014 local and European elections in the Republic of Ireland: second order or austerity voting?' *Representation*. http://dx.doi.org/10.1080/00344893.2015.1061043 (accessed 20 October 2016)

Labour Party (2011) *One Ireland: jobs, reform, fairness*, general election manifesto. www.labour.ie/download/pdf/labour_election_manifesto_2011.pdf (accessed 30 October 2016).

Labour Party (2014a) 'Address by Eamon Gilmore to Tom Johnson summer school', press release, 21 June. www.labour.ie/news/press/2014/06/21/tanaiste-address-to-tom-johnson-summer-school/ (accessed 22 October 2016).

Labour Party (2014b) 'Labour is delivering a sustained and shared recovery', press statement by Joan Burton, 15 May. www.labour.ie/news/press/2014/05/15/labour-is-delivering-a-sustained-and-shared-recove/ (accessed 20 October 2016).

Labour Party (2016) 'Standing up for a Social Europe', policy document. www.labour.ie/download/pdf//labour_irelands_standing_up_for_a_social_europe_hr.pdf (accessed 31 January 2017).

Ladrech, R. (2012) 'Party change and Europeanisation: elements of an integrated approach', *West European Politics*, 35 (3): 574–588.

Lavery, B. & O'Brien, T. L. (2005) 'For insurance regulators, trails lead to Dublin', *New York Times*, 1 April. www.nytimes.com/2005/04/01/business/worldbusiness/for-insurance-regulators-trails-lead-to-dublin.html (accessed 30 August 2016).

Morgan, A. (2008) 'Government must use new powers to clean up banking sector and protect national interests', Sinn Féin press statement, 7 October. www.sinnfein.ie/contents/13809 (accessed 30 October 2016).

Morgan, A. (2009) 'Sinn Féin cannot support nationalisation of hopeless, poison-ous institution', press statement, 20 January. www.sinnfein.ie/contents/14808 (accessed 20 October 2016).

Müller, W. C. & Strøm, K. (1999) *Policy, office, or votes: how political parties in western Europe make hard decisions*, Cambridge: Cambridge University Press.

Murphy, G. (2016) 'The background to the election', in M. Gallagher & M. Marsh (eds) *How Ireland voted 2016: the election that nobody won*, Basingstoke: Palgrave Macmillan, 1–26.

Nolan, A., Barry, S., Burke, S. & Thomas, S. (2014) *The impact of the finan-cial crisis on the health system and health in Ireland*, Copenhagen: WHO. www.euro.who.int/__data/assets/pdf_file/0011/266384/The-impact-of-the-financial-crisis-on-the-health-system-and-health-in-Ireland.pdf?ua=1 (accessed 31 August 2016).

OECD (2014) *Society at a glance 2014: OECD social indicators*, Paris: OECD Publishing. http://dx.doi.org/10.1787/soc_glance-2014-en (accessed 31 August 2016).

Oireachtas (2016) *Report of the Joint Committee of Inquiry into the Banking Crisis*, Volume 1, Dublin: Houses of the Oireachtas. https://inquiries.oireachtas.ie/banking/ (accessed 25 January 2017).

O'Malley, E. (2016) '70 days: government formation in 2016', in M. Gallagher & M. Marsh (eds) *How Ireland voted 2016: the election that nobody won*, Basingstoke: Palgrave Macmillan, 255–276.

Ó Riain, S. (2014) *The rise and fall of Ireland's Celtic Tiger: liberalism, boom and bust*, Cambridge: Cambridge University Press.

Ó Riain, S. (2017) 'Ireland's recovery: explanation, potential and pitfalls', in E. Heffernan, J. McHale & N. Moore-Cherry (eds) *Debating austerity in Ireland: crisis, experience and recovery*, Dublin: Royal Irish Academy, 219–234.

O'Toole, F. (2016) 'We should collect Apple's €13 billion and change Ireland', *Irish Times*, 30 August. www.irishtimes.com/opinion/we-should-collect-apple-s-13-billion-and-change-ireland-1.2773136 (accessed 30 August 2016).

Patterson, H. (2015) *The politics of illusion: a political history of Sinn Féin and the IRA* (3rd edn), London: Serif.

PBPA (2009) 'Lisbon Treaty is unchanged and must be rejected', press statement. http://archive.peoplebeforeprofit.ie/node/156 (accessed 30 October 2016).

PBPA (2012) 'Richard Boyd Barrett TD debates Simon Coveney (FG) on Austerity Treaty', press release, 30 May. https://richardboydbarrett.ie/2012/05/ (accessed 2 February 2017).

PBPA (2014) *For a people's Europe: yes to democracy, no to corporate rule*, European manifesto. http://michaelpidgeon.com/manifestos/docs/pbp/PBP%20EE%20 2014.pdf (accessed 2 February 2017).

Right2water (n.d.) 'Home page' and 'About our campaign'. http://right2water.eu/ (accessed 26 January 2017).

RTE (2013) *RTE News*, 6 April. www.rte.ie/news/2013/0405/379848-nessa-childers/ (accessed 30 October 2016).

Sinn Féin (2008) 'Sinn Féin – Ireland's voice in Europe', press release, 11 October. www.sinnfein.ie/contents/13853 (accessed 16 March 2019).

Sinn Féin (2009) 'Lisbon Treaty = a bad deal', press release, 15 September. www.sinnfein.ie/contents/17351 (accessed 1 February 2017).

Sinn Féin (2012) 'Sinn Féin launches campaign against Austerity Treaty', press release, 25 April. www.sinnfein.ie/contents/23022 (accessed 1 February 2017).

Sinn Féin (2014) *Putting Ireland first*, EP manifesto. www.sinnfein.ie/files/2014/EU_Manifesto_2014_Web.pdf (accessed 4 September 2015).

Sinn Féin (2015) 'A fair recovery is possible', policy document. www.sinnfein.ie/files/2015/FairRecoveryDoc_June2015_English_web.pdf (accessed 4 October 2015).

Sinn Féin (2016) *For a fair recovery*, general election manifesto. www.sinnfein.ie/files/2016/GE2016ElectionManifesto.pdf (accessed 1 February 2017).

Socialist Party (2009) 'Defend workers' rights and public services: No to Lisbon II', campaign leaflet. http://socialistparty.ie/2009/09/socialist-party-lisbon-leaflet/ (accessed 30 October 2016).

Socialist Party (2015) 'European Union: a Europe for the markets and corporations'. http://socialistparty.ie/2015/03/european-union-a-europe-for-the-markets-and-corporations/ (accessed 2 February 2017).

United Left Alliance (2011) *Candidate pledge and programme for the 2011 general election*. http://michaelpidgeon.com/manifestos/docs/ula/United%20Left%20Alliance%20GE%202011.pdf (accessed 16 March 2019).

6

The Cypriot left and the crisis: one step forward, two steps back

Yiannos Katsourides

Introduction

This chapter examines the Cypriot left in the period since the outbreak of the global financial crisis, a period that found the major party of the Cypriot left, AKEL, in government. A brief historical perspective is introduced in order to contextualise the discussion and highlight the particularities of the left bloc in Cyprus, which is dominated by a reformist communist party (March, 2008: 4). It then proceeds to scrutinise the Cypriot left's responses to the crisis in terms of government–opposition dynamics; the impact that these responses have had on the left's electoral fortunes and ability to mobilise; and the intra-bloc relations, especially amidst a scenery of advancing political de-alignment.

The Cypriot left presents a significant dissimilarity compared to other EU countries – at least until very recently with the rise of SYRIZA. The reformist communist party AKEL (Progressive Party of the Working People) is the largest left-wing party in the country, capturing approximately one third of the popular vote. It has a margin of more than 20% over the social democrats (EDEK – United Democratic Union of the Centre) and the minor Green party. This has historically enabled AKEL to define what is 'left', side-lining other leftist voices. Moreover, AKEL governed Cyprus from 2008–2013, with EDEK a junior coalition partner for the first two years. In this period, because of the severity of the economic crisis, European integration and especially EMU were increasingly politicised.

The left government initiated a string of light austerity measures from 2011[1] that culminated in a MoU with the troika in March 2013. This provided for the first time in the EU a bail-in.[2] Although a change of government took place one month before the bail-in took effect, the harsh austerity measures in the MoU were to a large extent blamed on AKEL's administration. Hence, the right returned to government in February 2013.

The chapter focuses on the Cypriot left during the economic crisis, examining its constituent units in terms of their responses to the crisis, their strategy and tactics in the party political arena and the impact the crisis had on their electoral fortunes and ideological standing. The analysis of the left bloc is unavoidably intertwined with broader developments in the EU and the overall political system of Cyprus.

A changing political system

The Republic of Cyprus was established in 1960 after 82 years of British rule. The constitution provides for a clear separation of powers. Executive power is exercised by the president, who appoints the cabinet. The president is not accountable to parliament, which plays a secondary role within the political system (Ker-Lindsay, 2008: 107). Cyprus went through a stormy 'childhood' that led to a Greek-junta-led coup against the elected President Makarios on 15 July 1974, followed by a Turkish invasion five days later. Cyprus is divided to this day and the unresolved Cyprus problem remains an open wound (Ker-Lindsay, 2011).

Cypriot politics has historically centred on the powerful left–right dimension. This was shaped in the 1940s, which emphasised socio-economic issues (Christophorou, 2006), but also accommodated the various positions on the Cyprus problem and issues of democracy especially in the aftermath of the 1974 events. This culminated in strong political identities. Historically, intra-party factions and new parties have rarely survived, and voter turnout has been very high; this phenomenon is best understood as a function of party identification. Moreover, there is widespread agreement that Cypriot politics embodies a corporatist and deeply 'partitocratic' form of political behaviour, with parties and their affiliated organisations, especially trade unions, exercising an all-embracing control over society (Charalambous, 2014).

Cypriot politics is marked by a peculiar consensus between social and political actors. This has essentially nullified any type of social protest.[3] This consensual culture can be attributed to two factors. First, there is a fear of re-radicalising political conflict, which is what led to the coup in 1974 and ultimately the division of the island. Second, the Code of Industrial Relations, which is based on the unofficial institution of tripartite cooperation and collective negotiations between the state, the trade unions and employers' associations, is essentially a social contract between labour and capital and creates a historic compromise (Sparsis, 1998). Cyprus's preparation for EU entry, which took place in 2004, along with an improving standard of living, further enhanced the consensual character of politics (Katsourides, 2003).

The strong presidential system in Cyprus means that party competition bows to the paramount logic of forming alliances for electing presidents (Ker-Lindsay, 2008). In this regard, all parties in Cyprus have been engaged in complex cycles of cooperation and conflict. Alliances were always formed based on power sharing but were justified by party positions on the Cyprus problem. However, these alliances, as well as the overall politics of the island, are now taking place in a more fluid environment. During the second round of Cypriot presidential elections in February 2018, parties and candidates failed for the first time to form alliances. Parties' influence on citizens is now weakening and there has been widespread disenchantment with, and profound distrust in, the major social and political institutions. This has led to a weakening of electoral alignments, and increased electoral volatility – all unusual for the highly politicised Cypriot society (Christophorou, 2012; Katsourides, 2016a). The entire political system is experiencing a severe legitimacy crisis amidst a plethora of political scandals (Anastasiou, 2014). The economic crisis served to magnify and accelerate the chronic deficiencies of Cypriot politics, and arguably presented opportunities for the left.

Past and present of the Cypriot left

The core of the party system is formed by four main parties: AKEL, founded in 1926; the social democratic EDEK, founded in 1969; the centre right Democratic Party (DIKO), founded in 1976; and right-wing Democratic Rally (DISY), founded in 1976. This pattern finally began to change in the mid-1990s when, among other factors, pure proportional representation was introduced (in 1995). Although a number of new parties emerged after the change in the electoral law, only one proved durable: the Green Party (1996). Until recently, a far-right party did not exist, but the National Popular Front (ELAM) – a sister party of the fascist Greek Golden Dawn – was founded in 2008 and entered parliament in 2016.[4]

The way the party system developed in Cyprus influenced the constellation of political forces both between and within ideological blocs. The left milieu in Cyprus currently comprises three major parties: AKEL, EDEK and the Greens, whereas a far left party never existed. For a long time, the left was united and dominated by AKEL.[5] The party pioneered the establishment of the trade union movement in Cyprus and has exercised considerable influence and leadership over this movement. The party maintained strong links with the Soviet Union, and it continues to proclaim itself in its statutes as Marxist-Leninist. AKEL's organisational structure is best described as a series of concentric circles with the party at the heart of various organisations.[6] The auxiliary organisations have considerable autonomy, but take ideological and political guidance from the party (Ellinas & Katsourides, 2013).

Despite its strong electoral presence since the 1940s, AKEL remained out of direct government participation until the early 2000s. This was a result of two factors. First, the party prioritised the solution of the Cyprus problem over its long-term aims for socialism; this perspective also took into account Cyprus' position within the western alliance. Second, other political forces treated AKEL as an outsider, excluding it from executive power. The party changed aspects of its strategy in the early 1990s. It dropped its opposition to the EU in 1995 (Charalambous, 2012), it began participating in coalitions at the local level and gradually made explicit its will to participate in government. It formed a winning alliance for the presidential elections of 2003 (Katsourides, 2012), and the new strategy came to full fruition in 2008 when AKEL's leader Demetris Christofias assumed the office of the president of the Republic. This process of transformation means that ideological radicalism and class politics have subsided significantly (Katsourides, 2016b).

AKEL has not faced any significant threat from the centre left, as prior to 1969 there was no Cypriot social democratic party, and EDEK was – and remains – fairly ineffectual. The party was set up as a democratic party with the aim of uniting centre left political forces and personalities in order to provide support to the President, Archbishop Makarios, in a period of intense political turbulence.[7] Gradually it adopted a 'third world' type of socialism and developed good relationships with the Greek PASOK and various Arab socialist parties (Stamatiou, 2013). Its political discourse was defined less by its proposals on social issues and more by the Cyprus problem, on which it took a more nationalistic perspective as a means to differentiate itself from AKEL. Unable to outflank AKEL in the late 1990s it became unsuccessfully involved in a process of mergers and coalitions with minor political forces aiming to reposition itself as a European social democratic party.[8] EDEK is affiliated with a number of organisations.[9]

The party has contested all presidential elections either alone or in coalition with AKEL or DIKO. Only once, in 1998, has the party supported a DISY

Table 6.1 Electoral performance of the Cypriot left prior to the crisis (%)

Party	National 1991	National 1996	National 2001	European 2004	National 2006
AKEL	30.6	33.0	34.71	27.89	31.13
EDEK	10.9	8.1	6.51	10.79	8.91
GREEN	-	1.0	1.98	0.86	1.95

Source: author's elaboration

candidate, which proved electorally very costly. EDEK has taken part in cabinet three times: for one year in the 1998–2003 right-wing DISY administration; for a full tenure in the 2003–2008 centre right DIKO-led government; and for two years in the 2008–2013 left-wing AKEL government. The electoral support of the party was traditionally low compared both to AKEL and its European counterparts, hovering between 6–10%. Despite its small electoral presence EDEK has nevertheless shown considerable endurance.

The Cyprus Green Party was founded in 1996 with the specific aim of fighting for the protection of the environment and to raise awareness of ecology problems. The party has tried to position itself as an alternative to the mainstream parties of both the left and right. However, the party has been preoccupied with the Cyprus problem, something that took away part of its claim to be different. Although this strategy at first did not bear fruit, something seemed to change in the mid-2010s, not unrelated to the multi-faceted crisis facing Cyprus (Pegasiou, 2013). Currently, the Greens are the youngest and the smallest party within the left. The Greens have their own youth organisation, but no ties with the trade union movement.

Cooperation between all three parties has been historically uneasy with many ups and downs. Arguably they are closer on policies dealing with the economy and welfare state (despite disagreements over issues such as privatisations) than they are on the Cyprus problem. In recent years tension between them has been growing, mostly because of their divergent positions on the Cyprus problem. This found its expression in their inability to form a second-round alliance to support a joint candidate in the 2018 presidential elections. Linkage with European party families and individual parties also reveals indications of ideological identity, and all Cypriot leftist parties are attached to one of the major European party families.

AKEL holds observer status at PEL and is an active member the GUE/NGL group, with one of the party's two MEPs taking the post of group vice-president in 2014. AKEL also has good relations with many parties of the socialist party family. Historically, AKEL had close ties with the Greek Communist Party (KKE) but confrontation erupted between them over the Cyprus problem and over the reformist character of AKEL.[10] Currently, AKEL is closer to SYRIZA. EDEK is a member of the S&D group in the EP and the Party of the European Socialists. The Greens are a member of the EGP – they have not held an MEP seat – and member of the Global Greens. Unlike AKEL's very close relationship with their European counterparts, both EDEK and the Greens have had difficult relations with their respective party families. In both cases this was due to different views regarding the Cyprus problem and not any other European issue. The Cypriot parties are considered to be more hard-line with regard to the Cyprus problem than their affiliated European organisations.

The Cypriot left and the crisis

Periods of crisis bring the left face to face with important strategic questions where it has to deal with pressing conjunctural demands on the one hand and strategic goals on the other. The resulting debates have often led to deep and paralysing divisions among leftists (Spourdalakis, 2013). While the economic crisis did not fundamentally change dominant economic or political paradigms, it arguably provided a fertile environment for left parties (Bruff, 2014; March & Rommerskirchen, 2015). The left's opposition to austerity and neoliberalism relates to its strategy on the issue of government participation. Although governing within the EU implies an acknowledgment that 'the basic conditions for government participation have been established by neo-liberalism and are not easily changed', at the same time 'the left faces the challenge of using the opportunity (i.e., the economic crisis) to fight for the fulfilment of a just society' (Daiber, 2010: 7, 9).

Although the economic crisis was evident in Cyprus as early as 2009, it did not really begin to affect the country deeply until after 2011, following the haircut on the Greek loan in October 2011. The 2011–13 financial crisis in Cyprus is closely related to the deep and prolonged recession in Greece. Cypriot banks were highly exposed to the Greek debt crisis, the Cypriot economy was downgraded to junk status by international rating agencies and the country lost access to international credit markets. Cyprus's 'hypertrophic' banking system could not absorb the increase of its non-performing loans in Greece and the 'haircut' of the Greek sovereign debt (Tombazos, 2014). The Cypriot state was unable to raise liquidity from the markets to support its huge financial sector, which was eight times greater than the country's GDP, and was forced to request assistance from the EFSF (Pegasiou, 2013).

The real impact of the crisis on the people of Cyprus was not felt until March 2013, following the bail-in agreement. Given the neoliberal character of the agreement – profitable public companies and ports were privatised, there were public spending cuts, and the labour market was deregulated further – the impact of the measures dictated to Cyprus was largely one-sided, with labour bearing the brunt (Katsourides, 2016a).

Cyprus experienced considerable social dumping, not all of which is attributable to the MoU. The banking sector experienced a sharp increase in non-performing loans, from 36% midway through 2013 to 55.2% in March 2015 and to 48.5% in October 2016 despite debt write-offs and loan restructuring, second only to Greece in the EU (Cyprusprofile, 2017). At the same time, all social indices showed deterioration. Unemployment increased from 11.8% in 2012 to 16.1% in 2014 (IMF, 2015: 35), and while showing signs of a small decrease in December 2015 (13.1%) it rose again to 14.3% in December 2016 (Eurostat, 2017). The number of people at risk of poverty or social exclusion rose to 244,000 (28.9% of the total population) in 2015 (Cyprus Statistical Service, 2016). Income inequality rose from 31% in 2012 to 34.8% in 2014.[11]

Within the EU the at-risk-of-poverty or social exclusion rate has grown from 2008 to 2015 in 15 member states, the highest increases being recorded in Greece (+7.6%) and Cyprus (+5.6%) (Eurostat, 2016). Cyprus's average household available income decreased by over 16% from €20,218 in 2012 to €16,944 in 2015 (Cyprus Statistical Service, 2016). The ratio of incomes between the richest 20% and the poorest 20% of the Cypriot population increased to 5.4 in 2014 (from 4.4 in 2009), before falling slightly in 2015, back to the EU average of 5.2. The widening inequality has been caused by faster income growth among the richest. The share of total income of the richest 10% of households rose by 15% from 2006 to 2015, while the income share of the poorest 10% over the same period declined slightly (European Commission, 2017).

The economic crisis found the Cypriot left in government. AKEL's leader Christofias headed a coalition with DIKO and EDEK and with the support of the Green Party. However, the coalition did not last for long and by 2011 it was dissolved. The main reasons were the divergent approaches of the parties regarding the negotiations for the solution of the Cyprus problem and other internal politics factors. The response to the economic crisis was pivotal, as the AKEL-led government was accused of not taking timely measures. Both collaborating parties favoured a tighter fiscal policy regarding public expenses and did not exclude privatisations or at least equity swap.

Christofias's economic policies in the early stages of his administration were mildly Keynesian: public spending increased, and the privatisation of state-run enterprises was categorically ruled out. This was not a very radical position; it was rather an old social democratic approach, albeit one no longer common in the EU. The party was reluctant to introduce radical proposals, both at home and in the European domain (Katsourides, 2012). As the economic crisis emerged, the government introduced several austerity measures that caused some tension with their affiliated trade union, PEO. These measures were not extremely harsh on the working class and the population in general, compared to those that were adopted in 2012. When AKEL's last remaining coalition partner DIKO departed the government in September 2011, there was enormous pressure to adopt more austerity measures and privatisations (Panayiotou, 2014: 42). As a result of the crisis, people's concerns shifted to the economy and to the personal consequences of the crisis rather than wider politics and the Cyprus problem. By 2012 the bail-in memorandum dominated party debates. Although the 2011 legislative elections did not produce any meaningful alteration in the party system or within the left bloc (Table 6.2) they verified earlier indications

Table 6.2 Electoral performance of the Cypriot left since the start of the crisis, 2009–2019 (%)

Party	National Elections			European Elections				
	2011	2016	(+) (−)	2009	2014	(+) (−)	2019	(+) (−)
AKEL	32.7	25.7	−7.0	34.9	27.0	−7.9	27.5	+0.5
EDEK	8.9	6.2	−2.8	9.9	7.7*	−2.2*	10.6*	+2.9*
GREENS	2.2	4.8	+2.6	1.5	7.7*	+6.2*	3.3*	−4.4*

Source: author's elaboration

Note: * In the 2014 European elections EDEK and the Greens contested on a joint
platform. The combined decrease was 3.67%. In 2019 EDEK ran alone
whereas the Greens presented a joint ticket with the Citizens Alliance.

that attachment to party and ideology was declining and abstention was rising (Christophorou, 2012).

The presidential elections in 2013 brought both numerical and qualitative changes in the party system. AKEL's tenure in government proved damaging for the party. Many believed that the government's application to the troika for financial help and the measures demanded by the lenders violated fundamental party positions, for example on privatisation, social cuts or changes in automatic price indexing. Although it condemned the troika stance, the government, in the absence of alternatives, gave in to them and the party voted for the bills in parliament (House of Representatives, 2012). In the 2013 elections, AKEL, traditionally the party with the strongest organisational mechanisms and very highly disciplined voters, found itself in a situation where 25% of its constituency voted contrary to party choice. Moreover, it had no allies. DISY, under Nicos Anastasiades, returned to power after ten years in opposition.

When the European elections took place in 2014, the campaign took on the character of an indirect vote of confidence in the austerity measures. It was the first time that 'Europe' played a small part in any type of election campaign in Cyprus. A left–right divide was visible with parties of the left and centre left emphasising arguments against privatisations and opposing the seizure of private properties due to non-performing loans. Anger at the EU was at an all-time high in Cyprus following the Eurogroup's decisions. This led to a major surge in public Euroscepticism. However, this was not reflected by questioning Cyprus's participation in the EU or the Eurozone in any party manifesto. It was mostly expressed by criticism of the current direction of the EU. EDEK and the Greens, for example, called for a vague 'progressive re-direction of the EU' away from neoliberalism, emphasising that the EU 'remains the context for solving the country's and the continent's problems' (Omirou, 2014).

Although European elections are usually characterised by punishment for the incumbent, in Cyprus voters penalised the former governing party AKEL for the 2013 March bail-in. While maintaining its two seats, AKEL lost 8% of its vote share and 37,000 voters compared to the previous European elections. The party's anti-austerity message was not persuasive because the public considered AKEL as the party that had actually invited the troika to Cyprus and voted in favour of most of the Memorandum-related legislation. EDEK in a joint ticket with the Greens managed to keep its seat, though it still lost a significant part of its electorate (Table 6.2).

The 2016 national elections revealed a shift in the Cyprus party system's ideological centre of gravity. The centre right, albeit more fragmented now, increased its vote share at the expense of the left. AKEL lost 7%, 42,000 voters and three seats compared to the 2011 elections despite now being in opposition. EDEK lost 2.75%, two seats and 14,381 voters. The Greens on the other hand were among the winners. They doubled their electoral share as well as their representation in the House, electing two deputies. In 2011, the combined left polled approximately 44%, whereas in 2016 their overall share dropped to approximately 37%. This could be related to the inability of the left to provide feasible alternatives for overcoming the economic crisis, instead reinforcing conservative reactions among the electorate.

As mentioned above, European issues have never been very significant in national or European elections. This was mostly due to AKEL's change of position in 1995 when it significantly de-radicalised its policies (Charalambous, 2012; Katsourides, 2014). The ambition to govern further solidified party positioning on European integration, and by 2008 when AKEL won power any radicalism on EU issues was greatly reduced in an effort to defuse their salience in political debates maintaining its anti-neoliberal stance (Katsourides, 2014).

Unavoidably, the economic crisis brought the EU issue onto the party's agenda. The crisis was conceptualised as an anticipated and inherent symptom of capitalism – a classic Marxist interpretation that puts the blame on the voracious thirst for profit (AKEL, 2013, 2014). Following the way the extreme austerity measures were inflicted upon Greece since 2010 the party criticised the neoliberal character of EU policies, claiming that they increasingly and negatively affected Cypriots' lives. This stance seemed to reflect a partial re-ideologisation of the EU issue and was a way to deflect criticism from the party's deficiencies and lack of radicalisation while in power. Re-radicalisation of party policies in all domains was immediate when it returned to opposition, thus highlighting the impact of government–opposition dynamics.

No longer tied to government, suffering significant electoral losses and fearing further partisan detachment, AKEL declared itself ready to fight against the troika and the Cypriot government's neoliberal policies (AKEL,

2014: 5). It proposed Cyprus's exit from the Eurozone (AKEL, 2013), and led the way in demonstrations and legislative bills against the MoU measures. The party submitted a bill calling for the postponement of privatisations until the end of 2017, it declared its intention to renationalise public companies and PEO sought to restore past workers' achievements (Kyritsis, 2015). PEO was largely unsuccessful at least initially but it had some minor success towards the end of 2016[12] – not unrelated to the upcoming presidential elections in February 2018. AKEL was met with scepticism and opposition by all other actors, which forced them to play down references to a Eurozone exit. AKEL's time in government negatively affected its ability and willingness to mobilise protest, and its efforts at re-ideologisation were seen by many as largely hypocritical (e.g. Cyprus-Mail, 2013).

The bail-in temporarily shook the Green Party's European commitment. However, in line with all the other parties, the party viewed the Cyprus problem as the main reason for supporting the country's full participation in the EU (Katsourides, 2014). Despite its positive stance towards the EU, the Greens criticised aspects of the Union, including the bias against labour forces, the democratic deficit and the lack of genuine green policies. The Greens were the only party not to support the legislative measures that enforced the agreement with the troika (House of Representatives, 2012) and they also voted against the bail-in agreement in April 2013. The party experimented for a while with a possible exit from the Eurozone as a possible way out of the troika but never endorsed such a proposal.

The party blamed equally the EU policies, the Cypriot government and the Cypriot banks for the way the economic crisis was manifested in Cyprus. Sometimes adopting a rather populist rhetoric and in compliance with the mainstream media discourse, they accused the public service and the left government of over-spending, wasteful practices and privileges focusing on the benefits and the salaries of public officials. While condemning the MoU, they believed that parts of it would help Cyprus to overcome chronic inefficiencies and would facilitate the modernisation of the banking sector. However, they voted down all government budgets, on account of their austerity measures and the cuts in social welfare.

EDEK also remained totally committed to European integration. The paramount motive for their support for the EU is the belief that the Union can help ensure a fair solution to the Cyprus problem. EDEK was supportive of EU social policies despite some occasional disagreements. A 'yes but' approach was EDEK's main strategic feature with regard to the government's agreement with the troika. While EDEK voted for the legislation, the party's political discourse was very critical of both the initial MoU (House of Representatives, 2012) and the bail-in agreement of March 2013. EDEK, like the Greens, accused both the then-left government of AKEL and the

EU for the way the economic crisis unfolded in Cyprus. In addition, the party announced a social dialogue with the aim of disengaging from the troika, but it never agreed with exiting the Eurozone.

Cooperation among the three parties during the crisis followed a specific pattern and developed in distinct directions depending on the level and issues of possible cooperation. The general pattern saw AKEL being isolated from the two other parties, EDEK and the Greens, with both trying to find some common ground on which to cooperate as a means of capitalising on AKEL's decay. This saw them eventually forming an electoral alliance in the 2014 EU elections and jointly supporting the same candidates at the 2013 and 2018 presidential elections. These efforts produced some good results, but also grievances and tensions. While maintaining their autonomy, EDEK and the Greens have cooperated on many occasions and issues in parliament, building on their similar positions on most issues including the Cyprus problem, the economy and the EU. This parliamentary cooperation even included AKEL in some instances, particularly on economic issues. In the December 2016 local elections cooperation between left parties did not follow any particular pattern, indicating their inability to agree consistently. However, the distance between AKEL and the other parties grew even further during the 2018 presidential elections with the parties disagreeing strongly over the issue of the Cyprus problem.

The above discussion indicates that each party of the left perceived the causes and proposed therapies for the crisis via the lenses of internal politics, and sought to benefit against each other. Although arguments emphasising the protection of national sovereignty and a critique of capitalism were voiced, particularly by AKEL, these did not inform actual policy proposals. All parties proposed solutions that were confined to those from the social democratic toolbox: market regulation, higher welfare spending, halting privatisations, and cutting down inequality. This created preconditions for cooperation, but it never actually materialised. Their differing perspectives on the Cyprus problem further hindered the prospects of cooperation between them, which constantly oscillated between partnership and rivalry.

In reviewing this period, it is also interesting to note the low levels of public mobilisation and protest politics despite the worsening economic and societal conditions (Katsourides, 2016a: 207–211). The absence of social protest can be explained by the capacity of the political and party system to absorb much of the tension and thus hinder protest. In addition, the Code of Industrial Relations neutralised nests of potential radicalisation. Finally, AKEL's participation in government had a negative impact on the party's willingness to mobilise protest as shown when the party moved to opposition. Only four large protests took place after the change in government in 2013. These were essentially staged by AKEL but were isolated and were confined to brief gatherings which were dismissed easily and quickly, and did not sustain any pressure on the government (Charalambous, 2014: 65). AKEL and PEO found themselves in the very peculiar situation of having to implement neoliberal policies against their long-established positions. This essentially short-circuited them as they could not challenge their own government. This created openings for other left actors.

The impact of the crisis on the Cypriot left

AKEL's experience offers valuable insight into the impact of the crisis and of government participation on the left. Notwithstanding the generalised neoliberal offensive against AKEL, the Christofias tenure seems to have reinforced a view held by some of the Cypriot left that AKEL was little more than yet another social democratic enterprise (Fischer & Economou, 2015). It was clear that AKEL's tenure of the executive had proved very costly: the government, the party and especially the President suffered heavy public disapproval. Even five years further on, polls suggested that public disapproval of AKEL's previous time in government was still the main reason for the party's failed candidacy in the 2018 presidential elections. Additionally, during Christofias's presidency the party and PEO were tied up in defusing members' and voters' grievances, emphasising parliamentary solutions and social dialogue.

Christofias's election highlighted the problem of AKEL's radical identity and the left's overall inability to develop an alternative proposal. The hard choice between the 'policy-office-vote' trichotomy of party goals was at the heart of this problem. For example, although the party did not change its stance on the EU during the Christofias administration, there was clearly tension between party rhetoric and government practice (Charalambous, 2012). The party strategy regarding the EU was primarily focused on taking positions that were viable in the short run and also different from those of the right; to a lesser extent, it targeted any type of rupture with existing economic and social relations. Especially while in government, the party disavowed its theoretical programme and accepted EU policies. In this regard, AKEL's stance towards the EU combines mild ideological criticism and pragmatism, the latter being the most obvious.

AKEL's actual impact while in government was minimal. The party failed to enact any structural or radical reforms that were carried beyond their short term of government participation. On some of the most important issues – for example, joining or remaining in the Eurozone or austerity measures – the party was unable to turn the tide. AKEL was largely exhausted by its defensive strategies aimed at preventing the worst. The desire to govern and the experience of governing had a moderating effect on the party's policies. In opposition AKEL's rhetoric and policy positions were more radical. This reveals that government/opposition dynamics played an important role in its strategy and policy. Marxism was valuable as a rhetorical and explanatory tool but of little use in designing public policy. Moreover, AKEL was clearly unprepared to take the reins of government (Katsourides, 2016b). In retrospect, Christofias's presidency can be judged in two opposing ways: as an attempt to withstand the pressures of neoliberalisation on the one hand, and as a de-radicalisation of party positions on the other.

The economic crisis did not affect only radical left parties such as AKEL. It also exposed European social democracy, revealing its inability to take advantage of a situation that on the surface appeared tailor-made for a critical view of free market capitalism (Bruff, 2014: 114). This was particularly applicable in the case of EDEK. Distancing itself in a timely fashion from AKEL's government in February 2009, the party could have taken advantage of AKEL's difficulties, particularly after the implementation of the first austerity measures in 2011. However, on the one hand EDEK continued to focus on the Cyprus problem even though this had taken a back seat in public discussions, and on the other hand pressed for more austerity. For example, the party's programmatic congress in 2010 called for the closure of some public companies and the gradual disposal of part of the share capital of others to private investors, and further reductions to public expenses (EDEK, 2010). This strategy proved ineffective, as the electoral results indicate. At the same time, AKEL's ideological move to the centre in previous years caught them out and they did not manage to respond.

The Green Party may have seen its vote share increase in 2016 but this is mostly due to the legitimacy crisis of the political and party systems of the country and particularly of the old, mainstream parties and less to the implications of the economic crisis *per se*. The economic crisis was a significant factor in magnifying and accelerating the legitimacy crisis of the mainstream parties but as the 2016 polls revealed, most of the votes that the Greens received were votes of protest against a group of parties – including AKEL – that looked increasingly similar.

The above is telling of a specific situation: most often, crises have revealed the inability of the left to stand up to these challenges. The left's strategy cannot be reduced to merely articulating demands and transferring them to the political system. The left cannot simply be the vehicle of various social groups claiming their demands. It cannot just project abstract demands and vague calls for a different and more just world without specifying *what* and *how*. The left has to aggregate social demands into a coherent programme of change that breaks with capitalism. It has to formulate public policies that are both alternative and viable. And it has to link these policies into a coherent programme of societal change. In so doing, the left has to take clear-cut positions on the most fundamental issues of our times: the role of the EU and NATO; the environment; the economic model it advises; how its positions and proposals will be achieved, and so on. This relates to the ability of the left to mobilise the necessary resources to come up with alternatives, which the Cypriot experience clearly denies.

As the Cypriot experience reveals, the most pressing and important among these questions is not just government participation but whether governing is a means to an end or a means in itself. Otherwise the left risks being considered as ideal for opposition but not for governing. While the crisis provided considerable scope for cooperation between them, there were no practical results. Moreover, the crisis and AKEL's participation in government exercised a paralysing effect on the party's mechanisms of resistance and mobilisation, thus impeding the overall ability and potential of the left to resist austerity and neoliberalism.

The decline of the mainstream left as expressed by AKEL could have contributed significantly to the success of other small parties, as it opened space on the political spectrum. But no other left party emerged during the crisis years that proved durable. Although many people that previously voted for the left were without their ideological homes – both AKEL and EDEK lost tens of thousands of voters from 2001 – no new left party successfully entered the political arena. Although from the mid-2000s a new, leftist public sphere emerged, their presence was confined mostly to ideological discussions and activities in the social media, whereas their membership remained very small. There is a niche market within the left bloc for possible entrepreneurs to exploit but none has done so yet effectively.

Notes

1 These included, for example, a freezing of salaries for two years in the public sector, a freezing of any new recruitment in the public service and a horizontal cut of public expenses by 10%.
2 The Cypriot bail-in differed from the bailout used in other cases in one fundamental way: it provided for the 'rescue' of the banking system with funds from shareholders, creditors and depositors of the two largest banks of the island instead of external recapitalisation.
3 There were no general strikes from 1980 until 2010 (Data Banks International, cited in Charalambous, 2014: 8).
4 For more on ELAM see Katsourides (2013).
5 AKEL was founded as the Communist Party of Cyprus (CPC) and renamed AKEL in 1941 (Katsourides, 2014; 2016b).

6 This includes one of the largest trade unions of Cyprus; organisations for youth, farmers and women; and cultural and athletic associations, which are present in every community and village in the country.
7 It was founded by Vassos Lyssarides, a politician and personal physician of Archbishop Makarios.
8 The party briefly adopted the name the Movement of Cypriot Social Democrats in 2000. However, the new venture failed to live up to the expectations of its initiators, and the old name was soon reinstated.
9 Notably the minor Democratic Progressive Working Movement (DEOK), a farmers' organisation (Agrotiki), the Socialist Women's Movement and the Socialist Youth (EDEN). These appear autonomous but in practice are fully controlled by the party (Protopapas, 2016: 82).
10 See the bitter exchange of letters between the two parties in AKEL's party newspaper *Haravgi* (8 November 2016).
11 Using the Gini index coefficient (Eurostat, 2015: 128).
12 For example, restoring the initial percentage of employers' contribution in workers' welfare funds.

Bibliography

AKEL (2013) *Political proposal for exiting the memorandum*, April, Nicosia: AKEL.
AKEL (2014) *Theses of AKEL's Central Committee for the Programmatic Congress*, 15–16 February, Nicosia: AKEL.
Anastasiou, A. (2014) 'Scandal fatigue settles over Cyprus', cyprus-mail.com, 30 November. http://cyprus-mail.com/2014/11/30/scandal-fatigue-settles-over-cyprus/ (accessed 20 March 2018).
Bruff, I. (2014) 'The rise of authoritarian neoliberalism', *Rethinking Marxism*, 26 (1): 113–129.
Charalambous, G. (2012) 'AKEL and the European Union', *Greek Political Science Review*, 38: 51–87.
Charalambous, G. (2014) *Political culture and behaviour in the Republic of Cyprus during the crisis*, PCC Report 2/2014, PRIO Cyprus Centre.
Christophorou, C. (2006) 'The emergence of modern politics in Cyprus (1940–1959)', in H. Faustmann & N. Peristianis (eds) *Britain in Cyprus: colonialism and post-colonialism 1878–2006*, Mannheim: Bibliopolis, 295–314.
Christophorou, C. (2012) 'Disengaging citizens: parliamentary elections in the Republic of Cyprus, 22 May 2011', *South European Society and Politics*, 17 (2): 295–307.
Cyprus-Mail (2013) 'The hypocrisy, opportunism and populism of the communist party are staggering', cyprus-mail.com, 10 October. http://cyprus-mail.com/2013/08/10/our-view-the-hypocrisy-opportunism-and-populism-of-the-communist-party-are-staggering/ (accessed 13 April 2018).
Cyprusprofile (2017) 'Cyprus NPLs drop to €24.1bn in October 2016', Cyprusprofile.com, 13 January. www.cyprusprofile.com/en/articles/view/cyprus-npls-drop-to-24.1bn-in-october-2016 (accessed 12 April 2018).

Cyprus Statistical Service (2016) *Population and social conditions, living conditions and social protection*, Nicosia: Ministry of Finance Statistical Service.

Daiber, B. (2010) 'Introduction', in B. Daiber & R. Kulke (eds) *The left in government: Latin America and Europe compared*, Brussels: Rosa Luxemburg Foundation, 7–20.

EDEK (2010) *Resolution of the Programmatic Congress for the economy and development*, 12 December, Nicosia: EDEK.

Ellinas, A. & Katsourides, Y. (2013) 'Organizational continuity and electoral endurance: the Communist Party of Cyprus', *West European Politics*, 36 (4): 859–882.

European Commission (2017) *Country report Cyprus 2017*, Brussels, 22 February, SWD (2017) 78 final.

Eurostat (2015) *Sustainable development in the European Union – 2015: monitoring report of the EU Sustainable Development Strategy*. http://ec.europa.eu/eurostat/web/products-statistical-books/-/KS-GT-15-001 (accessed 24 February 2019).

Eurostat (2016) 'The share of persons at risk of poverty or social exclusion in the EU back to its pre-crisis level: contrasting trends across Member States', press release, 17 October. https://ec.europa.eu/eurostat/documents/2995521/7695750/3-17102016-BP-EN.pdf/30c2ca2d-f7eb-4849-b1e1-b329f48338dc (accessed 16 March 2019).

Eurostat (2017) 'December 2016 euro area unemployment at 9.6%', news release, 31 January.

Fischer, L. & Economou, D. (2015) 'Cyprus at the crossroads', 26 May. www.jacobinmag.com/2015/05/cyprus-communists-SYRIZA-greece/ (accessed 4 June 2015).

House of Representatives (2012) *Proceedings from the discussions on Cyprus Agreement with the troika*, 15 December, Nicosia.

IMF (International Monetary Fund) (2015) 'Cyprus: eighth review under the Extended Arrangement under the Extended Fund Facility and request for modification of performance criteria – press release; staff report; and statement by the Executive Director for Cyprus', Country Report No. 15/271. www.imf.org/external/pubs/cat/longres.aspx?sk=43305.0 (accessed 4 June 2016).

Katsourides, Y. (2003) 'Europeanisation and political parties in accession countries: the political parties of Cyprus', EpsNet Plenary Conference, Paris, 13–14 June.

Katsourides, Y. (2012) 'Travelling against the tide: the Cypriot Communist left in the post-1990 era', *Perspectives on European Politics and Society*, 13 (2): 187–209.

Katsourides, Y. (2013) 'Determinants of extreme right reappearance in Cyprus: the National Popular Front (ELAM), Golden Dawn's sister party', *South European Society and Politics*, 18 (4): 567–589.

Katsourides, Y. (2014), 'The national question in Cyprus and the Cypriot Communist left in the era of British colonialism (1922–1959)', *Journal of Balkan and Near Eastern Studies*, 16 (4): 474–501.

Katsourides, Y. (2016a) 'Delegitimization accelerated: democracy, accountability and the troika experience in Cyprus', *Portuguese Journal of Social Science*, 15 (2): 195–216.

Katsourides, Y. (2016b) *The radical left in government: the cases of SYRIZA and AKEL*. Basingstoke: Palgrave Macmillan.

Ker-Lindsay, J. (2008) 'Presidential power and authority', in J. Ker-Lindsay & H. Faustmann (eds) *The government and politics of Cyprus*, Bern: Peter Lang, 107–124.

Ker-Lindsay, J. (2011) *The Cyprus problem: what everyone needs to know*, Oxford: Oxford University Press.

Kyritsis, P. (2015) 'Counterattack', *Haravgi*, 29 November, 6.

March, L. (2008) 'Contemporary far left parties in Europe: from Marxism to the mainstream?', *International Policy Analysis*, Friedrich-Ebert-Stiftung, November.

March, L. & Rommerskirchen, C. (2015) 'Out of left field? Explaining the variable electoral success of European radical left parties', *Party Politics*, 21(1): 40–53.

Omirou, Y. (2014) 'Speech by the President of EDEK in the official presentation of EDEK and the Greens candidates for the EP Elections', 23 February.

Panayiotou, A. (2014) *The first left presidency, 2008–2013*, Limassol: Cyprus Centre for East Mediterranean Studies.

Pegasiou, A. (2013) 'The Cypriot economic collapse: more than a conventional South European failure', *Mediterranean Politics*, 18 (3): 333–351.

Protopapas, V. (2016) 'Empty vessels? DIKO and EDEK's linkage with society', in G. Charalambous and C. Christophorou (eds) *Party–society relations in the Republic of Cyprus*, Abingdon: Routledge, 69–90.

Sparsis, M. (1998) *Tripartism and industrial relations: the Cyprus experience*, Nicosia: n.p.

Spourdalakis, M. (2013) 'Left strategy in the Greek cauldron: explaining SYRIZA's success', in L. Panitch, G. Albo & V. Chibber (eds) *Socialist Register 2013: the question of strategy*, London: Merlin Press, 98–120.

Stamatiou, G. (2013) *History of EDEK 1969–1974*, Nicosia: EDEK.

Tombazos, S. (2014) 'The vicious circle of Cyprus's economic crisis', 11th Annual Conference of Historical Materialism 'How Capitalism Survives', 6–9 November, London.

7

The Italian left and the crisis: the case of Matteo Renzi's Partito Democratico

Jorge del Palacio Martín

Introduction

In Italy, just like in the majority of southern European countries, the economic crisis that got underway in 2008 soon translated into a serious political, social and institutional crisis whose consequences led to major changes in the party system. Without a doubt, the most important change came in the 2013 elections with the breakthrough of a new political party that managed to capitalise on the protest vote against the system: the MoVimento Cinque Stelle (M5S, Five Star Movement), founded by the comedian Beppe Grillo. M5S then entered government after the 2018 general election.

The consolidation of the M5S as a governing alternative has had at least two major consequences for Italy's political system. In terms of elections, the emergence of the M5S has led to the end of a kind of bipolarism based on competition between left and right coalitions that has defined the historical period known as the Second Republic in Italy. Ideologically, the discourse of the M5S, based on the populist promise of relaunching democracy on a participative and anti-elitist basis, has largely shaped the political agenda of the leading parties in Italy on both ends of the political spectrum.

When analysing the impact of the ascent of the M5S on the Italian left, this chapter shall focus on the political project and leadership of Matteo Renzi, the secretary of the Partito Democratico (PD, Democratic Party) since 2013. The reason is twofold. On the one hand, he is of interest primarily because both his leadership as the secretary of the PD (since December 2013) and his tenure as the President of the Council of Ministers (February 2014 to December 2016) dovetails in time with the rise of Beppe Grillo's party and allows us to evaluate the impact of the rise of anti-politics in the PD.

On the other hand, the PD is the most important and representative party of the centre left in Italy, born in 2007 as the result of the merger of

Democratici di Sinistra (DS, Democrats of the Left) and Democrazia è Libertà – La Margherita (Democracy is Freedom – The Daisy). The birth of the PD was the culmination of a long and complex process of electoral alliances between two political traditions which, paradoxically, were enemies during the First Republic: the communists and the Christian democrats. It goes without saying that the PD is not the only party of the Italian left. In the 2013 elections the left-wing coalition Revoluzione Civile (Civil Revolution, CR), including the Partito della Rifondazione Comunista (Communist Refoundation Party) led by the former anti-mafia prosecutor of Palermo, Antonio Ingroia, competed with the PD and M5S for left-wing voters, but did not win any seats. One of the reasons for the failure of the CR is the success of the M5S in attracting left-wing anti-system support after the economic crisis, even though Grillo's political movement cannot be considered, as will be discussed later, a left-wing party.

Matteo Renzi has been considered an epitome of the 'Third Way' approach represented by Tony Blair and Bill Clinton. Renzi certainly aspired to transform the PD ideologically into a centrist party, following the New Labour model. However, his rise in Italian politics cannot be understood without paying attention to his strong anti-political discourse against the Italian political establishment. In fact, Matteo Renzi's career has largely been built on demands for a radical shift in the Italian political class, and even in his own party. Note that Renzi gave himself the nickname *il rottamatore* ('the scrapper'). Both elements clash with the political culture of the Italian left and should be contextualised within the twofold scenario generated by the financial crisis on the one hand and the ascent of the M5S and the success of its anti-political discourse on the other.

The case of Renzi's PD is fascinating in comparative terms: while the crisis led the radical left parties to success over social democratic parties in some southern European countries, this pattern did not hold in Italy. For example, in the 2014 European Parliament elections the PD earned 40.8% of the votes, becoming the party that garnered the most votes in Europe. However, this chapter will also examine how Renzi's political agenda to transform the PD and his leadership style sparked a great deal of resistance and criticism from within the party.

Even though Matteo Renzi resigned as Prime Minister after losing a referendum intended to push through a series of constitutional reforms held on 4 December 2016, the former mayor of Florence remained secretary of the PD and aspired to give a new impetus to his agenda with the support of the more than 40% of voters who approved his constitutional reform plan. The future of the left in Italy and the ideological nature of his project will largely depend on his success or failure.

The political effects of the financial crisis in Italy: The end of the Second Republic?

The period in Italian history that spans from 1948 to 1993 tends to be known as the First Republic, while the name Second Republic is reserved for the period after 1993 (Grilli di Cortona, 2007). The year 1993 is taken as the reference point because it is when the popular referendum that led to the abolition of the proportional electoral law used since the end of the Second World War was held, and it was replaced with a quasi-majoritarian electoral system. Despite the fact that the 1993 electoral law was changed again in 2005 in favour of a new proportional system plus a majority bonus,[1] the so-called Second Republic has been characterised by the prevalence of bipolar competition, which has generated alternating governments (Fabbrini, 2009).

In addition to the new election laws, another factor that facilitated the construction of the new bipolar competition is the effect of the trial known as *Tangentopoli* (Bribe City) on the party system, primarily because the corruption scandals delegitimised most of the main parties in the First Republic, which ended up disappearing (Fabbrini, 2009). This process made it possible for new parties and new coalitions to be created. Noteworthy among the new political actors were two parties destined to become the main referents for voters on both the right and left in the Second Republic: Forza Italia (FI) and the Partito Democratico della Sinistra (PDS, Democratic Party of the Left). The former was the personal party of Italian magnate Silvio Berlusconi, while the latter reflected the transformation of communist parties in Europe after the fall of the USSR. The PDS continued to develop, becoming the PD in 2007. Because of its importance in the development of the Second Republic, we should add that these parties were joined by the regionalist party Lega Nord (Ignazi, 2008) in 1992.

Pasquino and Valbruzzi (2015) state that even though the party system in the Second Republic can be regarded as bipolar in relation to its 'mechanics', it should be taken as multi-polar in its 'format'. Both authors stress that the bipolarism of the party system that emerged with the Second Republic gained ground via the growth of party fragmentation. In their own words, 'It has ended up creating an anomalous case of extreme bipolarism where a considerable number of parties has been constrained by, and encapsulated within, two competing governing coalitions. The kind of bipolarism that took hold in Italy meant the governments were condemned to instability because there were too many programmatic differences between coalition partners' (Pasquino & Valbruzzi, 2015: 443).

The elections held in February 2013 put an end to the particular bipolar logic that had prevailed in all of Italy's elections since 1996. Some authors

even believe that the 2013 elections may have signalled a new reconfiguration of the party system and may ultimately put an end to what is known
as the Second Republic. However, they also underscore that it is still too
early to confirm the change: 'Many of the ingredients of a major political
realignment are present. But one election is not enough to support the
conclusion that such a realignment has taken place' (D'Alimonte, 2013:
128). The analyses in this vein particularly spotlight the breakthrough of
the M5S, which managed to capture 25.6% of the vote in 2013 by exploiting
rejection of the system, thus becoming the third most powerful force in
the country. The M5S's outstanding performance in the 2012 municipal
and regional elections had led to predictions that Beppe Grillo's party
would fare well. In fact, the end results achieved by the party were far
above what the pre-election polls had predicted (Pasquino & Valbruzzi,
2015).

The 2013 election results not only revealed the M5S's exceptional breakthrough into the Italian party system and the shaping of a new tripolar
scenario; it also revealed the gradual decline of the two main coalitions of
the Second Republic. A comparison of the results of the 2013 elections with
the previous ones – 2006 and 2008 – illustrates a progressive erosion of the
coalitions that had alternated in power since 1996. Between the 2008 and
2013 elections, the two main coalitions lost more than 9 million votes. In
percentages, while in 2008 both coalitions were capable of capturing 84.4%
of the votes, in 2013 the total of votes for both parties combined was just
58.7%. Going back to the 2006 elections, we can see that the loss of votes
by the two main coalitions dates from earlier. In 2006, the two main electoral
coalitions earned over 99% of the votes.

In short, the two main coalitions organised around Forza Italia (or its
subsequent transformations) and the PD (or its predecessors) lost a total of
40.8% of their voters since 2006. If we do the same with the traditional
political blocs rather than specific parties, the result confirms the thesis.
From 2006 to 2013, the centre left bloc lost 41% of its voters, while the
centre right lost 30% (Maggini, 2013).

In the opinion of some analysts, the M5S was the virtual winner of the
elections held in 2013, and not only because of its spectacular results in its
first ever national elections. The party 'is the largest party in almost one-half
of the provinces (50 out of 109) and it is the only one with a truly national
base. Unlike its major rivals it gained more or less the same percentage of
votes in the North, the Centre and South' (D'Alimonte, 2013: 119).

Inasmuch as the M5S capitalised on the protest vote against the system,
one of the reasons that can explain the end of bipolarism and the growth
of Grillo's party is the increase in Italians' mistrust of political parties and
representative institutions. We can clearly see that trust in Italian political

institutions is on the wane from 41% in 2005 to 24% in 2013 in one survey (Diamanti et al., 2013). In a 2015 report the parties and parliament are the institutions that generate the least confidence in Italians, earning only 10% (the parliament) and 5% (parties). What is more, 48% of those surveyed believe that democracy can work without parties. In 2008, this figure stood at 38% and in 2014 it reached 50% (Diamanti et al., 2015). It is also important to note that in the 2013 elections, voter turnout reached its lowest level since the restoration of democracy in Italy after the Second World War. Turnout was 75.2%, 5.3 points lower than in 2008, and far from the historical peaks of over 93% in 1958 and 1976.

It could be argued that citizens' mistrust of parties is a global and not exclusively Italian phenomenon. The decline in voter turnout and the decrease in affiliation with the traditional parties is a pattern that can be found in all western democracies (Mair, 2013). In this sense, the declining electoral returns of the main Italian parties, the increase in Italians' mistrust of their representative institutions and the drop in voter turnout are not caused exclusively by the economic crisis. However, the crisis and its political and institutional consequences have served to spur the dynamics of disaffection that were already present in Italian political life.

For this reason, when explaining the rise of the M5S and the electoral erosion of the right and the left in Italy, we cannot lose sight of the effect of the resignation of Silvio Berlusconi as President of the Council of Ministers of Italy and the formation of the technocratic government of Mario Monti in November 2011 in the midst of the financial crisis.[2] Italy was facing a difficult economic situation in the summer of 2011, with Berlusconi being urged by the ECB and the IMF to take exceptional measures to lower public debt, which totalled 120% of GDP, to stop the increase in the risk premium, and to restore confidence in the markets. In July, Berlusconi's government approved a package of economic measures aimed at achieving economic adjustments of €77.9 billion in 2014.

However, the package of measures was designed to be implemented in three phases, leaving the bulk of the adjustments until after the 16th legislature, and thus did not have the desired soothing effect. The economic situation was so dire that Berlusconi's government received a letter signed by Jean-Claude Trichet and Mario Draghi asking the Italian government to take urgent measures to guarantee the country's fiscal sustainability.[3] This forced Berlusconi's government to propose a new package of austerity measures. However, even though the government's measures were approved on 14 September, the decision-making process revealed the government's weakness. Only 308 of the 340 deputies from the centre right voted in favour of the new package.[4] Nor did they stop Standard & Poors from lowering the Italian credit rating from A+ to A. On 12 November, Berlusconi, whose credibility had been seriously compromised in both Italy and the international community, resigned (Chiaramonte & D'Alimonte, 2012).

The formation of the Monti government cannot be disassociated from the political effects of the economic crisis in southern Europe. The Greek debt crisis turned the financial crisis into a problem of sovereign debt in the Eurozone's peripheral economies and it finally caused the quasi-simultaneous downfall of four governments of southern Europe in 2011: Portugal, Spain, Italy and Greece (Bosco & Verney, 2012). The main feature of the new Monti government was that none of its members, most of them university professors and civil servants, represented any party or had served in an elected post. Despite having a sound reputation around Europe as an economist, Monti himself lacked experience in Italian political life (Bosco & Verney, 2012). It was a government of technocrats.[5]

The main goal of Monti's government was to deal with the economic crisis, and it remained in power with the support of all the parliamentary groups except the Lega Nord. Most notably, both Berlusconi's Popolo della Libertà and the PD supported the government, which meant implicit acceptance of austerity policies proposed by the European Union. In fact, Pasquino and Valbruzzi accurately note that the bipolarism of the Second Republic did not end with the 2013 elections, but with the formation of Monti's technocratic government. This is crucially important because it ushered in a new stage of cooperation between the main left and right parties (Pasquino & Valbruzzi, 2015). In this way, an opportunity arose in late 2011 to capitalise on opposition to Monti's government, and the M5S took advantage of it better than any other party, as the 2013 elections revealed.

The technocratic government of Monti also had a major impact on attitudes towards the European Union in Italy. A 2016 survey shows clearly that trust in the European Union among Italians fell sharply from 57.5% in 2008 to 29% in 2016. The survey shows a slight recovery in trust in the EU from 2011 to 2012 (from 36.6% to 43.5%), but the 2013 elections triggered a return to declining trust in the EU, from 43.5% in 2012 to 27% in 2014 (Diamanti et al., 2016). The outstanding performance of the M5S was also the result of the success of Grillo's party in exploiting this growing lack of confidence of many Italians in the European Union through a strongly Eurosceptic discourse.

The M5S and the challenge of anti-politics

The impact of the crisis on the southern European countries also resulted in a window of opportunity for new parties and movements, especially for those that saw the economic and political crisis as an opportunity to take electoral advantage of the citizens' loss of trust in the traditional parties. This is the context that explains the rise of the Bloco de Esquerda in Portugal, Podemos in Spain, the M5S in Italy and SYRIZA in Greece.

Even though they all make use of a populist rhetoric, the essential difference between the Bloco de Esquerda, Podemos and SYRIZA on the one hand and the M5S on the other is that the Italian party cannot clearly be identified as a leftist party, especially because it rejects the left–right dimension of competition. The M5S is clearly a party that encompasses some demands that could be part of the political agendas of the radical left. For example, the M5S supports direct democracy and an anti-growth philosophy (Bordignon & Ceccarini, 2015). Furthermore, even Beppe Grillo himself tried to run in the PD primaries albeit unsuccessfully (Biorcio, 2015). However, inasmuch as its protest against the system also includes the political parties, unions and illegal immigration, we could state that the M5S has kept its doors open to right-wing voters as well. In fact, both the M5S's current electorate and its potential voters are rather evenly distributed among the left (36.3%), the centre (27.3%) and the right (20.8%) (Emanuele & Maggini, 2015).

The M5S has been defined as 'a strange animal … in the zoo of Italian politics' (Corbetta & Gualmini, 2013). Yet despite its heterodoxy, Bordignon and Ceccarini claim that it is possible to identify four main features that define Beppe Grillo's movement. Firstly, the M5S challenges the concept of representative democracy as opposed to a pure or unmediated democracy organised on the internet. Secondly, it is a post-ideological movement that rejects the categories of left and right. Thirdly, it is a hybrid organisation that combines horizontal elements with strong leadership that holds much of the power. And finally, it brandishes a radical discourse against what it regards as two castes: the political elite and the media (Bordignon & Ceccarini, 2015). Likewise, Grillo's leadership style exemplifies the characteristics of populist leadership for at least three reasons. Firstly, Grillo always appeals to the people as the main source of legitimacy. Secondly, his rhetoric is anti-political in that he has turned the traditional parties into his main adversaries. And thirdly, the founder of the M5S seeks direct contact with the party's followers, avoiding any mediation (Tarchi, 2015).

Obviously, the economic context is not irrelevant in the rise of the M5S, primarily because it generated the conditions for the success of a discourse that protests against the system. In fact, condemnations of the misuse of public resources by politicians was one of the main topics exploited by Grillo's rhetoric. However, unlike the parties that capitalised on the protest vote in southern Europe, the M5S does not make criticism of the capitalist economy its main playing field. Furthermore, Grillo's attempt to situate his party in the liberal group within the European Parliament in January 2017

Table 7.1 Italian general election results (in % of vote) and government coalition, 2005–2017

Election year	U/PD	RC/SA/ SEL/LU	M5S	FI/PdL	LN	Left parties combined (U/PD and others)	National government (led by party mentioned first)
April 2006	31.27	5.84	-	23.72	4.58	49.81	L'Ulivo & Others
April 2008	33.18	3.08	-	37.38	8.30	40.63	PdL & LN
Feb 2013	25.43	3.2	25.56	21.56	4.09	29.55	PD & Others
March 2018	18.76	3.39	32.68	14.00	17.35	26.25	M5S & LN

Source: Ministero dell'Interno (n.d.)
Notes:
L'Ulivo (Democratici di Sinistra, DS, + Margherita): 2006 / Partido Democratico (PD): 2008, 2013, 2018
Rifondazione Comunista (RC): 2006 / La Sinistra Arcobaleno (SA): 2008 / Sinistra Ecologia Libertà (SEL): 2013/ Liberi e Uguali (LU): 2018
Movimiento Cinque Stelle (M5S): 2013, 2018
Forza Italia (FI): 2006, 2018 / Popolo della Libertà (PdL): 2008
Lega Nord (LN): 2006, 2008, 2013, 2018

illustrates the huge ideological gulf between the M5S and other parties protesting against the system, in spite of their common ground.[6]

As Roberto Biorcio and Paolo Natale have stated, the main challenge that the M5S poses to the Italian parties is its anti-politics: a radical criticism of the traditional political class and the professionalisation of politics. In fact, Grillo's decision not to equip the M5S with an organisational structure outside of the internet revealed his desire to break with the classical way of understanding and engaging in politics. It established a new relationship between society, political parties and forms of participation and representation (Biorcio & Natale, 2013). In this way, the M5S challenged the right–left ideological clash that had prevailed in the Second Republic, and instead introduced dialectics of the 'people vs. caste', 'politics vs. anti-politics' and 'old politics vs. new politics'.

The 2013 elections and Matteo Renzi's rise to the leadership of the PD

Even though the PD won the 2013 elections, the victory led to a crisis for the main party on the Italian left. The PD and its main coalition party, Sinistra Ecologia e Libertà (SEL, Left, Ecology and Freedom), managed to secure a majority in parliament but not the Senate. Therefore, Pier Luigi Bersani,

Table 7.2 European Parliament election results in Italy (% of vote), 2004–2019

Election year	U/PD	RC/AET/Sin	M5S	FI/PdL	LN	Left parties combined (U/PD&Others)
2004	31.08	6.06	-	20.93	4.96	46.21[a]
2009	26.12	3.39	-	35.26	10.21	40.64[b]
2014	40.81	4.04	21.16	16.81	6.15	44.85[c]
2019	22.74	1.75	17.06	8.78	34.26	24.49[d]

Source: Ministero dell'Interno, n.d.
Notes:
Altra Europa con Tsipras (AET): 2014
[a] L'Ulivo+RC+Verdi+Comunisti Italiani+Di Pietro-Occhetto+Socialisti Uniti
[b] PD+RC+SEL+Lista Di Pietro-Italia dei valori
[c] PD+AET
[d] PD+Sin

the coalition candidate from the left, was unable to form a government by himself. Bersani refused to negotiate with the centre right and even designed an alternative governing platform in an attempt to enlist the support of the M5S. However, Grillo rejected any kind of cooperation and Bersani was forced to step down as the secretary of the PD after two months of dramatic negotiations that highlighted his inability to form a government.

After Bersani's failure, Enrico Letta, who had been the vice-secretary of the PD, was charged by the President of the Republic, Giorgio Napolitano, with forming a new government. Letta did manage to do so, but only by resorting to the 'grand coalition' formula; that is, with the support of the majority of parliamentary forces, including Berlusconi's Popolo della Libertà and Scelta Civica, Mario Monti's party. However, Letta's new government did not manage to quieten the critics of the PD who asked for a thorough overhaul of the party, its strategy, its organisation and its objectives. The clearest picture of the crisis underlying the PD's bitter electoral victory came in the vote for the new President of the Republic, when 101 PD deputies did not back the candidacy of one of the party's founding fathers, Romano Prodi (Seddone & Venturino, 2015).

The crisis created in the centre left by the resignation of Pier Luigi Bersani as the secretary of the PD led to another contest for the office of the party secretary, which is open to party members and sympathisers. In the spotlight in this election was Matteo Renzi, the young mayor of Florence, who won the election for the post of secretary of the PD, held on 8 December 2013, with a resounding 67.6% of the votes. Renzi had already challenged the party's old guard back in 2012, when he announced that he would take on the PD's general secretary in coalition primaries to decide on the centre left prime ministerial candidate for the 2013 general election. Even though Renzi lost to Bersani in the second round, he performed quite well and was perceived by the party members and sympathisers of the PD as the future leader of the Italian centre left (Vicentini, 2015).

Despite its short history, one of the features of the PD is the instability of its leadership. Matteo Renzi became the fifth secretary of a party that had only been founded in 2007. The main consequence of this instability, which contrasts with Berlusconi's uncontested leadership on the right, is that no secretary had the time and resources to equip the PD with a lasting, stable and recognisable party model (Pasquino, 2014).

Matteo Renzi's leadership

Matteo Renzi's meteoric career peaked when he replaced Enrico Letta and formed a government on 22 February 2014. Renzi thus became the youngest Prime Minister in the history of the Italian Republic. His election as the new leader of the PD was a huge challenge to the political culture of the Italian left. His leadership style clashes with the organisational and ideological values of the Italian left. For example, his political agenda was based on both a Third Way conception of social democracy and the very idea of scrapping the Italian political establishment. This promise also included a challenge to the old guard of his own party (Seddone & Venturino, 2015).

Despite the challenge that Renzi's leadership posed to the Italian left, his characteristics largely match the kind of leadership typical of the Second Republic. According to Fabio Bordignon, this kind of leadership has six characteristics. Firstly, it is a post-ideological leadership that rejects the left–right dimension of political competition. Secondly, it is an anti-political leadership, 'proposing his movement as the authentic interpreter of the *will of the people* as opposed to political establishment'. Thirdly, it is a personal leadership that 'takes the role of political representative above all as a person [...], rather than as an expression of some collective entity'. Fourthly, it is leadership by an outsider, 'who made his way outside the ordinary recruitment circles of the elite in opposition to the oligarchies and traditional political apparatus'. The fifth characteristic is that it is an inspirational leadership based on the leader's charisma and communicative skills. The sixth is that it is an innovative leadership in which the leader becomes 'the potential reformer (or refounder) of the political system so as to give voice to the people, indicating new procedures and new infrastructures to foster the popular will' (Bordignon, 2014: 3).

The main inspiration for this model of leadership is Silvio Berlusconi, and it has been adopted by almost all the new parties in the Second Republic, with differing levels of intensity. Note that the sentiment of rejection of the traditional political class that followed the crisis unleashed between 1992 and 1994 paved the way for the advent of a new, charismatic kind of leadership that questioned the centrality of the parties as instruments of political representation and instead fostered the advent of strong leaders. In short, it led to an intense personalisation of politics, whose corollary is the birth of the 'personal party' (Calise, 2010). However, until the arrival of Matteo Renzi, the Italian centre left had remained distant from the personalisation of politics.

To understand why the Italian centre left had resisted the personal leadership style typical of the Second Republic, it is interesting to observe the process of the founding of the PD. It was born in 2007 as a product of the merger between the Democrats of the Left and the Daisy. The provenance of the former was the Partito Comunista Italiano (PCI, Italian Communist Party), while the latter came from the Democrazia Cristiana (DC, Christian Democracy). Most importantly, the PD was founded as a reformist, progressive party that was the culmination of a long, complex process of electoral alliances (Bordandini et al., 2008). In this sense, both the communist and Christian democratic political cultures are the antithesis of the personal party. Clearly, neither the DC nor the PCI lacked strong leaders; however, these never abandoned the idea of the party as the expression of a collective identity. And this anti-personal attitude, which is present in former communist and former Christian democratic culture, is best expressed in the bylaws of the PD, which set a limit of two terms per secretary (Pasquino & Venturino, 2014).

However, the arrival of Matteo Renzi as the secretary of the PD brought the Italian centre left closer to the personal leadership style typical of the Second Republic. Yet it is worth underscoring that the PD is not a 'personal party' like Forza Italia or the M5S, as its bylaws do not allow the leader to totally control the party organisation, nor are its internal workings driven by loyalty to the leader, and the party organisation is not weakly institutionalised by design (Kostadinova & Levitt, 2014).

Just like the majority of contemporary leaders, Renzi used a storytelling strategy to reinforce and characterise his political image. Through his books and speeches, Renzi created a story of his political career as a relentless struggle against the country's ruling class. Paradoxically, Renzi has always been a professional politician, but his frequent clashes with the PD elite lent an air of truth to his story about his 'outsider' status. Anti-political discourse is a powerful, effective tool as an instrument of opposition, as its goal is to distinguish the new leader from the establishment and present him as the representative of a silent majority that traditional politics has silenced (Campus, 2006). In Renzi's case, the two key concepts around which he articulated his story were *la rottamazione* ('the demolition') and *cambiamento* ('change'). In his narrative, simple yet extraordinarily effective, the replacement of the ruling class becomes the *sine qua non* for Italians' progress (Ventura, 2015).

Therefore, in Renzi's political language for the Italian left, progressivism is equated with the desire for innovation and change, while conservatism is equated with a resistance to change and ultimately the defence of the status quo. We could say then that Renzi innovated the Italian left's discourse to adapt it to a public opinion that is highly critical of the political class and predisposed to anti-political discourse, as shown by the successful election results of the M5S. In fact, Renzi's ability to adapt the PD's discourse to the prevailing anti-political rhetoric has led some to define Renzi's style as 'institutional populism' (Tarchi, 2015). Renzi himself accepts he used a strategy to adapt to the dominant anti-political consensus in Italy after the crisis, replying when asked about his radical tone against the political elites of the country: 'If it hadn't been for the metaphor of the *rottamazione*, they wouldn't even have listened to me. That word was nothing other than a nod to the rules of modern communication' (cited in Ventura, 2015: 11).

Another of Renzi's innovations was to introduce into the discourse of the Italian left concepts and ideas from the Third Way popularised by Tony Blair, a politician for whom Renzi never hid his admiration. Renzi tried to distance himself from state-centred conceptions of politics and promote a social democratic order that is favourable to market politics. Hence, in his speeches on change and innovation, Renzi's rhetoric introduces key words from business jargon, such as efficiency, speed and merit, as positive values for politics (Bordignon, 2014).

Matteo Renzi's reforms

One of the most important reforms of Renzi's government was the package of measures targeted at reforming the job market, known as the Jobs Act. Renzi's purpose was to liberalise the job market in order to make it less rigid. The reform also led to the elimination of article 18 of the Italian Workers' Statute, which obliged companies with more than 15 employees to reinstate unfairly dismissed workers. Because of the strong symbolic content of this article, the Jobs Act unleashed open warfare between Renzi and the unions, which the PD leader equated with the part of the establishment that rejects any changes and is to blame for Italy's economic crisis.

However, the Renzi government's main project was constitutional reform, which sought to meet four main objectives:

1) To eliminate the pure bicameralism established in the 1948 Constitution, which stipulates that both the Chamber of Deputies and the Senate have the same legislative authorities.
2) To turn the Senate into a regional chamber with legislative authority limited to constitutional reforms and/or laws.
3) To strengthen the state over the regions and to eliminate the provinces.
4) To eliminate the National Economy and Labour Council (CNEL), a consultative body of the government, the chambers and the regions called for in article 99 of the Constitution.

Renzi's government advocated the reform by underscoring the need to simplify Italy's bureaucratic system, streamlining the decision-making process, lowering the costs of the political class and ameliorating the shortcomings of Italian governance, which has translated into 64 different governments in 17 legislatures, in which only two prime ministers have managed to complete their terms.[7] The support for this constitutional reform, which sought to improve governability, was the new electoral law called Italicum, which was approved in May 2015. This gave a super-majority of 55% for any party that wins 40% in the first or second round. Approved before the constitutional referendum, the law was part of the Renzian strategy to introduce a new majoritarian constitutional environment.

Although the reform could have been approved by parliament, from the start Renzi announced his intention to submit it to a referendum and give the people their say. The No vote prevailed in the referendum held on 4 December 2016, with 59.1%, compared to 40.9% who supported it. This led Renzi to step down as Prime Minister, as he had promised to do if the referendum failed. Italicum, the new electoral law approved by Renzi's government, was later amended by the Italian Constitutional Court.

During the PD National Assembly, held on February 2017, Matteo Renzi decided to relaunch his political career by resigning as secretary of the party and announcing his intention to run for the next party leadership election. In the new primaries, in April, Renzi was re-elected secretary of the PD with 69.2% of the votes. However, Renzi's landslide victory was overshadowed by the foundation of two new parties, also in February 2017. The first one was a left-wing split from the PD called Articolo 1 – Movimiento Democratico e Progressista, headed by Roberto Speranza and backed by historic leaders of the Italian left such as Pierluigi Bersani and Massimo D'Alema. The second one, Campo Progresista, was launched by the former mayor of Milan, Giuliano Pisapia. The birth of those two parties, besides the possibility of a common electoral strategy including other minor parties from the left, could be considered the expression of a response to Renzi's project to transform the PD into a more centrist, liberal and personal party.

Conclusion

Matteo Renzi's arrival as the secretary of the PD signalled a clash with the political culture of the Italian left. However, his transformation into the leader of the main leftist party in Italy cannot be disassociated from the political context sparked by the economic and financial crisis. This context has fostered the emergence of intensely personal and radically anti-political leaders, as shown by the fact that the M5S became the second most powerful party after the 2013 elections.

Renzi's leadership gave the PD a spectacular victory in the 2014 European elections, earning 40.8% of the votes, more than 2 million more votes than in the 2013 general elections (Segatti et al., 2015). Furthermore, his most important action was to include the PD in the Progressive Alliance of Socialists and Democrats, the political group of the Party of European Socialists (PES) in the European Parliament, for the first time. However, it is also true that from the time that Renzi became the secretary of the PD, the perpetual threat of schism loomed over the party. According to Bordignon, 'Renzi's predilection for quick decision-making, which bypasses the intermediation of parties and unions, is viewed with unease – if not as a symptom of authoritarian tendencies – in a party in which the collective dimension is still important' (Bordignon, 2014: 8). In this sense, the campaign for the constitutional referendum clearly exemplified the division Renzi has sown within the PD.

In any event, Renzi's leadership has once again foregrounded the debate on two different narratives of party legitimacy. Pasquino and Valbruzzi have quite accurately noted that two different visions of the party model coexist within the PD. The first, represented by Bersani and the 'old guard', defends a cleavage representation party, 'well-defined notions of group interests to which members are expected to defer'. The second, represented by Veltroni and Renzi, is 'a purely election-oriented vote-seeking political party, according to which the voters, not the members, are the organization's bottom line' (Pasquino & Valbruzzi, 2017: 282–283).

In this sense, Matteo Renzi appeared on the Italian scene as a politician capable of taking the PD far beyond the party's political confines and electoral capabilities. However, any attempt to transform the PD into a party with a majoritarian vocation (Renzi has flirted with the idea of creating a 'Party of the Nation') remains doomed to collide with those who uphold the other model of a leftist party that also exists within the PD. Despite the fact that he resigned as Prime Minister, Matteo Renzi remained secretary of the PD after the Italian 2018 general elections.

The PD led by Matteo Renzi came third with 18.76% of the votes, below the 25.43% of votes achieved by his predecessor Pier Luigi Bersani and very far from the 40.81% of the votes achieved by Renzi himself in the 2014 European elections. After this result Renzi announced his resignation as secretary of the PD giving way to a renewal process of the party in the context of an Italy led for the first time by a government formed by two populist challenger parties: M5S and Lega. It should be stressed that the post-Renzi PD, led by Nicola Zingaretti, became the second largest party in the 2019 European election with 22.74% of the votes. This result put the PD ahead of populist M5S, but the spectacular rise of Salvini's Lega, for the first time Italy's biggest party and a dominant force by winning 34.26% of the votes, shows that the Italian centre-left remains far from able to challenge Italy's populist cross-party consensus.

Notes

1 A party or list gaining 40% of the vote or better receives 340 out of the 630 seats, with the remaining 290 seats distributed proportionally among remaining parties.
2 Monti is a renowned economist who had been European Commissioner for the Internal Market (1995–1999) and European Commissioner for Competition (1999–2004).
3 Trichet was president of the ECB at the time, Draghi (who took over as President of the ECB in November 2011) was Chair of the Financial Stability Board.
4 Centre left MPs from the PD (206) and Italia dei Valori (22) as well as centre right MPs from Futuro e Libertá (22) and Christian Democrats-UDC (34) voted against.
5 This was not the first time that Italy had handled a political and economic crisis by resorting to a technical government, as there was the precedent of the government of Lamberto Dini in 1995–1996. Dini served in the IMF (1959–1979) and later became the director general of the Bank of Italy and was Treasury minister in the first Berlusconi government.
6 M5S MEPs sit with the Eurosceptic Europe of Freedom and Direct Democracy group in the EP.
7 Alcide De Gasperi (1948–1953) and Silvio Berlusconi (2001–2006)

Bibliography

Biorcio, R. (2015) *Il populismo nella politica italiana: da Bossi a Berlusconi, da Grillo a Renzi*, Milano, Mimesis.

Biorcio, R. & Natale, P. (2013) *Politica a 5 stelle: idee, storia e strategie del movimiento di Grillo*, Milano, Feltrinelli.

Bordandini, P., Di Virgilio, A. & Raniolo, F. (2008): 'The birth of a party: the case of the Italian Partito Democratico', *South European Society and Politics*, 13 (3): 303–324.

Bordignon, F. (2014) 'A leftist Berlusconi for the Italian Democratic Party?', *South European Society and Politics*, 19 (1): 1–23.

Bordignon, F. & Ceccarini, L. (2015) 'The Five-Star Movement: a hybrid actor in the net of the state institutions', *Journal of Modern Italian Studies*, 20 (4): 454–473.

Bosco, A. & Verney, S. (2012) 'Electoral epidemic: the political cost of economic crisis in southern Europe, 2010–11', *South European Society and Politics*, 17 (2): 129–154.

Calise, M. (2010) *Il partito personale: I due corpi del leader*, Roma, Laterza.

Campus, D. (2006) *L'antipolitica al governo: De Gaulle, Reagan, Berlusconi*, Bologna, Il Mulino.

Chiaramonte, A. & D'Alimonte, R. (2012) 'The twilight of the Berlusconi era: local elections and national referendums in Italy, May and June 2011', *South European Society and Politics*, 17 (2): 261–279.

Corbetta, P. & Gualmini, E. (eds) (2013) *Il partito di Grillo*, Bologna, Il Mulino.

D'Alimonte, R. (2013) 'The Italian elections of February 2013: the end of the Second Republic?', *Contemporary Italian Politics*, 5 (2): 113–129.

Diamanti, I., Ceccarini, L., Bordignon, F., Di Pierdomenico, M. & Gardani, L. (2013) *Gli italiani e lo stato – rapporto 2013*. Report commissioned by *La Repubblica*. www.demos.it/a00935.php (accessed 1 May 2017).

Diamanti, I., Ceccarini, L., Bordignon, F., Di Pierdomenico, M. & Gardani, L. (2015) *Gli italiani e lo stato – rapporto 2015*. Report commissioned by *La Repubblica*. www.demos.it/a01211.php (accessed 1 May 2017).

Diamanti, I., Ceccarini, L., Bordignon, F., Di Pierdomenico, M. & Gardani, L. (2016) *Gli italiani e lo stato –rapporto 2016*. Report commisioned by *La Repubblica*. www.demos.it/a01341.php (accessed 10 June 2017).

Emanuele, V. & Maggini, N. (2015) 'Il partito della nazione? Esiste e si chiama Movimento 5 Stelle'. http://cise.luiss.it/cise/2015/12/07/il-partito-della-nazione-esiste-e-si-chiama-movimento-5-stelle/ (accessed 1 May 2017).

Fabbrini, S. (2009) 'The transformation of Italian democracy', *Bulletin of Italian Politics*, 1 (1): 29–47.

Grilli di Cortona, P. (2007) *Il cambiamento politico in Italia: dalla prima alla seconda Repubblica*, Roma, Carocci.

Ignazi, P. (2008) *Partiti politici in Italia*, Bologna, Il Mulino.

Kostadinova, T. & Levitt, B. (2014) 'Towards a theory of personalist parties: concept formation and theory building', *Politics and Policy*, 42 (4): 490–512.

Maggini, N. (2013) 'La perdita di consenso dei partiti italiani e il successo di un nuovo attore politico', in L. De Sio, M. Cataldi & F. Di Lucia (eds), *Le Elezioni Politiche 2013*, Dossier CISE N°4, 69–74.

Mair, P. (2013) *Ruling the void: the hollowing of western democracy*, London: Verso.

Ministero dell'Interno (n.d.) *Archivio Storico delle Elezioni*. http://elezionistorico. interno.it/ (accessed 1 May 2017).

Pasquino, G. & Venturino, F. (eds) (2014) *Il Partito Democratico secondo Matteo*, Bologna: Bononia University Press.

Pasquino, G. & Valbruzzi, M. (2015) 'The impact of the 2013 general election on the Italian political system: the end of bipolarism?' *Journal of Modern Italian Studies*, 20 (4): 438–453.

Pasquino, G. & Valbruzzi, M. (2017) 'The Italian Democratic Party: its nature and its secretary', *Revista Española de Ciencia Política*, 44, July. https://recyt.fecyt.es/index.php/recp/article/view/59480/html_46 (accessed 1 September 2017).

Seddone, A. & Venturino, F. (2015) 'The Partito Democratico after the 2013 elections: all change?', *Journal of Modern Italian Studies*, 20 (4): 474–490.

Segatti, P., Poletti. M. & Vezzoni, C. (2015) 'Renzi's Honeymoon effect: the 2014 European election in Italy', *South European Society and Politics*, 20 (3): 311–331.

Tarchi, M. (2015) *Italia populista: dal Qualunquismo a Beppe Grillo*, Bologna, Il Mulino.

Ventura, S. (2015) *Renzi & Co: il racconto dell'era nuova*, Soveria Monelli, Rubbetino.

Vicentini, G. (2015) 'From foreign body to the party leadership and beyond: Explaining Matteo Renzi's path to power through the evolution of his primary election voters', *Contemporary Italian Politics*, 7 (2): 127–143.

8

The financial crisis and the curse of Latvian left parties

Karlis Bukovskis and Ilvija Bruge

Introduction

'The left' is close to being a derogatory term in Latvian politics. Although social democratic ideas are clearly visible in policies and opinions, an association with 'the left' has been and continues to be more damaging than good. This is based partly on the lack of a traditional ideological division of political parties since an independent democratic party system was re-established in Latvia in 1991. It is also related to the continuous political self-mismanagement of the political parties located on the left. As a result, a country that was among the most heavily hit in the world by the 2008 economic crisis did not see a social democratic (or socialist) resurrection on the political scene or emergence of intellectual alternatives to the ruling neoliberal economic ideology.

This chapter provides a short explanation of the fall of the Latvian left from historical prominence to modern infamy, followed by an analysis of the surprising lack of resurrection of the left in spite of harsh austerity measures imposed in the country, and the impact of the Latvian cross-ideological consensus on the future of the EU. As a result, three central arguments will be presented in the context of the financial crisis and the left. First, Latvian politics saw a self-induced relabelling of some parties from ethnic issues to social democratic ones. Second, some social democratic politicians and their policies were incorporated into government. Third, economic social democracy became a part of catch-all programmes of Latvian political parties.

For the purposes of this chapter, Latvia's left could be grouped as follows: 1) social democratic oriented nationalist politicians; 2) the Social Democratic Party, Harmony,[1] with its satellite, the Socialist Party of Latvia; and 3) the Latvian Green Party.[2] The predominant trend in the Latvian political arena has been constant reshuffling of political parties with new ones emerging before every election and old ones merging or becoming defunct. Moreover, the classical division between party lines based on economic ideology has not existed in Latvia since Latvia left the Soviet Union, although it was present during the period of independence from 1918 until 1940. The Latvian left–right cleavage has been based on ethnic rather than economic principles, with left parties traditionally associated with pro-Russia and Russian minority positioning as opposed to Latvian national and pro-NATO policies.

The ongoing struggle for acceptance of Latvia into the world community, and concerns regarding the policies of Russia, have kept this political division on the table for more than two decades. And even the financial crisis of 2008–2010 that resulted in high unemployment, increasing income inequality and austerity measures implemented by the government, did not change this. The rebirth (or birth) of Latvian social democracy has not happened although there has been a general demand in the society for a greater catalogue of state services. This stems from the dominance of traditional neoliberal national governments and policies. Parties like Harmony have used social democratic ideas to criticise Latvian parties, creating an opposition stance to the government. It is also typical of the catch-all approach in Latvian politics.

The fall of the Latvian left

While Latvia has re-invented for itself or copied from western partners many diverse ideas, it has not been able to transpose western economic ideological cleavages to national politics. But it was not always like that. The Latvian social democratic movement started organising itself as representatives of workers at the end of the nineteenth century and in 1904 the Latvian Social Democratic Workers Party (LSDSP) had already been established. LSDSP became a prominent player in Latvian politics during the parliamentary period of 1918–1934 with substantial representation in the Constitutional Assembly (1920–1922), gaining 39% of popular support (57 seats) and leading the race in all the consequent national parliament (Saeima) sessions until the coup d'état in 1934 – 30 seats in 1922; 32 seats in 1925; 25 seats in 1928, and 21 seats in 1931 (the last Saeima until the restoration of independence). Although LSDSP participated only in two short-lived coalition governments and mostly remained in opposition throughout the parliamentary period, it was among the first parties to be banned during the authoritarian period and re-established itself during the Soviet period as an important political force of Latvian exile activists.

LSDSP was part of the Socialist International during the period and, as recalled by one of its main activists, Atis Lejiņš, the Latvian party's exclusion

Table 8.1 National election results in Latvia, 1998–2014

Election Year (seats/%)	People's Harmony Party	LSA/ LSDSP	PCTVL	Greens and Farmers	Harmony	Other elected parties	National Government (coalition)
1998	16 / 14.12%	14 / 12.81%				People's Party (24 / 21.19%); Latvian Way (21 / 18.05%); TB/LNNK (17 / 14.65%); New Party (8 / 7.31%)	26.11.1998–16.07.1999: Latvian Way (*Vilis Krištopans*); TB/LNNK; New Party; LSDSP (since 05.02.1999) 16.07.1999–05.05.2000: People's Party (*Andris Šķēle*); Latvian Way; TB/LNNK 05.05.2000–07.11.2002: Latvian Way (*Andris Bērziņš*); People's Party; TB/LNNK; New Party
2002			25 / 19.0%	12 / 9.4%		New Era Party (26 / 23.90%); People's Party (20 / 16.60%); LPP (10 / 9.50%); TB/LNNK (7 / 5.40%)	07.11.2002–09.03.2004: New Era Party (*Einars Repše*); Greens and Farmers; TB/LNNK; LPP 09.03.2004–02.12.2004: Greens and Farmers (*Indulis Emsis*); People's Party; LPP 02.12.2004–07.11.2006: People's Party (*Aigars Kalvītis*); Greens and Farmers; LPP; New Era Party
2006			6 / 6.03%	18 / 16.71%	17 / 14.42%	People's Party (23 / 19.56%); New Era Party (18 / 16.71%); LPP/LC (10 / 8.58%); TB/LNNK (8 / 6.94%)	07.11.2006–20.12.2007: People's Party (*Aigars Kalvītis*); Greens and Farmers; LPP/LC; TB/LNNK 20.12.2007–12.03.2009: LPP/LC (*Ivars Godmanis*); People's Party; Greens and Farmers; TB/LNNK 12.03.2009–03.11.2010: New Era Party (*Valdis Dombrovskis*); People's Party; Greens and Farmers; TB/LLK; Civic Union
2010				22 / 19.68%	29 / 26.04%	Unity (33 / 31.22%) National Alliance (8 / 7.67%)	08.11.2010–25.10.2011: Unity (*Valdis Dombrovskis*); Greens and Farmers

2011	13 / 12.22%	31 / 28.36%	ZLP (22 / 20.83%) Unity (20 / 18.83%) National Alliance (14 / 13.88%)	25.10.2011–22.01.2014: Unity (*Valdis Dombrovskis*); ZLP; National Alliance 22.01.2014–05.11.2014: Unity (*Laimdota Straujuma*); ZLP; National Alliance; Greens and Farmers
2014	21 / 19.53%	24 / 23.0%	Unity (23 / 21.87%) National Alliance (17 / 16.61%) LRA (8 / 6.66%) NSL (7 / 6.85%)	05.11.2014–11.02.2016: Unity (*Laimdota Straujuma*); Greens and Framers; National Alliance Since 11.02.2016: Greens and Farmers (*Māris Kučinskis*); Unity; National Alliance

Source: CVK (nd)

Party abbreviations:

Civic Union – consisted of split-off members from New Era Party and TB/LNNK

Greens and Farmers – Union of Greens and Farmers – member of the Alliance of Liberals and Democrats for Europe Group

Harmony – Concord Centre (since 2014 – Social Democratic Party 'Concord') – member of Progressive Alliance of Socialists and Democrats

Latvian Way – member of the Alliance of Liberals and Democrats for Europe Party

LPP – Latvia's First Party – member of the Alliance of Liberals and Democrats for Europe Party

LPP/LC – Latvia's First Party / the Latvian Way (election alliance)

LRA – Latvian Association of Regions

LSA/LSDSP – Latvia's Union of Social Democrats / Latvian Social Democratic Workers Party

National Alliance – 'All For Latvia!' – 'For Fatherland and Freedom/LNNK' – member of the European Conservatives and Reformists group

New Era Party – Member of the European People's Party Group

NSL – For Latvia from the Heart PCTVL – Union of Political Organizations 'For Human Rights in a United Latvia' – member of the Greens/European Free Alliance

People's Party – member of the European People's Party Group

TB/LNNK – 'For Fatherland and Freedom/LNNK' – member of the Union for Europe of the Nations (until 2009)

Unity – Member of the European People's Party Group

ZLP – Reform Party also known as 'Zatler's Reform Party'

from this western-based organisation was high on the Soviet leadership's agenda (Lejiņš, 2017). The Soviet regime managed to exclude LSDSP from the youth section, but with the active involvement of former Austrian Chancellor Bruno Kreisky the Latvian party managed to remain in the main section of the organisation. The party became not only the main centre for Latvian social democracy for almost half a century, but also an important lobby for Baltic independence.[3]

With the collapse of the Soviet Union and Latvia's transition to a market economy, society was looking for a smoother transition than 'shock therapy'.[4] Leaders of the national movement like Dainis Īvāns and Jānis Jurkāns[5] favoured a social democratic approach (Lejiņš, 2017). But the internal struggles, short-term interests, growing competition from other political parties, and unsuccessful media appearances resulted in LSDSP losing their political momentum. Internal quarrels and differences in attitudes towards party membership, stances on ethnic issues and relations with Russia and western countries ended with them not receiving sufficient support to enter the national parliament until the 1998 elections.[6]

It was the Latvian Social Democratic Association and active leadership of Juris Bojārs that allowed Latvian social democrats to enter the Saeima with 14 (out of 100) places and later 14 places (out of 60) in the Riga municipality. Internal struggles continued to be destructive and one such with Egils Baldzēns led to the Latvian Social Democratic Union[7] splitting away in 2002. Consequently, LSDSP lost the national elections, receiving only 7 seats in the Riga municipality in 2005, and other visible leaders like Atis Lejiņš and Ansis Dobelis left the party in 2010. Lejiņš became a member of the Saeima for a liberal party, 'Unity', and Dobelis started a social democratic association entitled Progressives in 2011. Ansis Dobelis admitted that discrepancies with LSDSP leader Jānis Dinēvičs and different stances not so much on economic issues as on social and political values and egali-tarianism as well as relations with Russia have severely damaged the social democratic movement in Latvia (Dobelis, 2017). Finally, experts indicate that voters in the twenty-first century more often look at actual work done by particular parties instead of the emphasis on plans and promises, which was more typical of the 1990s. The problem with the Social Democratic Party (as well as Latvia's Socialist Party) is that they do not have anything to show, especially on the national level (Kolodzieja, 2013).

Harmony emerged as a victor from this internal struggle and, mired in allegations of corruption, the Social Democratic Party collapsed. While a social democratic party consisting of a younger generation is still a possibility, it is the Social Democratic Party 'Concord' (Harmony) that has taken the vacant social democrat slot in the Latvian political arena. A combination of political manoeuvring and constant voter support, mainly from Russian-speaking

Latvian voters, has allowed the party to be a permanent and influential political force in the Latvian arena. But it is the interest in attracting ethnic Latvian voters that has been pushing Harmony to re-emphasise its social democratic beginnings. The chairman of the party and Mayor of Riga Nils Ušakovs declared that 'We don't talk about ethnic issues; … I believe that, in the long run, the politics in our city and our country needs to be based on ideological values, not ethnicity' (Lyman, 2014). Ušakovs's popularity due to his charisma, conciliatory approach to ethnic relations and popular policies,[8] in addition to regular criticisms of the neoliberal national governments, have allowed Harmony to reach out to like-minded voters.

At the same time, as noted by another leader of Harmony, Jānis Urbanovičs, it is unlikely that Latvian politics and voters will be able to grow out of ethnic-based divisions and into having parties based on economic ideology and with proper intellectual ambitions (Urbanovičs, 2017). This claim is rather realistic taking into account the emotional response and insecurity stirred up in Latvian society by Russia's actions in Crimea and eastern Ukraine since 2014. Moreover, Harmony's attempts to shift its image away from ethnic policies is heavily impeded by its official collaboration agreement with the party United Russia and the Communist Party of China. The party is trying to become a legitimate part of western social democracy by means of allying itself with the European Parliament's S&D,[9] though it is not a member of the Party of European Socialists. Its relations to the Kremlin remain an issue of concern both in Latvia and among western social democrats (Friedrich-Ebert-Stiftung, 2016; Lejiņš, 2017).

The financial crisis and 'social demand'

The rise of Harmony as the only social democratic party in the Latvian political arena, especially since the start of the financial crisis, is no accident. But it is also not evidence of true ideological shifts either. The party has constantly been in opposition in the national parliament to neoliberal oriented Latvian national parties and numerous governments. Although Harmony has had a strong representation and rhetoric in Riga and some other municipalities, indicating an emphasis on social policies, its natural position has always been criticism of government policies, including fiscal policy and annual national budgets from the opposition benches. Not being part of the coalition government, Harmony has not had an opportunity to directly rule on social or economic policies on the national level. But neither Harmony's active self-promotion, nor the harsh experiences of the financial crisis in Latvia, nor expectations of a large part of the population have managed to shift the political party discourse away from ethnic cleavages. The current left parties are doomed to remain perpetual opposition parties and new social democratic parties will be unsuccessful due to social democratic undertakings of the liberal government and overall populism and 'catch-all-ism' in the party system.

Latvia was among the hardest hit countries during the financial crisis. In the period from 2008–2010 the country's GDP contracted by 23% in total and unemployment figures increased to 19.5% in 2010 according to Eurostat statistics (Eurostat, 2017a). After the rapid growth of 2004–2007 (Kattel & Raudla, 2013: 426–449), coinciding with Latvia's accession into NATO and the European Union and the rapid increase of foreign direct investment and internal consumption, Latvia hit the wall of the bursting real estate bubble and bailout of Parex Bank – the second largest bank in the country owned by Latvians. There were three consecutive neoliberal governments led by Valdis Dombrovskis from 2009. These introduced austerity measures at the request by the IMF and the European Commission. There were heavy cuts to the number of public servants and agencies (the public service was downsized by approximately 14,000 positions), a 10% reduction of pensions (with reimbursement after the Constitutional Court decision), the closing of 29 out of 49 hospitals (Aslund, 2010: 37), cutting social benefits, including unemployment and maternity allowances, and reducing public spending on healthcare and educational programmes (for more information see Austers, 2016). These 'internal devaluation' policies resulted in a rather quick macroeconomic recovery (for more discussion see Aslund, 2010; Aslund & Dombrovskis, 2011; Eihmanis, 2018), but the severe cuts in government budget spending of almost 14% naturally had a significant impact on the welfare of the general society.

Latvian society came out of the financial crisis with the Gini coefficient at 37% in 2011 (Hansen, 2011), with unemployment only in 2015 falling below 10% (Central Statistical Bureau, 2016a), with continued mass emigration for job opportunities in Ireland, the United Kingdom, Norway and other European countries reaching approximately 13% of population since Latvia joined the EU. The average monthly wage (€762) in the country returned to pre-crisis levels only in April 2014 (Kas jauns, 2014b). Although one of the central undertakings of the Latvian governments since the 'grand plan' of meeting the Eurozone membership requirements has been decreasing socio-economic inequalities in the country, with then Prime Minister Dombrovskis announcing plans for an increased minimum wage and non-taxable incomes (Financenet, 2013), no rapid decrease of inequality has taken place. According to Eurostat data and recommendations by the European Commission and the Organisation of Economic Co-operation and Development (LSM, 2016), the inequality issue still remains one of the most serious concerns. In 2015, 30.9% of the Latvian population were still living at risk of poverty (Eurostat, 2016: 2), and the Gini coefficient was 35.4% (Eurostat, 2017b).

Low support for increasing non-taxable income or social benefits to social groups at risk is argued to be too costly to the state budget. Introduction of a progressive taxation system instead of Latvia's classical flat personal income tax has been constantly postponed due to widespread criticisms from different sides (Progresīvie, 2015). The Ministry of Finance in 2015 came closest to introducing progressive taxation with a plan to start diversifying the tax burden from 2016, but the idea was shelved for an indefinite time period due to criticisms that there would be an additional bureaucratic burden and lack of immediate effects on the poor. Calculations by Jānis Hermanis of the Latvian Employers Confederation demonstrate the poverty risk index for households in Latvia in 2015 was 21.8% with single senior (over 65 years old) households leading the statistics with 74%, followed by 60.3% for single female households and 46.1% for single male households (Hermanis, 2017).

Another visible economic problem that Latvia is facing is the minimum wage. The minimum wage since January 2017 has reached €380 before taxes. Although gradual increases have occurred annually, Latvia is still in the group of the EU countries with the lowest minimum wage rates. The political unwillingness to increase the minimum wage more rapidly traditionally stems from arguments about the inability of enterprises to pay an increased wage and the danger of them going bankrupt. Especially Latvian regional businesses have been arguing that a speedy increase in minimum wage requirements would result in job losses or going out of business altogether. Hence, the threat of increasing unemployment and consequently government expenditures on social benefits, together with willingness to be cost competitive in labour against the other two Baltic states, results in slow increases in the minimum wage.

This eternal problem is strongly tied to another structural problem – the high number of small or micro-enterprises in the country and the low number of large companies in Latvia. The lack of widespread merger or acquisition trends, in combination with lower taxation to micro-enterprises (with a €720 monthly wage cap) introduced during the financial crisis, have led to a race to the bottom in terms of the salaries offered for low added value jobs. As a result the economic and social discrepancies are appearing more vividly between different Latvian regions. It is not only that the GDP per capita is more than three times higher in Riga than in Latvia's poorest regions, namely, €20,222 in Riga compared to €6,061 in Latgale (Hermanis, 2016), a steep divergence since membership in the EU. It is also about significant average wage differences between the Latvian regions; with Latgale leading with the lowest income levels of €409 per month after tax deduction and the population of Riga earning almost €663 (Central Statistical Bureau, 2016b). These post-financial crisis economic trends therefore show a need for increased social spending and wealth distribution policies that address practical needs among large parts of the Latvian population. Hence this would be an opportunity for left parties to gain political popularity points on social democratic or even socialist ideology.

Moreover, a ground-breaking discovery made by the research centre SKDS in 2012 showed that, although 'only 16 percent of the Latvian population think of themselves as left oriented (only 4 percent think of themselves as fully left oriented), in reality more than a half (55%) of Latvian people should be considered as left oriented (moreover 12 percent should be considered as radical left)' (SKDS, 2012: 5). The data clearly indicates that the majority of the Latvian population wishes for greater redistribution and solidarity in social policies, although they would not prefer to be called or seen as left. This demonstrates the deep-rooted misalignment of left–right economic principles in Latvian political culture. This discrepancy was especially evident among Latvians identifying themselves as liberals (47%).

Discrepancies between ideological labels and self-identification and the stigmatisation of 'the left' has resulted in many parties or politicians trying to avoid association with socialist or even social democratic ideas or labels. At the same time, as mentioned, recognition of the need for social policies or even classical social democratic notions like progressive taxation is visible also in the liberal government policies. Moreover, even liberal oriented political parties identify themselves as promoters of exclusively liberal social values, rather than liberal economic principles.[10] With the societal demand for domestic solidarity and greater social services identified by the aforementioned SKDS research, it is at the same time impossible for politicians to avoid introducing economic equality and justice issues in their programmes and electoral promises.

In spite of these reasons, the financial crisis did not provide left parties with a new momentum. During the three elections[11] only Harmony increased its representation in the 100-seat parliament between 2010 and 2011 from 29 to 31 representatives, an increase that was lost in the 2014 national elections when only 24 places were acquired. The quasi-left Greens and Farmers Union received 22 places in 2010, 13 in 2011 and 21 in 2014 for reasons more related to change of the old political elite rather than economic arguments. No other left parties were part of the parliament, and Harmony remained in opposition during all coalition governments.

This result and these trends are clearly the conclusions also of Ammon Cheskin and Luke March. 'Latvia's radical left has shown no notable ideological or strategic response. Existing [radical left parties] did not secure significant political gains from the crisis, nor have new challengers benefitted' (2016: 231). Their research was largely focused on the Socialist Party of Latvia, whose success in all elections largely depended on it running as part of Harmony, as well as For Human Rights in United Latvia, which has not received popular support in national elections since the 2010 elections and has transformed itself into a purely ethnic party under the title Latvian Russian Union.

Other researchers have arrived at harsher conclusions when evaluating the situation with the Latvian left parties. For instance, Ivars Ījabs's general conclusion on the current political party system in Latvia is that 'Parties in Latvia do not define the agenda, but just follow it' (Ījabs, 2017). This idea is supported by Jānis Urbanovičs of Harmony who admits that politicians in Latvia are creating a demand that they themselves cannot fulfil in the form of social democratic promises: 'There is no ideological party in Latvia' (Urbanovičs, 2017). Similarly, Egils Baldzēns believes that there are various internal and external influences in Latvia and parties are often just adjusting to those (Baldzēns, 2017). The same characterisation of the Latvian political party scene is given also by Arnis Kaktiņš who underlines the extremely blurred and incoherent ideological positioning of all of the Latvian political parties: 'The elite simply has not carried out a self-reflection on their ideological belongingness' (Kaktiņš, 2017).

Ivars Ījabs, when discussing the low support for social democratic ideas in Latvia, highlights the low levels of solidarity in Latvian society that go hand in hand with the fact that 'there is a demand for social democratic action, not social democratic ideology in Latvia' (Ījabs, 2017). One of the young social democratic leaders in Latvia, Ansis Dobelis, when discussing the poor results of left parties during the economic crisis states that 'in spite of the fact that people care about the healthcare system, education and income, the ethnic division comes first when a party must be chosen; [moreover, in Latvia] parties are not long-term projects, they lose their popularity as soon as their leaders lose theirs; [also] the crisis did not give any boost to the left because media were liberally oriented for austerity' (Dobelis, 2017). His claim is closely related to both a shortage of openly economically left oriented mass media, as well as general criticism of government policies stemming from a lack of social assistance and spending. Latvian mass media, similar to the political parties in opposition, criticise governments for lacking social expenditure, but naturally without providing a comprehensive plan for alternative economic governance. Therefore, besides the acknowledgment that the 'average Latvian is a social democrat' (Urbanovičs, 2017), the social democratic ideology is part of the left, but as Jānis Ikstens also stresses: 'In [Latvian] politics the Left is seen as Soviet and Russian

[and] that leads to negative stereotypes' (Kolodzieja, 2013). Some go even further, stating that in Latvia social democracy in public discourse is seen as synonymous with communism (Dinēvičs, 2017).

In spite of public perceptions, among the most visible public proponents of leftist ideas are the trade unions and especially the Free Trade Union Confederation of Latvia (LBAS). Although their status as a social partner and part of National Tripartite Cooperation Council (NTSP) provides them with direct influence on national, including budgetary policies (LIKUMI, 1998), the popularity of trade unions is rather low. As leader of LSDSP Jānis Dinēvičs estimates: 'If LBAS unites only 17% of the labour force [of Latvia], we cannot speak of influence of trade unions. The only exceptions could be the Latvian Trade Union of Education and Science Employees Latvian Trade Union of Health and Social Care Employees' (Dinēvičs, 2017). It is admitted that LBAS functions as a strong mechanism for promotion of social programmes, increase of salaries and workers' rights in the country. The provisions of the Labour Law in Latvia are seen as one of the most visible achievements. But a rather subtle self-evaluation is given also by the current president of LBAS Egils Baldzēns, stating that the influence of trade unions in modern Latvia is far from perfect. The veteran social democrat politician also denied that the influence of social democratic policies via LBAS and NTSP is substituting the need for social democratic parties in Latvia (Baldzēns, 2017). Igors Pimenovs of Harmony also stresses that 'Trade unions are very important [for building up social democratic ideas in Latvia], but their development is only in the very early stage. Mutual trust between politicians and trade unions is essential and it improves with every year' (Pimenovs, 2017). This statement correlates with the slow development and general misconception about the trade unions in Latvia as being seen as bureaucratic structures and hence distrusted in Latvia (Dobelis, 2017). Therefore, Latvia's experience shows that trade unions are not a strong force in support for left parties. LBAS and individual organisations generally operate as autonomous units without lasting party connections. This correlates with a general observation on Latvia's political system, that it is dominated by extreme individualism (Dobelis, 2017).

Finally, Latvia's unique situation with the left, especially during the financial crisis, is strongly related to the fact that liberal parties tend to include principles in favour of higher wages, better working conditions, social responsibility, improved public healthcare, higher social benefits and other such principles in their electoral programmes and promises. Liberal parties tend to include the principles not only due to societal demands and needs, but also in order not to push away voters with lesser income, who would otherwise potentially vote for Harmony. The fact that 'social democrats are in all political parties' (Baldzēns, 2017) and 'social democracy works through all parties' (Lejiņš, 2017) creates a situation in which the appearance of a new social democratic party on the Latvian stage is complicated. For instance, the most recent issues like an increase in non-taxable minimum and child benefits have been led by Atis Lejiņš, a Latvian exile with a long experience of western social democratic movements, who attempted to reshape LSDSP into a western social democratic party before joining and being elected to national parliament from the strongest pro-western, liberal-values-promoting party, Unity. The tendency for all political parties to have active social democratic members is indirectly recognised also by the former president of LBAS, Pēteris Krīgers, stating that parties tend to forget the socially responsible promises that they made before the elections (Tvnet, 2011).

If the case of the Latvian left can be seen as unique, then also the situation with the political advocates of environmental ideas is also rather interesting. The Latvian Green Party is as economically left as every other liberal Latvian party that has been part of the national governments. The Latvian Green Party classically collaborates with the Latvian Farmers Union, and they are represented together in the national parliament. The Union of Greens and Farmers (ZZS) has been in and out of ruling coalitions since 2002. The party is not considered left, neither in accordance with the 'Latvian standard' as it is an ethnically Latvian party, nor economically left as it does not have a clear economic policy. As Augusts Brigmanis puts it: 'Municipalities are the all-important factor in securing electoral victory, and Greens and Farmers Union is a municipality party; it is hard to win elections based just on green ideas' (Brigmanis, 2017). The chairman of the Latvian Farmers Union, one of the two oldest parties in Latvia along with the LSDSP, points out that there is a demand for social justice in the country, but it is Harmony that tries to appeal to the niche of employees.

The ZZS must be considered the ultimate catch-all party as it tries to appeal to various kinds of ideas, including often having public disagreement among its members even on essential issues, like Latvia's membership of NATO. Economically, the Greens and Farmers Union is about state involve-ment, control rather than redistribution (Ījabs, 2017). As Edgars Tavars puts it: 'There should not be capital concentration, and economic security in national states should prevail, as the open market global approach has lost. [...] Environmentally we appeal for eternity of issues, not only sustain-ability' (Tavars, 2017). This economic nationalism of the Latvian Green Party does not go further than calling for more protectionist policies. Therefore, the Latvian Green Party should be considered as quasi-left at most. Due to a lack of heavily polluting industries, the environmental issues in Latvia's green ideas are rooted in environmentalism as a starting point for national independence movements during the Perestroika period and 'an awkward understanding of green farming and the farmer's lifestyle' (Pimenovs, 2017). This combination has allowed the Latvian Green Party to acquire a constant representation in the national parliament with 4 seats after the 2010 and 2011 elections and 6 seats since 2014.

Therefore it is visible that the deep financial crisis and its legacies have not shifted the political rhetoric into economy-based debates. In spite of Harmony and attempts to change the discourse, the ethnic/geopolitical-orientation-based system has remained the same. While some incorrectly argue that the state of Latvia's economy does not allow for social democratic redistribution (Līcītis, 2012), others rightly point out that 'high-levels of shadow economy prevent the implementation of social democratic policies' (Baldzēns, 2017), pointing towards the funds that were not acquired which could theoretically have been used for social policies. Hence, although Latvia's social system could be in need of left policies, the political party system and political culture prevent it from happening.

The pro-European left and national interests

The positioning of the Latvian left parties towards the European Union is unusual. All parties, regardless of their stance on ethnic issues, have declared themselves to be pro-EU. Though some of their politicians occasionally are tempted to criticise the European Union's policies, especially since the refugee crisis started, no party has openly called itself Eurosceptic or demanded Latvia's exit from either the Eurozone or the European Union (for more information see Austers, 2016). Curiously, it is the Greens and Farmers Union that have had the most critical positions towards the EU, while ethnically pro-Russian Harmony, including the Socialist Party of Latvia, has not expressed vocal opposition to the EU, even during the financial crisis.

The pro-European position of the parties is related to Latvia's geopolitical interests as a small country. Latvian political parties keep supporting the European project in the name of a wide range of perceived national interests: geopolitical security, shared values and the prospects of economic welfare (for more detail see Bukovskis, 2016). The main support comes from the pro-European position of the Latvian population. But both Latvians and the Russian speaking minority see the EU as a long-term perspective and project regardless of its current problems. This is also reflected in the party positions on the future of the EU or Economic and Monetary Union. Interestingly, although Latvia's left do not always have a clear cut plan for the Latvian economy, they tend to still see the future of the EU in more extensive social policies. 'The EU house cannot be other than social democratic if it does not want to collapse', states Jānis Urbanovičs (2017). Similarly, argues

Egils Baldzēns, the EU must develop the Social Rights Pillar (Baldzēns, 2017). A different opinion is that of LSDSP's J. Dinēvičs, who states that globalisation is currently failing, national state values are coming back and therefore social democracy should adjust to these new challenges. 'If the EU wants to preserve itself it should build a system in which differences in EU countries' thinking does not impede their progress' (Dinēvičs, 2017). A similar 'EU refurbishment' approach is characteristic also of the Latvian Green Party, where it is believed that preservation of the EU is necessary as a common good, but that it should give more 'breathing space' to nation states (Tavars, 2017).

This is the most critical the Latvian politicians are on the European Union. The membership euphoria that was characteristic of Latvian politics from 2004 started disappearing only in 2015 after Latvia successfully managed its presidency of the Council of the European Union, and for this first time approached the perspective of budgetary expenditure on solidarity with Greece. But 'it was not the Greek sovereign debt crisis, but the refugee crisis that damaged Latvia's attitude towards the European Union' (Lejiņš, 2017). In the case of the Third Economic Adjustment Programme for Greece, politicians agreed to the plan after discovering that it did not involve any direct payments from the national budget. Hence solidarity with Greece was supported as part of Latvia's overall pro-EU policy, with the Cabinet of Ministers supporting the plan on 18 August 2015 and the Saeima European Affairs Committee voting on 17 August 2015, though with a strong emphasis that no debt relief should take place. After the vote only Igors Pimenovs of Harmony expressed views that the programme will deepen Greece's problems: '[New conditions] will enhance the risks of business stagnation and will not facilitate the economic development of Greece' (LSM, 2015). Solidarity with Greece put Latvia in a complicated dilemma as assistance was needed by a country, the living standard of which is higher than that of Latvia's population. The issue disappeared from the agenda with the rise of the refugee crisis, though it could cause challenging national debates if it should return to attention. The political anxiety regarding the assistance to Greece was only the prelude to a storm that started with the refugee crisis. The support for relocation of all the planned refugees to Latvia was adopted by the Saeima European Affairs Committee on 18 September 2015 only after most of the Harmony members from the opposition voted together with Unity on the matter, while coalition partners from the National Alliance and also ZZS objected (Skaties.lv, 2015).

This was not the first case of Harmony supporting the coalition in EU-related projects. An important illustration of such covert support is Harmony's position on the introduction of the euro in Latvia. Initially, during the 31 January 2013 vote on the Law 'on the introduction of the euro', Harmony as an opposition party voted against the law together with another then-opposition party – ZZS. Both parties argued that they supported the introduction of the euro, but at a later date than 2014 – due to the ongoing financial crisis in Europe and Latvia's 'insufficient' economic development levels. Both parties argued that more discussions should take place and instead of a simple majority vote, two thirds of parliament should support the government's decision to start the introduction procedures. ZZS alone proposed that the euro should only be introduced when, for instance, the minimum wage, the average wage, unemployment figures and GDP per capita had reached a certain level; while members of Harmony asked for introduction of the euro only when at least 2% of GDP is spent on research and development and trade balance is no more than minus 10% (Delfi, 2013). After the parliamentary vote with 52 members of Saeima supporting, 40 against and two abstaining, the decision to introduce the euro was made, while individual politicians started campaigning for organising a referendum on the issue. However, despite the significant levels of public scepticism, neither ZZS nor, most notably, Harmony used this opportunity of populism. Neither of them supported any further legal or political battles over the issue (Diena, 2013), thus *de facto* supporting the government's plan to introduce the euro from 2014.

Therefore, Latvian parties seldom hold debates on EU issues or express their positions on such matters. Most of the argumentation and public explaining is done by the Ministry of Foreign Affairs or line ministries. The positions are drafted by the government and respective ministries, while the European Affairs Committee adopts the positions often with little or no discussions receiving additional media circulation. There is general consensus on the importance of Latvia's EU membership, with more complex issues of deepening the EMU or economic governance rarely being addressed in the wider public sphere. The EU issues are also not used as a driving force for political publicity unless they gain widespread exposure in other EU countries, like the Transatlantic Trade and Investment Partnership (TTIP) negotiations, refugee crisis, etc. Hence the political parties do not have clearly formulated programmes or positions on the way the economic govern-ance of the EMU is shaped. In the 2019 European elections, Latvia's political parties continued to lack clear programmatic positions on the future of the EMU's economic governance structure. This is a clear indication that while the debate is ongoing, it continues to lack serious depth.

Conclusion

The example of the Latvian left parties demonstrates the complex ideational environment that a lack of clear economic ideologies creates. The left–right cleavage based on ethnic and historical divisions with stigmatisation of left and even of social democratic policies has resulted in the emergence of a post-ideological party system in Latvia. Ideologies are seen as somewhat anachronistic as voters tend to vote for specific issues or personalities with concrete achievements instead of ideological perspectives. Latvia's left parties are cursed by three factors: 1) an ideological mismatch in society's self-evaluation, 2) post-financial crisis social needs and economic capacities of the state budget, and 3) traditional party divisions along the geopolitical preferences. All three factors make party choices even more complex in the face of generational change and following the emergence of political cleavage between liberal and conservative social values.

In addition, global technological development, mechanisation and advancement of workers' rights have eradicated the classical voter base of social democratic and socialist forces – the workers. Income inequality is becoming more of an issue to be addressed throughout the European Union, especially in the aftermath of the financial crisis. But, this is not providing enough ground for re-emergence of social democratic movements as the ruling liberal parties tend to recognise the need to address inequality issues in order to preserve their popular support. Latvian society therefore seems to claim a need for social policies rather than political parties promising social policies. The financial crisis did not change the political landscape in Latvia as it did not change the pro-European predisposition of the parties. But it is in the aftermath of the current financial crisis, fuelled with populism that the left parties tend to look for a European Union that is more socially inclusive and yet nationally specific with respect to its messages.

Notes

1 The Latvian word is Saskaņa, which the party website translates as 'Concord'. However, 'Harmony' has become the more common English translation, and is used in this chapter.
2 A new party, Progressives (Progresīvie) was founded in 2017 with some left-wing, environmentalist and pro-EU activists (Tvnet, 2017).
3 LSDSP was excluded from the Socialist International in 2014. In 2014 Harmony was admitted as a consultative member and is lobbying to become a full member from Latvia.
4 Eglitis and Lace (2009) discuss the challenges of economic progress in post-community Latvia.
5 Jānis Jurkāns later founded a party that transformed into today's Harmony.
6 Bennich-Björkman (2009) examines party formation in post-communist Latvia; Ikstens (2007) looks at the EU and Latvia's political parties.
7 Later renamed the Social Democratic Union (Sociāldemokrātu savienība) and Social Democratic Party (Sociāldemokrātiskā partija) and terminated in 2010.

8 Such as providing all non-working pensioners with free public transportation in the Latvian capital; also special rates allocated to people with special needs, pupils, students and some other groups in accordance with Riga municipality binding rules No. 89, issued 24 August 2010 (LIKUMI, 2010).
9 Currently one of Latvia's nine MEPs, Andrejs Mamikins, is part of the S&D group. Additionally, see for instance the endorsement of the President of the European Parliament Martin Schulz of Nils Ušakovs before the Latvian national elections of 2014 (Kas jauns, 2014a).
10 This trend was clearly argued during an anonymous interview with founders of a new liberally oriented political party in January 2017.
11 Including one election that was a result of a positive outcome of a referendum on dissolution of a parliament in 2011.

Bibliography

Aslund, A. (2010) *The last shall be the first: the East European Financial Crisis*, Washington, DC: Peterson Institute for International Economics.

Aslund, A. & Dombrovskis V. (2011) *How Latvia came through the financial crisis*, Washington, DC: Peterson Institute for International Economics.

Austers, A. (2016) 'The case of Latvia: popular Euroscepticism in *Impasse*' in K. Bukovskis (ed.) *Euroscepticism in Small EU Member States*, Riga: LIIA. http://liia.lv/en/publications/euroscepticism-in-small-eu-member-states-546 (accessed 10 June 2017).

Bennich-Björkman, L. (2009) 'The communist past: party formation and elites in the Baltic states', *Baltic Worlds*, 2 (3–4): 26–36. http://balticworlds.com/the-communist-past-party-formation-and-elites-in-the-baltic-states/ (accessed 28 September 2018).

Bukovskis, K. (2016), 'Latvia: supporting the right cause and deepening the EMU', in V. Pertusot (ed.) *The European Union in the fog: building bridges between national perspectives on the European Union*, IFRI, 11 April. www.ifri.org/en/publications/publications-ifri/ouvrages-ifri/european-union-fog-building-bridges-between-national (accessed 10 June 2017).

Central Statistical Bureau (2016a) 'Bezdarbnieku īpatsvars' 23 February. www.csb.gov.lv/statistikas-temas/px_tabulas/bezdarbnieku-ipatsvars-43464.html (accessed 10 June 2017).

Central Statistical Bureau (2016b) 'Darba samaksa – Galvenie rādītāji', 6 November. www.csb.gov.lv/statistikas-temas/darba-samaksa-galvenie-raditaji-30270.html (accessed 10 June 2017).

Cheskin, A. & March, L. (2016) 'Latvia's "Russian left": trapped between ethnic, socialist, and social-democratic identities', in L. March & D. Keith (eds) *Europe's radical left: From marginality to the mainstream?*, London: Rowman and Littlefield, 231–253.

CVK (nd) 'Saiema elections', Riga: Centrālā Vēlēšanu Komisija/Central Election Committee. Available online at: https://www.cvk.lv/en/elections/saeima-elections (accessed 20 July 2019).

Delfi (2013) 'Saeima pieņem eiro ieviešanas likumu: pret nobalso arī viens koalīcijas deputāts' (15:25), 13 January. www.delfi.lv/news/national/politics/saeima-pienem-eiro-ieviesanas-likumu-pret-nobalso-ari-viens-koalicijas-deputats-1525.d?id=43016970 (accessed 10 June 2017).

Diena (2013) 'Saskaņas centrs sola neparakstīties par referenduma rosināšanu saistībā ar eiro ieviešanu', 4 February. www.diena.lv/raksts/latvija/politika/_saskanas-centrs_-sola-neparakstities-par-referenduma-rosinasanu-saistiba-ar-eiro-ieviesanu-13991644 (accessed 10 June 2017).

Eglitis, D. S. & Lace, T. (2009) 'Stratification and the poverty of progress in post-communist Latvian capitalism', *Acta Sociologica*, 52 (4): 329–349.

Eihmanis, E. (2018) 'Cherry-picking external constraints: Latvia and economic governance, 2008–2014', *Journal of European Public Policy*, 25 (2): 231–249.

Eurostat (2016) 'The share of persons at risk of poverty or social exclusion in the EU back to its pre-crisis level, 2008 and 2015', Luxembourg. http://ec.europa.eu/eurostat/documents/2995521/7695750/3-17102016-BP-EN.pdf/30c2ca2d-f7eb-4849-b1e1-b329f48338dc (accessed 10 June 2017).

Eurostat (2017a) 'Unemployment rate – annual data', Luxembourg. http://ec.europa.eu/eurostat/tgm/table.do?tab=table&init=1&language=en&pcode=tipsun20&plugin=1 (accessed 10 June 2017).

Eurostat (2017b) 'Gini coefficient of equivalised disposable income – EU-SILC survey', Luxembourg. http://ec.europa.eu/eurostat/tgm/table.do?tab=table&init=1&language=en&pcode=tessi190&plugin=1 (accessed 10 June 2017).

Financenet (2013) 'Dombrovskis vēlētos nākamgad palielināt neapliekamo minimumu', 12 June. http://financenet.tvnet.lv/viedokli/467735-dombrovskis_veletos_nakamgad_palielinat_neapliekamo_minimumu (accessed 10 June 2017).

Hansen, M. (2011) 'On inequality Latvia is still Nr.1!' IR, 7 January. www.irlv.lv/2011/1/7/on-inequality-latvia-is-still-nr-1 (accessed 10 June 2017).

Hermanis, J. (2016) 'GDP per capita in Latvian statistical regions', Twitter post by Jānis Hermanis (Expert on Economic development at Employers' Confederation of Latvia), 30 December. https://twitter.com/J_Hermanis/status/814847182020804609 (accessed 10 June 2017).

Hermanis, J. (2017) 'Nabadzības riska indekss pēc mājsaimniecības tipa (%)', Twitter post by Jānis Hermanis (Expert on Economic development at Employers' Confederation of Latvia), 2 February. https://twitter.com/J_Hermanis/status/827221729697214465 (accessed 10 June 2017).

Ikstens, J. (2007) 'Does Europe matter? The EU and Latvia's political parties', in P. G. Lewis & Z. Mansfeldová (eds) *The European Union and Party Politics in Central and Eastern Europe*, Basingstoke: Palgrave Macmillan, 86–106.

Kas jauns (2014a) 'Eiroparlamenta prezidents Martins Šulcs: Ušakovs ir cerība Latvijai, un es viņu atbalstu', 19 September. www.kasjauns.lv/lv/zinas/165578/eiroparlamenta-prezidents-martins-sulcs-usakovs-ir-ceriba-latvijai-un-es-vinu-atbalstu (accessed 10 June 2017).

Kas jauns (2014b) 'Ekonomiste: "Strādājošo cilvēku pirktspēja atgriezusies pirmskrīzes līmenī"', 29 August. www.kasjauns.lv/lv/zinas/163657/ekonomiste-stradajoso-cilveku-pirktspeja-atgriezusies-pirmskrizes-limeni (accessed 10 June 2017).

Kattel, R. & Raudla, R. (2013) 'The Baltic Republics and the crisis of 2008–2011', *Europe-Asia Studies*, 65 (3): 426–449.

Kolodzieja, K. (2013) 'Eksperti: Sociāldemokrātija mūsdienās ir stereotipu apvīta', *LSM*, 1 May. www.lsm.lv/lv/raksts/zinju-analiize/analize/eksperti-socialdemokratija-musdienas-ir-stereotipu-apviita.a55772/ (accessed 10 June 2017).

Līcītis, E. (2012) 'Mūsu zemes proletārieši – nesavienojas', *Latvijas Avīze*, 3 May. www.la.lv/musu-zemes-proletariesi-nesavienojas/ (accessed 10 June 2017).

LIKUMI (1998) 'Regulation of National Trilateral Cooperation Council', *Cabinet of Ministers*. http://likumi.lv/doc.php?id=50778 (accessed 10 June 2017).

LIKUMI (2010) 'Rīgas domes saistošie noteikumi Nr.89 Rīgā 2010.gada 24.augustā (prot. Nr.38, 4.§). Par braukšanas maksas atvieglojumiem Rīgas pilsētas sabiedriskā transporta maršrutu tīklā', 24 August. http://likumi.lv/doc.php?id=215859 (accessed 10 June 2017).

LSM (2015) 'Latvija atbalstīs palīdzību Grieķijai, bet iebildīs pret parāda norakstīšanu', 17 August. www.lsm.lv/lv/raksts/latvija/zinas/latvija-atbalstis-palidzibu-griekijai-bet-iebildis-pret-parada-norakstisanu.a141835/ (accessed 10 June 2017).

LSM (2016) 'OECD norāda uz lielu nevienlīdzību un iedzīvotāju skaita sarukumu Latvijā', 31 March. www.lsm.lv/lv/raksts/latvija/zinas/oecd-norada-uz-lielu-nevienlidzibu-un-iedzivotaju-skaita-sarukumu-latvija.a175988/ (accessed 10 June 2017).

Lyman, R. (2014) 'Mayor of Latvian capital tries to bridge old divide', *New York Times*, 12 December. www.nytimes.com/2014/12/13/world/europe/nils-usakovs-mayor-of-riga-aims-to-move-beyond-ethnic-politics.html (accessed 10 June 2017)

Progresīvie (2015) 'Nodokļu sistēmas progresivitāte – ceļš uz rietumnieciskāku sabiedrību', 5 August. www.progresivie.lv/2015/08/05/nodoklu-sistemas-progresivitate/ (accessed 10 June 2017).

Skaties.lv (2015) 'Saeimas komisija, pateicoties opozīcijai, atbalsta pozīciju 526 bēgļu uzņemšanai', 18 September. http://skaties.lv/zinas/latvija/politika/saeimas-komisija-pateicoties-opozicijai-atbalsta-poziciju-526-beglu-uznemsanai/ (accessed 10 June 2017).

SKDS (2012) 'Latvijas iedzīvotāju ideoloģiskais portrets', *Pasaules uzskats: pašnovērtējums un realitāte*, Populares Latvija, March.

Tvnet (2011) 'Krīgers: Partijas aizmirsušas savus priekšvēlēšanu solījumus', 6 October. www.tvnet.lv/zinas/viedokli/394593-krigers_partijas_aizmirsusas_savus_prieksvelesanu_solijumus (accessed 10 June 2017).

Tvnet (2017) 'Par biedrības "Progresīvie" partijas dibināšanu nobalso 220 biedri', 25 February. www.tvnet.lv/zinas/latvija/649132-par_biedribas_progresivie_partijas_dibinasanu_nobalso_220_biedri (accessed 10 June 2017).

Interviews

Baldzēns, E. (2017) Authors' interview with Egils Baldzēns, President of the Free Trade Union Confederation of Latvia (LBAS), January.

Brigmanis, A. (2017) Authors' interview with Augusts Brigmanis, member of Saeima, January.

Dinēvičs, J. (2017) Authors' interview with Jānis Dinēvičs, Leader of the Latvian Social Democratic Workers Party, January.

Dobelis, A. (2017) Authors' interview with Ansis Dobelis, Chairman of the non-governmental organization Progresīvie, January.

Friedrich-Ebert-Stiftung (2016) Authors' interview with a representative of Friedrich-Ebert-Stiftung in Latvia, December.

Ījabs, I. (2017) Authors' interview with Ivars Ījabs, Political Scientist, Associate Professor at the University of Latvia, January.

Kaktiņš, A. (2017) Authors' interview with Arnis Kaktiņš, Sociologist, Director of SKDS, January.

Lejiņš, A. (2017) Authors' interview with Atis Lejiņš, member of Saeima, January.

Pimenovs, I. (2017) Authors' interview with Igors Pimenovs, member of Saeima, January.

Tavars, E. (2017) Authors' interview with Edgars Tavars, member of Saeima, January.

Urbanovičs, J. (2017) Authors' interview with Jānis Urbanovičs, member of Saeima, January.

9

Navigating through troubled times: the left and the euro crisis in Finland

Tapio Raunio

Introduction

The campaign for the 2015 Eduskunta elections saw a clear divide between the two traditional parties of the left, the Social Democrats (SDP) and the Left Alliance (VAS), and the rest. The centre right parties, the main employers' organisation, the Confederation of Finnish Industries (EK), economists, and even the overall public mood seemed to favour cuts to public spending that would make the Finnish economy more competitive. Since the onset of the financial crisis Finland had experienced almost constant economic decline, with worsening public debt amidst job market uncertainty: one month ahead of the election the unemployment rate stood at 10.3%. A report by the powerful Ministry of Finance had indicated the need to achieve €6 billion of savings during the 2015–2019 electoral period, but SDP and VAS disagreed. Social Democrats advocated a more moderate speed of adjustment while the Left Alliance was the only Eduskunta party against cuts to public spending, arguing instead in favour of public investments financed with more foreign loans (Arter, 2015).

SDP finished fourth with 16.5% of the vote, its worst ever performance in Eduskunta elections, while the Left Alliance managed 7.1% of the vote, down 1%. The collective vote share of the leftist parties has declined dramatically in recent decades. Whereas Social Democrats and the predecessor of Left Alliance, the Finnish People's Democratic Union (FPDU), won over 45% of the vote between them in all but one election between 1945 and 1966 (when they won 48.3% of the vote together), by 2015 the electoral strength of the left had decreased to 23.6%. FPDU's decline began in the late 1960s and support for the Left Alliance has declined gradually since 1995. VAS has found it difficult to cater to the needs of both traditional working class voters and more urban new 'green left' supporters, and hence it is probable that in 2015 many in the latter group switched to the Green League (VIHR) which won 8.5% of the vote. The cabinet formed after the election brought together the agrarian/liberal Centre Party, the conservative National Coalition and, significantly, the populist and Eurosceptic Finns Party, whose rise affected both the support of the leftist parties and national debates on the European Union.

The vanishing electoral strength of left-wing parties is also bad news for trade unions, whose influence has depended strongly on the Social Democrats leading or being at least a partner in the ruling coalition. The weaker support means that leftist parties and the unions are increasingly on the defensive in Finland, with initiatives and discourse of the centre right parties and business interests dominating the agenda. This chapter argues that the response of the Finnish left to the euro and financial crisis must be understood in light of these domestic developments, with the positions of SDP, VAS and the Greens clearly influenced by the changing tides of party politics, the shape of the national economy and the domestic politicisation of Europe. The next section examines the decline of the left and the politicisation of European integration through the euro crisis, with the third section in turn exploring the ideological response of the left to the crisis. The concluding discussion looks ahead, arguing that the severe challenges facing the left and the unions are far from over.

The decline of the left and rise of populism

The shape of the Finnish party system, with no party as a rule winning more than 25% of the votes in Eduskunta elections, facilitates ideological convergence between all parties (Table 9.1). Finnish parties are strongly office-seeking, and cabinets are typically surplus majority coalitions that bring together parties from the left and the right. The dividing line between government and opposition has increased in significance as a result of recent constitutional reforms, but the pragmatic and consensual style of politics still largely prevails, particularly in EU and foreign policy (Arter, 2009; Karvonen, 2014; Ruostetsaari, 2015).

The fragmentation of the party system has increased since the start of the euro crisis. In two recent Eduskunta elections (2011, 2015), the rise of the Finns Party produced a situation where the party system has four quite equally sized large parties. The three-front model of Lipset and Rokkan (1967), where the relationship between trade unions and parties reflects underlying social cleavages, is still relevant but also under threat in Finland: the Centre Party represents agrarian or rural interests, the National Coalition the interests of the bourgeoisie or the capital, but SDP and VAS are now competing for the working-class vote with the Finns Party. While the Finns Party is not organisationally strong inside the main blue-collar confederation

Table 9.1 Distribution of votes in Eduskunta elections, 1945–2019 (%)

	SDP	Cent	Cons	Left	Green	RKP	Christ	Pop	Lib	Others
1945	25.1	21.3	15.0	23.5	–	7.9	–	–	5.2	2.0
1948	26.3	24.2	17.1	20.0	–	7.3	–	–	3.9	1.2
1951	26.5	23.2	14.6	21.6	–	7.3	–	–	5.7	1.1
1954	26.2	24.1	12.6	21.6	–	6.8	–	–	7.9	0.6
1958	23.2	23.1	15.3	23.2	–	6.5	–	–	5.9	2.8
1962	19.5	23.0	15.0	22.0	–	6.1	–	2.2	6.3	5.9
1966	27.2	21.2	13.8	21.1	–	5.7	0.5	1.0	6.5	2.9
1970	23.4	17.1	18.0	16.6	–	5.3	1.1	10.5	6.0	2.0
1972	25.8	16.4	17.6	17.0	–	5.1	2.5	9.2	5.2	1.2
1975	24.9	17.6	18.4	18.9	–	4.7	3.3	3.6	4.3	4.3
1979	23.9	17.3	21.7	17.9	–	4.3	4.8	4.6	3.7	1.8
1983	26.7	17.6	22.1	13.5	1.4	4.9	3.0	9.7	–	1.1
1987	24.1	17.6	23.1	13.6	4.0	5.6	2.6	6.3	1.0	2.1
1991	22.1	24.8	19.3	10.1	6.8	5.5	3.1	4.8	0.8	2.7
1995	28.3	19.8	17.9	11.2	6.5	5.1	3.0	1.3	0.6	6.3
1999	22.9	22.4	21.0	10.9	7.3	5.1	4.2	1.0	0.2	5.0
2003	24.5	24.7	18.6	9.9	8.0	4.6	5.3	1.6	0.3	2.5
2007	21.4	23.1	22.3	8.8	8.5	4.6	4.9	4.1	0.1	2.2
2011	19.1	15.8	20.4	8.1	7.3	4.3	4.0	19.1	–	1.9
2015	16.5	21.1	18.2	7.1	8.5	4.9	3.5	17.7	–	2.5
2019	17.7	13.8	17.0	8.2	11.5	4.5	3.9	17.5	–	5.9

Source: Ministry of Justice, 2019
Party abbreviations:
Cent – From 1907 to 1965 Agrarian Union, thereafter the Centre Party
Christ – From 1966 to 2002 Finnish Christian League, thereafter the Christian Democrats
Cons – National Coalition
Green – Green League
Left – From 1945 to 1990 Finnish People's Democratic Union (FPDU), from 1991 on
    Left Alliance
Lib – From 1918 to 1950 National Progressive Party, from 1951 to 1965 Finnish
    People's Party, from 1965 to 1983 Liberal People's Party. In the parliamentary
    election of 1983 the Liberal People's Party was a member organization of the
    Center Party. From 1987 to 2002 Liberal People's Party, thereafter the Liberals
Pop – From 1958 to 1966 Small farmers' Party, from 1966 to 1995 Finnish Rural
    Party, thereafter The Finns Party
SDP – Social Democratic Party
Swe – Swedish People's Party

SAK (the Central Organization of Finnish Trade Unions), in terms of party choice the Finns was the largest party among SAK members in the 2015 elections. Moreover, in 2015 SAK members were more likely to identify with the Finns Party than with either of the two traditional leftist parties (Tiihonen, 2015; 2016).[1]

Table 9.2 Distribution of votes in Eduskunta and EP elections, 2007–2019 (%)

Party	2007 Eduskunta	2009 EP	2011 Eduskunta	2014 EP	2015 Eduskunta	2019 Eduskunta	2019 EP
Centre Party	**23.1**	**19.0**	**15.8**	19.7	21.1	**13.8**	13.5
National Coalition	22.3	**23.2**	**20.4**	**22.6**	18.2	**17.0**	20.8
Social Democrats	**21.4**	17.5	19.1	12.3	**16.5**	17.7	14.6
Left Alliance	8.8	5.9	8.1	9.3	7.1	8.2	6.9
Green League	8.5	**12.4**	7.3	9.3	8.5	11.5	16.0
Christian Democrats	4.9	4.2	4.0	**5.2**	**3.5**	3.9	4.9
Swedish People's Party	**4.6**	**6.1**	**4.3**	**6.8**	**4.9**	4.5	6.3
The Finns Party	4.1	9.8	19.1	12.9	17.7	17.5	13.8
Others	2.2	1.9	1.9	1.9	2.5	5.9	3.1
TOTAL	100	100	100	100	100	100	100

Source: Ministry of Justice, 2019

Note: Governing parties are in bold. For example, at the time of the 2007 elections the ruling coalition consisted of the Centre, SDP, and the Swedish People's Party. At the time of the 2019 EP elections, Finland was yet to appoint a new cabinet after the April Eduskunta elections.

Centre right parties have held the majority of Eduskunta seats since the 1966–1970 electoral period, often with a comfortable margin. The prospect of a government consisting of only left-wing parties has not been realistic for several decades, and all cabinets formed since the 2003 elections have been led by centre right parties (Table 9.2). Social democracy has not been as strong in Finland as in the other Nordic countries, but SDP was the largest party in all Eduskunta elections from 1907 to 1954 and from 1966 to 1999 (except for 1991). Their peak was achieved in the 1995 elections with 28.3% of the vote, the highest vote share for a single party after the Second World War. But since the turn of the century, the SDP have not finished first in any election.

The dilemma facing SDP is of course typical for centre left parties across Europe. At its core are two interlinked questions: whether to defend traditional leftist economic goals or endorse more market-friendly policies, and who the party represents. This debate about the party's ideology and identity flared up after the 1991 elections, which ushered in a centre right coalition, and coincided with the serious recession of the early 1990s. With unemployment reaching at worst nearly 20% of the workforce, SDP and the trade unions began to emphasise the virtues of budgetary discipline and monetary stability alongside traditional social democratic goals such as universal social policies and job creation. Since trade with the Soviet regime had accounted for around 15–20% of overall national trade, the demise of the communist bloc increased trade dependence on the EU countries. As a result, internal party debates about ideology, the possibility of joining the EU and the need to restore economic well-being became closely entangled. In those circumstances, the gradual move towards the right was made as much out of necessity as out of deliberate choice. However, when in government[2] SDP has implemented economic reforms that have definitely frustrated many of its left-leaning supporters (Raunio, 2010; Mickelsson, 2015).[3] At the European level, SDP is a member of the Party of European Socialists and its MEPs sit in the Socialists & Democrats group.

The Left Alliance, founded in 1990, can be categorised as belonging to the 'new left' (Gomez et al., 2016; Fagerholm, 2017). Bringing together a variety of leftists and former communists, the party leadership advocates 'green left' ideological moderation, though its working-class voters more closely linked to trade unions oppose such centrist moves (Zilliacus, 2001). The party was in government from 1995 to 2003, but the experience was troublesome for both the party leadership and the rank-and-file (Dunphy, 2007; 2010). The Left Alliance entered another heterogeneous cabinet following the 2011 elections, but after an uneasy three years left the National Coalition-led 'six pack' cabinet in the spring of 2014 due to differences over economic policy. The Left Alliance belongs to the Party of the European Left and its MEP sits in the GUE/NGL group.

The Green League is quite centrist and refuses to be categorised as a left-wing party. It served in the government from 1995 to 2002 (when it left the cabinet due to disagreements over nuclear energy), from 2007 to 2011 and from 2011 to 2014 when it again exited the government over nuclear policy (Paastela, 2002; Bolin, 2016). The electorate of the party is diverse, bringing together more old-school radicals, 'green left' voters and younger liberals for whom environmental concerns are clearly just part of the overall green ideology (Zilliacus, 2001). Nonetheless, following the 2015 elections party chair Ville Niinistö lamented the decline of the left as the Social Democrats and Left Alliance share many of the values or concerns of the Greens, especially the fight against poverty and moral questions such as gender-neutral marriages (Raunio, 2015b). The Green League is a member of the European Green Party and in the European Parliament its representatives are in the Greens-EFA group.

The decline of the left presents a challenge for the trade unions, particularly for SAK. From the mid-1990s the SDP-led cabinets of Paavo Lipponen (1995–2003) emphasised the importance of collective wage bargaining and corporatism, not least because the cooperation of the trade unions was seen as essential in order to meet EMU criteria and to maintain budgetary discipline once in the Eurozone.[4] The main employers' organisation EK decided unilaterally to abandon tripartite collective wage talks in 2007 when Finland was governed by a centre right coalition (Bergholm & Bieler, 2013). However, since 2011 centralised wage agreements have been re-introduced, no doubt thanks to the fact that SDP re-entered the government after the 2011 elections. While the system of collective wage talks is not as comprehensive as before, many labour market agreements and laws are effectively decided in tripartite negotiations between the employers' federations, the trade unions and the government. Trade union density has also risen over the decades, and over 70% of the workforce belongs to unions. When SDP is not in the government, trade unions are immediately hurt (Raunio & Laine, 2017).

All three leftist parties have faced internal divisions over Europe, but such internal opposition has weakened over time. The significance of the formation of the 'rainbow' government in 1995 should not be underestimated, for it paved the way for Finland's entry to the Eurozone and ensured a broad backing for a national European policy that was strongly shaped by the social democratic Prime Minister Lipponen. In the membership referendum held in 1994 75% of SDP, 55% of Greens and 24% of VAS voters had supported joining the Union. In fact, the Green League and the Left Alliance were so divided over membership that they chose not to adopt official positions on the issue. Joining the government in 1995 meant that both parties had to align themselves almost overnight as pro-integrationist parties.

This adaptation was more difficult for the Left Alliance, which has also adopted a much more Eurosceptic discourse when in opposition. The Greens have made a more radical change, and it can perhaps even be considered now as the most pro-integrationist of all the Finnish parties. The Social Democrats have been solidly pro-EU since the late 1990s, but significantly it belongs to that section of the social democratic party family that had basically achieved much of its domestic policy goals, particularly the extensive welfare state regime (Marks & Wilson, 2000), and hence SDP – as well as VAS and VIHR – have balanced their pro-European policies with the need to protect the national welfare state policies.[5] As the results of elections to the EP suggest (Table 9.2), a sizeable part of the leftist electorate probably still views integration more as a threat than an opportunity. Overall, during EU membership right-wing parties and the Greens have performed better than SDP and VAS in EP elections (Raunio, 2016a).

The domestic consensus and the crisis

Until the euro crisis Finland's integration policy was characterised as flexible and constructive. This pro-integrationist approach enjoyed broad domestic elite approval. However, the divisive nature of the EU membership referendum held in 1994, in which 57% voted in favour of joining the EU, indicated that the commitment to integration which prevailed among the political parties was not shared to the same extent by the electorate. There was thus a notable lack of congruence between citizens and political parties, with most parties considerably more supportive of the EU than their supporters (Mattila & Raunio, 2005; 2012). In addition, the rules of the national EU coordination system, based on building broad domestic elite consensus behind closed doors, including often between the government and opposition parties, contributed to the depoliticisation of European issues (Hyvärinen & Raunio, 2014).

The domestic politicisation of the euro crisis, coinciding with the 2011 Eduskunta election campaign, certainly changed the nature of national EU discussions and even affected European-level decision-making. In the run-up to the 2011 elections, the problems affecting the Eurozone triggered heated debates, and the EU – or more precisely the role of Finland in the bailout measures – became the main topic of the campaign. The more Eurosceptic parties (the Finns Party, the Christian Democrats and the Left Alliance) and the main opposition party, the Social Democrats, led the attack on the government. The Social Democrats, perhaps not to be outdone by the Finns Party's EU critique, adopted a high-profile position against lending money to Greece without any securities (bilateral collaterals), and the opposition parties in general voted against the aid measures. The Finns Party had a particularly strong electoral incentive to capitalise on the crisis. It is the only party represented in the Eduskunta that has consistently been opposed to European integration, though without ever explicitly demanding Finland's exit from the EU or the Eurozone. It is also the only party which has systematically used the EU as a central part of its campaigns and political discourse (Raunio, 2012).

The election result was nothing short of extraordinary. The Finns Party[6] won 19.1% of the votes, a staggering increase of 15% on the 2007 elections and the largest ever increase in support achieved by a single party in Eduskunta elections.[7] In light of the election campaign, the 'six-pack' National Coalition-led government that entered into office in the summer of 2011 came under serious political pressure to 'defend national interests' more strongly in Brussels. Finland became the only EMU member state to demand bilateral lending guarantees on its bailout payments. It also rejected to begin with the ESM's 85% majority vote decision-making rules, demanding unanimity instead. And Finland blocked, together with the Netherlands, the entry of Bulgaria and Romania into the Schengen area. Overall, the success of the Finns Party clearly pushed the other parties in the direction of more EU critical discourse (Raunio, 2015a).

The main effects were nonetheless felt at home, with the euro crisis producing more contestation and debates in the government and especially in the plenary and the EU committee of the Eduskunta (Hyvärinen & Raunio,

2014; Raunio, 2016b).[8] Although problematic for the government (and occasionally by extension for EU decision-making), these developments were good news in terms of democracy and the level of public discussion. The plenary debates about the Eurozone were really the first time that the government was forced to justify and defend its EU policies in public – and when the opposition attacked the cabinet publicly over its handling of European matters.

The increased contestation influenced government formation. In 2011, the Finns Party was close to joining the cabinet, but according to Timo Soini, the long-standing party chair, it was impossible to participate in a government that was committed to further Eurozone rescue measures. However, after another strong election result in 2015 Soini guided his party into the new right-leaning cabinet. Similarly, Prime Minister Juha Sipilä needed to look over his shoulder, given that the Centre had been divided internally over European integration ever since EU membership entered the domestic political agenda in the early 1990s. The European section of the government programme is certainly more critical of integration than the programmes of previous cabinets, with the programme emphasising that each Eurozone member state is responsible for its own economy and 'EMU should not be developed through such deepening of economic coordination which would lead to an expansion of joint responsibility'. Sipilä's cabinet is thus 'opposed to increasing Finland's liabilities in handling the euro crisis' and argues that 'if the European Stability Mechanism must still be used, it should be done within the framework of the mechanism's current capacity and capital structure'.[9] Hence it was not surprising that in the summer of 2015 Finland was among those countries that were most critical of a new Greek bailout package.[10] In the end the government swallowed the bitter pill and accepted the bailout deal, not least because it realised that under ESM rules Finland could not block decision-making alone.

Despite the domestic politicisation of Europe via a more Eurosceptic discourse, and occasional awkward moments in Brussels, Finnish governments have continued to support the various moves towards closer economic integration. Economic factors played a key role in the decision to join the Union, and, if anything, the euro crisis seems to have further convinced at least the political and economic elites of the values of the internal market and monetary stability. Finland has supported tight budgetary discipline, emphasising that the success of the single currency and European economy depends on the performance of national economies. But while Finnish governments have consistently supported euro area rescue and coordination measures from bailout payments to Fiscal Compact and the banking union, they have certainly needed to pay closer attention to the mood at home.

Ideological responses to the financial crisis

The developments outlined in the previous section have clearly impacted on the positions of Social Democrats, the Left Alliance and the Greens towards the financial and euro crises. Multiparty coalitions limit the freedom of manoeuvre of individual cabinet parties, and hence government–opposition dynamics are evident in the behaviour of the parties. The rise of the Finns Party in turn resulted in the leftist parties adopting a more critical discourse towards the euro area coordination instruments. There is nonetheless also quite strong consistency, with all three parties essentially holding on to their policy stances throughout the 2007–2015 period.[11]

Throughout the period under analysis, the Social Democrats remained solidly in favour of integration, especially because of its positive impact on economic growth, job creation, security policy and international solidarity. Nonetheless, the discourse was very different from 2007 to 2011 when the party was in opposition. Throughout the euro crisis period the Social Democrats have stressed repeatedly that EMU is important and that the rescue of individual Eurozone countries is the right strategy, but that the burden of bailouts and other coordination instruments should not be borne by citizens alone.

SDP's 2009 EP election programme was particularly critical. Arguing that the 'neoliberal bubble has burst' and calling for more control and regulation of the markets, the party declared the need for a more human Europe: 'In the European Parliament the direction of politics is decided between the two largest party groups, the Social Democrats and the Conservatives. The main alternatives are also in Finland Social Democrats or a market oriented right. The consequences of bourgeois politics are known here in Finland and in the majority of European countries. This is what we want to change'. The importance of protecting national public services and labour market policies was also highlighted: 'Like the other Nordic countries, Finland has a lot to offer to the European Union. The Nordic model has provided security and well-being to citizens and has also been an economic success story. We want to make the EU also an area of well-being and economic success that is based on the needs of the people' (Suomen Sosialidemokraattinen Puolue, 2009).

SDP also at various times put forward other reform proposals. These included the democratisation of the International Monetary Fund and turning it into an organ that controls financial markets, establishing an EU agency for overseeing credit-rating firms, and that the EU should combat tax havens and the unfair pay and reward schemes of the managers of large companies. The 2014 EP election manifesto welcomed the banking union, seeing it as a step in the right direction (Suomen Sosialidemokraattinen Puolue, 2014).

When the euro crisis broke out, the Finns Party was rising in the polls, particularly among working-class voters. Hence it was not surprising that SDP felt the need to respond to the challenge, with party chair Urpilainen declaring that no Finnish money should be sent to Greece or other euro area countries without bilateral guarantees of return payment. Once this position was adopted, it became the focus of the party's public campaign together with the more general line of demanding that banks and private investors also share the burden of the bailouts. SDP has also underscored throughout the crisis period that each member state is responsible for its own economy and that control of banks and the financial sector needs to be strengthened both nationally and at the EU level. The wisdom of bilateral collaterals has been widely criticised, and the fact that no other member state demanded such special treatment suggests that such criticism is justified. Nonetheless, when the Social Democrats – and the Left Alliance and the Greens – entered the cabinet in the summer of 2011, the positions of leftist parties found their way into the government programme.

Three core objectives for the government were identified as reduction of poverty, inequality and social exclusion; consolidation of public finances; and the strengthening of sustainable economic growth, employment and competitiveness. Regarding EU policy, the programme repeated Finland's commitment to integration and stated that 'Finland will work towards strengthening the social dimension of the European Union'. The programme also spoke in rather general terms about the need to stabilise the European economy and promised that 'Finland will strive to expedite the introduction of a geographically extensive international tax on financial transactions that impacts activities of a speculative nature. The ultimate goal should be a global tax, but a system implemented at the EU level can be considered as an initial phase'. Domestically the government renewed collective wage bargaining with the unions, and, referring to social dialogue at the EU level, the programme underlined that 'Finland strives for better functioning labour markets and strengthened minimum protection of workers' terms of employment'. On the Eurozone coordination instruments, the programme stated: 'Before making any decisions, the Government will assess whether decisions made under the EFSF or the possible ESM are justifiable for Finland and for the citizens of the Member State in crisis. The Government will also evaluate whether the adjustment programme planned for the Member State affected will help resolve its problems. Accordingly, Finland will approve the establishment of the ESM, provided that the conditions set by Finland can be met'.[12]

As explained in the previous section, Finland approved the establishment of the ESM despite failing with the demand that decisions must be unanimous. And while initially favouring the Commission proposal on developing a financial transactions tax, the Finnish government decided in the autumn of 2012 against participating in the further development of such a proposed tax in contrast to the views of the Social Democrats, the Left Alliance and the Greens. Nonetheless, the SDP could now approve bailout packages as the bilateral guarantees were in place and as banks and private investors were, at least according to the party, involved in sharing the burden.

Between 2007 and 2011 the Social Democrats argued in favour of public investments while claiming that the measures of the centre right government were benefiting the rich and hurting the poor. And when in the government from 2011 to 2015, the party defended its record by saying that, while cuts to public spending clearly were needed, the inclusion of leftist parties in the cabinet had ensured that the reforms were implemented in a more balanced and fair manner. Overall, equality and fairness are concepts that keep appearing in the various party documents and speeches. Interestingly, at no point did the SDP, or the Left Alliance and the Greens, really share the often alarmist predictions of right-wing politicians, bankers and economists about the health of the national economy. An explanation might be that, while several economic indicators, including those regarding public debt, industrial output or exports, sent clear signals of a turn for the worse, unemployment did not increase that much.[13]

The Left Alliance is clearly located to the left of the Social Democrats on the political spectrum, and this shows in the positions and discourse of the party. Criticism of markets and 'neoliberal' policies is much stronger, and the party is considerably more willing to commit money to public services. Throughout the period under analysis VAS believed in investments and saw that the cuts were simply making matters worse and favouring the rich. Being a junior partner in the National Coalition-led cabinet proved very difficult for the party from the beginning, with party chair Paavo Arhinmäki first defending the decision to enter the government but in the end leading his party back to opposition in the spring of 2014.

Internal divisions over Europe are also evident in party positions. For example, in its 2009 EP election programme the party stressed the need for active international and European cooperation in order to fight for an 'alternative, better Europe' that was 'not so dominated by business interests'. Hence, the party saw a need for a fundamental reform of the international and the European economy, with more resources invested in improving the well-being of the citizens and the environment. The party also stated that the EU should be developed as an association of independent member states; argued in defence of the Nordic welfare state model; and against the further militarisation of the Union (Vasemmistoliitto, 2009). The 2014 EP election manifesto essentially repeated similar themes, with strong criticism of markets and European and global capitalism. According to the party, power had shifted during the crisis from the debtor countries to non-elected bodies such as the Commission, the ECB and the IMF – resulting in an EU that had become an unnecessary 'austerity union'. Interestingly, VAS also recommended a new referendum about national EU policy (Vasemmistoliitto, 2014).

When in opposition VAS voted against the bailout packages, and after joining the cabinet in 2011 the party continued to criticise the measures, essentially for the same reasons as the Social Democrats. The party argued forcefully that banks and private investors must also bear the burden and not just ordinary Greek or Portuguese citizens. Linking the bailout loans to increasing Finnish public debt, the Left Alliance saw it as irresponsible to be saving foreign banks when the national economy was doing badly. VAS put forward quite a lot of reform proposals, with many of those echoing the ideas of the Social Democrats – including a ban on tax havens and bank secrecy, better banking regulation, by introducing a Tobin tax, for example. The EU should also aim at setting minimum standards of taxation for companies and capital in order to avoid a 'race to the bottom', the debts of Greece and other recipients of bailouts should be renegotiated, and the ECB should provide cheap loans to member states. Such measures would contribute to both European and global solidarity and fairness. Overall, the Left Alliance seems to pay more attention to issues dealing with the international economy than the Social Democrats.

The Green League was in government from 2007 until the autumn of 2014. Programmatically the party continued to emphasise environmental issues, with economic policy receiving much less attention than is the case with either SDP or VAS. The Greens are strongly supportive of integration, but – in line with overall green ideology – argue that the EU needs to adopt policies that facilitate sustainable development. The Greens contend that neoliberal policies have privileged the few at the expense of the welfare of the citizenry and the state of the environment. They argue that tax havens should be banned, and banks and global financial markets should be subject to democratic regulation. The Greens would also like to see more transparent and participatory modes of decision-making. In the 2014 EP elections the party continued its critique of neoliberal policy approaches, including the TTIP, arguing that short-sighted greed is behind the global financial crisis which in turn fuelled anger and alienation. Like the Left Alliance, the Greens pointed out that the current policies increase inequality and hence undermine solidarity in Europe. As part of the governing coalition, the party voted in favour of the bailout packages and other Eurozone stabilisation instruments.[14]

There are many similarities between the positions of the Social Democrats and the Left Alliance. Particularly when in opposition both parties criticised the Finnish governments and the EU over 'neoliberal' policies that favour big banks and corporations. Both parties demand stronger EU-level or global regulation of financial markets, banks and creditors. In terms of domestic politics, SDP and VAS recognised the accumulation of foreign debt and the need to restore competitiveness, and differ from the centre right in so far as they see public investments as a key strategy for restoring economic growth. This applies particularly to the Left Alliance, and as stated in the introduction, may have cost the party votes in the 2015 elections. The Greens share many of the goals of the two traditional left parties, but talk much less about the economy and their critique was clearly more moderate due to its status as a government party from 2007 to 2014.

The tone of the debate in Finland was strongly influenced by the rise of populism. As the 2011 elections approached and the Finns Party was making significant advances in the polls, SDP and the Left Alliance adopted a tougher discourse about protecting national interests, with the Social Democrats demanding bilateral collaterals for bailout payments and especially the Left Alliance being strongly critical of a perceived bias towards the interests of 'big banks' in the bailout packages.[15] At the same time the findings offer at least some comfort for those who question whether parties still matter. The inclusion of SDP, VAS and VIHR in the cabinet formed in 2011 was clearly reflected in the government programme and in the policies pursued by the government domestically and in Brussels during the 2011–2015 legislative period.

Concluding remarks: the left on the defensive

The euro crisis destabilised Finnish integration policy. The outbreak of the euro crisis coincided with the campaign for the 2011 Eduskunta elections and revealed the fragile basis of the domestic (elite) consensus over Europe. That consensus was fragile because public opinion has consistently been more critical of integration than political parties. Moreover, most Finnish parties are internally divided over the EU, and hence there was always potential for dissent and electoral gains for a party with a more critical view of European integration. The politicisation and the success of the Finns Party have influenced domestic EU discourse, which is certainly more cautious, downplays any moves towards further centralisation and emphasises the role of national interests. Yet at the same time the Finnish government, with some reservations, supported the implementation of the various Eurozone coordination instruments and bailout packages (Raunio, 2015a).

The crisis clearly affected the parties on the Finnish left. In terms of votes, the left saw its electoral support decline during the crisis while Social

Democrats and the Left Alliance saw their combined vote decline from 30.2% of the vote in the 2007 Eduskunta elections to only 23.6% in 2015 – the lowest ever vote share of left-wing parties in Finland. Clearly both parties are struggling to maintain their core voters and much depends on whether the Finns Party manages to retain its popularity. However, including the Greens among the left-wing parties brings the vote share of the left to 32.1% in the 2015 elections, and the Greens achieved their best ever result in the 2017 municipal elections with 12.5% of the vote.

More troublesome for the left has been the general direction of domestic debate in Finland. The global and European uncertainty together with serious domestic fiscal challenges have brought about increasing criticism of leftist economic solutions. Whereas from the 1960s onwards leftist parties, particularly the Social Democrats, and trade unions closely linked to them, were often behind important and popular socio-economic reform initiatives in Finland, today they mainly focus on defending the status quo, with the initiatives coming from the centre right parties or business interests. The current economic climate, including the accumulation of high levels of national public debt and the associated need to cut public expenditure, is far from ideal for advocating traditional left-wing policies and this situation is unlikely to change in the next few years or at least not before the next Eduskunta elections scheduled for 2019. The agenda is thus strongly set by the political right, with Finland's political left on the defensive.

At the same time the crisis has nonetheless revealed ideological differences between the Finnish parties and has offered the left-wing parties the opportunity to distance themselves from the 'austerity' policies of their right-wing competitors. As Finnish coalition governments typically bring together parties from both the right and the left, the ability to pursue such goals depends primarily on the balance of power within the government and the Eduskunta. But even if the pendulum swings to the left in the next elections, the Social Democrats and the Left Alliance face hard ideological choices over economic policies. Both parties need also to react to the success of the Greens, and at least for the Social Democrats the likely path is further towards the political centre.

Notes

1 In SAK the Social Democrats are the dominant party, but VAS remains strong in select unions. In the Finnish Confederation of Professionals (STTK) the largest unions consist of nurses, health and social care professionals, and clerical employees. STTK is overall much less penetrated by party politics than SAK, and nowadays the distribution of party support among STTK members reflects quite well the distribution of party support among the population as a whole. The Confederation of Unions for Professional and Managerial Staff in Finland

(AKAVA) represents workers with university, professional or other high-level education. In AKAVA the strongest party is the National Coalition, but like STTK, it is internally much less prone to party political battles than SAK (Raunio & Laine, 2017).

2 SDP was the leading coalition party from 1995 to 2003 and the second largest party in 2003–2007 and 2011–2015.

3 Such frustrations surfaced in spring 2014 when SDP elected a new leader, with Antti Rinne narrowly beating the incumbent party chair Jutta Urpilainen. Rinne, a trade union leader with no previous parliamentary experience, was very much perceived as the 'trade union candidate', and his victory was interpreted by many as reflecting a yearning of part of the rank-and-file for a return to more leftist politics after two decades of politics during which the party had, both voluntarily and under strong external and budgetary constraints, embraced more market-friendly policies.

4 SDP leadership knew quite well that without support from SAK, its pro-EU policy would have shaky foundations. Bearing in mind the economic recession and the trade dependence with EU countries, it was not very surprising that SAK came out in favour of EU membership. SAK was initially against EMU, fearing that it might weaken the corporatist system of collective wage bargaining, but changed its opinion – partially as a result of the SDP-led government agreeing to so-called buffer funds in 1997. This active pro-European policy of the SAK has certainly made the management of EU-related issues, and in particular on the internal market and single currency, much easier for the SDP leadership to deal with (Raunio, 2010).

5 As argued by Marks and Wilson (2000: 443): 'To the extent that social democratic parties have been able to achieve their goals at the national level (for example, by creating national Keynesianism, strong welfare states and a highly institutionalised industrial relations system), we hypothesise that they will regard the deepening of market integration in Europe as a threat'.

6 The party adopted its current name, translated as the Finns Party, in August 2011. Until then it had been known as the True Finns. Please note that the Finnish name of the party has since its establishment been 'Perussuomalaiset'. In 2011 the party formally adopted its English name 'The Finns Party' as it felt that the old English name 'True Finns' was not really representative of the party. According to the party leader, Timo Soini, the new simpler name is intended to emphasise the fact that the party represents ordinary citizens. Soini also felt that the old name had an extreme right or nationalistic slant to it. The exact translation of the Finnish name of the party, *Perussuomalaiset*, would be 'common Finns' or 'ordinary Finns'.

7 In addition to the euro crisis, the Finns Party benefited from the economic downturn that began in 2008 and from an election finance scandal that hurt the Centre Party particularly. According to surveys, voters were drawn to supporting the party because they wanted societal change and to shake up both established patterns of power distribution and the direction of public policies, especially concerning immigration and European integration (Borg, 2012).

8 In addition to the euro crisis inspiring long and heated plenary debates, the euro crisis also featured in interpellations that have become the standard form of confidence vote. Before 2010 only two interpellations were EU-related, but between 2010 and 2015 the opposition tabled six crisis-related interpellations. The first of these was signed by the Left Alliance, while the other five were put forward by the Finns Party. Voting became more common in the Grand Committee (the EU committee), with the losing opposition minority also adding its dissenting opinions to the committee reports and minutes. Most of the contestation was initiated by the Finns Party, and the clear majority of the votes and dissenting opinions were on euro crisis-related issues (Raunio, 2016b).

9 *Finland, a land of solutions*. Strategic Programme of Prime Minister Juha Sipilä's Government, 29 May 2015. Government Publications 12/2015. http://valtioneuvosto.fi/en/sipila/government-programme (accessed 1 March 2019).

10 According to many sources Finland was the country most opposed to the deal, with Soini supposedly even threatening to leave the government should Finland agree to new loan arrangements. See, for example, Francis (2015), YLE Uutiset (2015).

11 The analysis is based on a close reading of the positions adopted by SDP, VAS and the Greens between 2007 and 2015. The analysed documents were: the manifestos for the 2007, 2011 and 2015 Eduskunta elections, the manifestos for the 2009 and 2014 EP elections; plenary debates on national budgets, euro area coordination measures, and other relevant parliamentary sessions where the financial crisis or national economy was debated; the speeches and writings of leading party figures and MEPs; and position papers adopted by the three parties on either the economy in general or on the EU or the euro area. I am grateful to Mari Kettunen and Taru Ruotsalainen for their research assistance.

12 Programme of Prime Minister Jyrki Katainen's Government, 22 June 2011.

13 In January 2008 it stood at 6.8%, in 2009 at 7.0%, in 2010 at 9.5%, in 2011 at 8.2%, in 2012 at 7.8%, in 2013 at 8.7%, in 2014 at 8.5% and in January 2015 at 8.8% (Statistics Finland, Labour force survey, www.findikaattori.fi/en/34, accessed 1 March 2019).

14 In the 2009 and 2014 EP elections the Green League campaigned on the basis of the common manifesto of the European Green Party (EGP).

15 Particularly in the Social Democrats there were voices, not least its MEPs, that criticised the party for its inward-looking discourse that placed national interests ahead of what is best for the whole EU.

Bibliography

Arter, D. (2009) 'From a contingent party system to party system convergence? Mapping party system change in postwar Finland', *Scandinavian Political Studies*, 32 (2): 221–239.

Arter, D. (2015) 'A "pivotal centre party" calls the shots: the 2015 Finnish general election', *West European Politics*, 38 (6): 1345–1353.

Bergholm, T. & Bieler, A. (2013) 'Globalization and the erosion of the Nordic model: a Swedish–Finnish comparison', *European Journal of Industrial Relations*, 19 (1): 55–70.

Bolin, N. (2016) 'Green parties in Finland and Sweden: successful cases of the North?', in E. van Haute (ed.) *Green Parties in Europe*, London: Routledge, 158–176.

Borg, S. (ed.) (2012) *Muutosvaalit 2011*, Helsinki: Oikeusministeriön julkaisu.

Dunphy, R. (2007) 'In search of an identity: Finland's Left Alliance and the experience of coalition government', *Contemporary Politics*, 13 (1): 37–55.

Dunphy, R. (2010) 'A poisoned chalice? The Finnish Left Alliance and the experience of government office', in J. Olsen, M. Koß & D. Hough (eds) *Left parties in national governments*, Basingstoke: Palgrave Macmillan, 69–86.

Fagerholm, A. (2017) 'What is left for the radical left? A comparative examination of the policies of radical left parties in western Europe before and after 1989', *Journal of Contemporary European Studies*, 25 (1): 16–40.

Francis, D. (2015) 'Tiny Finland could complicate new Greek bailout deal', *Foreign Policy*, 13 July. http://foreignpolicy.com/2015/07/13/the-biggest-roadblock-to-a-greek-deal-could-be-tiny-finland/ (accessed 1 March 2019).

Gomez, R., Morales, L. & Ramiro, L. (2016) 'Varieties of radicalism: examining the diversity of radical left parties and voters in western Europe', *West European Politics*, 39 (2): 351–379.

Hyvärinen, A. & Raunio, T. (2014) 'Who decides what EU issues ministers talk about? Explaining governmental EU policy co-ordination in Finland', *Journal of Common Market Studies*, 52 (5): 1019–1034.

Karvonen, L. (2014) *Parties, governments and voters in Finland: politics under fundamental societal transformation*, Colchester: ECPR Press.

Lipset, S. M. & Rokkan, S. (1967) 'Cleavage structures, party systems and voter alignments', in S. M. Lipset & S. Rokkan (eds) *Party systems and voter alignments: cross-national perspectives*, New York: The Free Press, 1–64.

Marks, G. & Wilson, C. J. (2000) 'The past in the present: a cleavage theory of party response to European integration', *British Journal of Political Science*, 30 (3): 433–459.

Mattila, M. & Raunio, T. (2005) 'Kuka edustaa EU:n vastustajia? Euroopan parlamentin vaalit 2004', *Politiikka*, 47 (1): 28–41.

Mattila, M. & Raunio, T. (2012) 'Drifting further apart: national parties and their electorates on the EU dimension', *West European Politics*, 35 (3): 589–606.

Mickelsson, R. (2015) *Suomen puolueet: Vapauden ajasta maailmantuskaan*, Tampere: Vastapaino.

Ministry of Justice (2019) *Information and result service*. https://tulospalvelu.vaalit.fi/indexe.html (accessed 16 March 2019).

Paastela, J. (2002) 'Finland', *Environmental Politics*, 11 (1): 17–38.

Raunio, T. (2010) 'The EU and the welfare state are compatible: Finnish Social Democrats and European integration', *Government and Opposition*, 45 (2): 187–207.

Raunio, T. (2012) '"Whenever the EU is involved, you get problems": explaining the European policy of The (True) Finns', *Sussex European Institute Working Paper*, 127.

Raunio, T. (2015a) 'Finland: an end to domestic consensus, in E. E. Zeff & E. B. Pirro (eds) *The European Union and the member states* (3rd edn), Boulder: Lynne Rienner, 243–257.

Raunio, T. (2015b) 'The Greens and the 2015 elections in Finland: finally ready for a breakthrough?', *Environmental Politics*, 24 (5): 830–834.

Raunio, T. (2016a) 'Finland', in D. M. Viola (ed.) *Routledge Handbook of European Elections*, Abingdon: Routledge, 396–413.

Raunio, T. (2016b) 'The politicization of EU affairs in the Finnish Eduskunta: conflicting logics of appropriateness, party strategy, or sheer frustration?', *Comparative European Politics*, 14 (2): 232–252.

Raunio, T. & Laine, N. (2017) 'Finland: strong party-union links under challenge', in E. Haugsgjerd Allern & T. Bale (eds) *Left-of-centre parties and trade unions in the twenty-first century*, Oxford: Oxford University Press, 93–111.

Ruostetsaari, I. (2015) *Elite recruitment and coherence of the inner core of power in Finland: changing patterns during the economic crises of 1991–2011*, Lanham, MD: Lexington Books.

Suomen Sosialidemokraattinen Puolue (2009) *Euroopan parlamentin vaalien vaaliohjelma 2009.* www.fsd.uta.fi/pohtiva/ohjelmalistat/SDP/414 (accessed 1 March 2019).

Suomen Sosialidemokraattinen Puolue (2014) *Oikeudenmukainen Eurooppa – laitetaan Eurooppa töihin.* www.fsd.uta.fi/pohtiva/ohjelmalistat/SDP/991 (accessed 1 March 2019).

Tiihonen, A. (2015) 'Etujärjestöjen, puolueiden ja yhteiskuntaluokkien suhde Suomessa 2000-luvulla', Master's thesis, political science, University of Tampere.

Tiihonen, A. (2016) 'Etujärjestöjen, puolueiden ja äänestäjien väliset suhteet', in K. Grönlund & H. Wass (eds) *Poliittisen osallistumisen eriytyminen – Eduskunta-vaalitutkimus 2015*, Helsinki: Oikeusministeriön julkaisu, 321–342.

Vasemmistoliitto (2009) *Parempi Eurooppa on mahdollinen.* www.fsd.uta.fi/pohtiva/ohjelmalistat/VAS/819 (accessed 1 March 2019).

Vasemmistoliitto (2014) *Kohti hyvinvointiunionina – Vasemmiston EU-vaaliohjelma 2014.* www.fsd.uta.fi/pohtiva/ohjelmalistat/VAS/1236 (accessed 1 March 2019).

YLE Uutiset (2015) 'Stubb: Finland is not alone in opposing Greek bailout', 12 July. https://yle.fi/uutiset/osasto/news/stubb_finland_is_not_alone_in_opposing_greek_bailout/8149043 (accessed 17 March 2019).

Zilliacus, K. O. K. (2001) '"New Politics" in Finland: the Greens and the left wing in the 1990s', *West European Politics*, 24 (1): 27–54.

10

Take a walk on the left side: the impact of austerity politics in France

Antonella Seddone and Julien Navarro

Introduction

The crisis and recession of the late 2000s and early 2010s impacted France as much as other western democracies, producing destabilising effects for the political system as a whole (Hernández & Kriesi, 2015; Morlino & Raniolo, 2017). Austerity policies were adopted in response to the financial crisis, but inevitably redefined the domestic policy agenda with quite remarkable consequences on electoral behaviour and citizens' satisfaction with politics as well as on governments' strategies in building political support (Hübscher & Sattler, 2017; Talving, 2017). Particularly in the Eurozone, the common economic and financial agenda defined in Brussels was perceived as an imposition to which *obtorto collo* all EU countries had to adapt. Ideological distinctions faded away in the name of the priorities imposed by the financial crisis. As a result, the dynamics between government and opposition were re-articulated in the light of these external pressures (De Giorgi & Moury, 2015; Moury & De Giorgi, 2015).

France offers a privileged field of observation for assessing the political consequences of the crisis and recession. When the crisis hit the country in 2008, the right-wing party UMP (Union pour un Mouvement Populaire) was in power with Nicolas Sarkozy as President and François Fillon as Prime Minister. This conservative majority had to tackle the most immediate effects of the economic downturn, in particular a slowdown in growth and soaring unemployment. The crisis further eroded the President's already low popularity (Turgeon et al., 2015); it also shifted the media coverage of the government's economic policies (Gerstlé & François, 2011). Though in opposition, the left also had to face the challenges of the economic and financial crisis by finding an alternative policy response and convincing people that it would be more effective than the government. But instead of strengthening the French left, the crisis only exacerbated the already existing divisions within its own ranks as to fundamental economic policy choices. This makes the French case especially interesting if the aim is to understand whether and to what extent the economic downturn has affected the left, its political actors and their attitudes towards the European Union.

The effects of the economic crisis go beyond questions of GDP growth or public debt. In France as in other countries, national policy agendas were altered, ideological paradigms were challenged, new political actors emerged (quite often with marked populist traits) and there was a growing public disaffection with politics. No matter if they were inevitable or indispensable, austerity measures were not entirely understood by citizens and this fuelled feelings of antipolitics and increasing Euroscepticism (Serricchio et al., 2013; Rozenberg, 2016), offering new political opportunities for radical parties both from the right or the left side of the political spectrum (Kriesi & Pappas, 2015; Moffitt, 2015; Bosco & Verney, 2016).

The French left is historically characterised by a marked internal dialectic about both the market economy and European integration. The economic crisis highlighted these deep divisions among different sections of the left and reignited competition between left-wing parties, offering new political opportunities for radical parties (Ducange, 2015; Damiani & De Luca, 2016). This proved very problematic when the Socialists returned to power in 2012. There was an attempt to 'take a walk on the left side', but this rapidly ran into problems. And the 2017 elections further highlighted the fragmentation and disagreements of the French left.

This chapter analyses the challenges and changes facing the French left. The next section introduces the major left-wing political families in France, and offers a brief account of their political dynamics. The third section will focus on the electoral performance of the French left during the crisis period, using an analysis based on economic voting theory. The fourth section investigates developments on the ideological right–left scale and on EU issues, working with data from the Manifesto project and analysing the manifestos from the 2017 elections.

United we stand, divided we fall

The French left is composed of a myriad of political parties. Its great ideological heterogeneity very often results in divisiveness and a high level of internal conflict. In particular, the extreme fringes often engage in a heated dialectic against the more moderate parties of the left, the Socialist Party in particular. The economic crisis highlighted these ideological differences, exacerbating conflicts and widening the distances (Ducange, 2015). Three main party families held seats at national level in the 2007–2017 period: (1) the French

Communist Party (PCF – Parti Communiste Français), which since 2008 has been in a federation of radical left parties and movements,[1] called the Left Front (FdG – Front de Gauche); MEPs sit in the GUE/NGL group, but not all constituent groups in the Left Front are members of the Party of the European Left – just the PCF and the Left Party;[2] (2) a Green movement (EELV – Europe Écologie Les Verts), promoting environmental issues and a member of the European Green Party; (3) the Socialist Party (PS – Parti Socialiste), the largest party of the French left, and a member of the Party of European Socialists. The following section briefly summarises the positions of these three major groups prior to the onset of the crisis, especially in relation to their stances on European integration.

The PCF was created in 1920, when a majority of members resigned from the French Section of the Workers' International (SFIO) to set up the French Section of the Communist International. The adherence to Marxist theories led the party towards openly anti-capitalist positions and constant support for the so-called 'popular democracies'. Inevitably, therefore, the collapse of the USSR put into question the PCF's fundamental principles and promoted a broad reorganisation. The anti-capitalism was replaced by criticism of neoliberalism, and in particular, the party developed a Eurosceptic position (Moss, 1998). The PCF (and subsequently the Left Front) was one of the main critics of the European integration process, especially the Maastricht Treaty of 1992, which was seen as a project advancing free-market policies. In the 1997 PS-led *gauche plurielle* government of Lionel Jospin, the PCF held three ministries. However, the dominance of the PS veiled the PCF, and the party continued its slow but very steady electoral and membership decline. This led to a new set of reforms, culminating in the creation of the Left Front (Damiani & De Luca, 2016).

EELV constitutes another electoral cartel, formed in 2010 and bringing together the Greens (Les Verts) with parties and movements sharing similar views on the economy and energy issues. The breakthrough for the Greens came in 1989 when they won 11% in European Parliament elections. They were initially reluctant to be described in traditional left–right terms, rejecting any ideological label and pursuing a purist Green agenda. However, several authors clearly identify EELV as a left-wing party (Sainteny, 2000; Repaire, 2016). In particular, their social views are close to those of the radical left, addressing the problems of poverty and unemployment (Price-Thomas, 2016). For a long time, it was closer to a movement than a party, with an inclusive and heterogeneous organisation. This made the party seem quite divided and conflictual, with various leaders not always in agreement. Just after the end of the Mitterrand era, the Greens chose to openly stand on the left (Close & Delwit, 2016; Villalba, 2016). In 1997, they opted for a strategic alliance with the Socialists. The success of this alliance resulted in their participation in Jospin's *gauche plurielle* government in 1997–2002, when there was one Green minister. The two parties coordinated with each other again in 2002, even if not formally organised in an alliance, but the relationship between PS and the Greens started to creak in 2007 due to discordant positions on policy issues related to energy and nuclear power. The Socialists were no longer identified as privileged partners; instead, the Greens showed greater interest in other forms of political cooperation. The economic crisis offered new opportunities for the division, with the Greens increasingly critical of austerity policies and of the EU, seen as over-assertive and invasive in domestic political dynamics.

The third significant component of the French left is the Socialist Party,[3] which can trace its origins to 1905 and the foundation of the SFIO. The Socialist party was transformed under the leadership of François Mitterrand, and in 1981 he became the first socialist President of the Fifth Republic (Kuhn & Murray, 2013). His style of leadership was quite pragmatic and efficient, and included a coalition with the PCF (Bachelot, 2011). The early months of the Mitterrand presidency were associated with an ambitious policy programme,[4] but although the party never really turned itself into a modern social democratic movement in the way most European socialist parties did, it moved away progressively from more ambitious socialist models. Pressures due to European integration were particularly significant in this respect (Clift, 2005; Daley, 2014). The acceleration of the EU integration process produced a new ideological cleavage for the party, focusing on the financial constraints of the EU and problems concerning sovereignty (Milner, 2004; Hanley, 2016). Thus, a general Europhile mood co-existed with quite ambiguous – even critical – attitudes towards the EU. In the aftermath of the Mitterrand era, the PS has struggled to find heirs capable of uniting the party, and its support has wavered. The nadir came in 2002, when Jospin failed to make the second round of the presidential election. The party was devastated by a severe internal crisis, struggling to find a balance between the different visions. The old divisions within the party came to light again, by revealing a quite divided and conflictual intra-party arena. Even if – being in the opposition – the party was mainly concentrated on contesting right-wing policy choices, from an internal point of view it was divided. This was epitomised by the outright split in the PS over the European Constitutional Treaty (Marthaler, 2012).

In conclusion, it is evident that the French left is quite heterogeneous. It is also characterised by strong ideological perspectives and competition both between different left-wing parties and within them. This has not prevented occasional pan-left cooperation from emerging, such as the *gauche plurielle* government of Lionel Jospin. However, the polarisation among the left focuses strongly on issues of acceptance of or opposition to neoliberal market reforms, and this is very strongly framed in terms of attitudes towards European integration. The social democratic left have tended to prioritise support for the EU, and some critics would say that they do so at the cost of accepting neoliberalism. The more radical left parties and groups see the EU as endorsing neoliberal policies, and have therefore tended towards Euroscepticism.

The economy of voting: the ups and downs of the left

The electoral dynamics of the French left during the crisis can be interpreted through economic voting theory. According to this theory, voters tend to consider the economic situation as a factor orienting their preferences in elections; they implement a dynamic of sanction or reward towards the government. In a nutshell, when the economy goes bad, voters tend to punish the incumbents (Lewis-Beck & Stegmaier, 2007). France represents a very stimulating case study. Several studies confirm that the economic health of the country can affect the electoral behaviour of French voters (Lewis-Beck & Nadeau, 2000; Nadeau et al., 2012). This suggests that the victory of the PS in 2012 should not be interpreted as a renaissance of the left; it must rather be understood as the consequence of the ineffective leadership of President Sarkozy in handling the immediate effects of the crisis (Hewlett, 2012), a point further emphasised by the calamitous problems faced by the PS in the 2017 elections.

The major macroeconomic indicators confirm the seriousness of the financial crisis and its deep impact on the French economy (see Table 10.1). GDP fell sharply in 2009, and despite some recovery, it has not regained the growth rates of the mid-2000s. Other macroeconomic figures, such as the public debt and inflation indicators, confirm the continuing consequences of the financial crisis on the real economy. More significantly, indicators of unemployment show the severe impact of the crisis not just on the French economy but also its society. This was probably the most sensitive political issue in the public debate. Unemployment had been stubbornly high during the previous three decades, but rose again at the end of Sarkozy's presidency and reached new summits during Hollande's term (10.4% in 2015). It was one of the key issues in both the 2012 and 2017 electoral races. The outcome of the elections has thus to be interpreted in the light of French economic performance.

The 2012 elections were the first after the onset of the economic crisis, and the victory of the left is the result of a critical economic conjuncture and a negative judgement about Sarkozy's achievements. Sarkozy's approach to the crisis had attempted to secure a close connection with Germany in

Table 10.1 French economic situation, 2006–2015

	2006	2007	2008	2009	2010	2011	2012	2013	2014	2015
GDP (% change year)	2.37	2.36	0.2	-2.94	1.97	2.08	0.18	0.64	0.63	1.26
Inflation (annual %)	1.68	1.49	2.81	0.09	1.53	2.11	1.95	0.86	0.51	0.03
Debt (% GDP)	76.9	75.66	81.58	93.2	96.83	100.7	110.44	110.92	120.33	121
Unemployment rate (%)	8.45	7.66	7.06	8.74	8.87	8.81	9.4	9.91	10.3	10.36

Source: Armingeon et al., (2016)

managing the crisis at an EU level (Cole, 2012). In contrast, the idea behind the election campaign of Hollande was to clearly set out a difference from Sarkozy's approach, promoting new and alternative recipes for addressing such an adverse economic situation. Hollande's programme was based on policy proposals focused on growth rather than austerity, increasing taxes on the richest sectors of society and creating jobs in education and the private sector (Hewlett, 2012).

Focusing just on votes it could be argued that the PS strategy worked, but this would be a superficial and naïve interpretation. A closer look suggests that support for the PS was incidental, and was primarily the result of dissatisfaction towards the centre right government and the worries about the economic crisis. In the first round, Hollande received 28.6% of the votes, just 1.4% ahead of Sarkozy (Table 10.2). The other left-wing candidates were: Jean-Luc Mélenchon for the Left Front, Eva Joly for EELV, and two Trotskyist candidates, Philippe Poutou and Nathalie Arthaud. Added all together, these left-wing candidates were far from reaching the absolute majority (43.8%). However, Hollande was eventually elected in the second round with 51.6%, the second lowest score in the history of the Fifth Republic.[5] Not by chance, therefore, opinion polls immediately registered a loss of approval for President Hollande who had to face the reality of the difficulties of implementing policies for growth in a time of austerity (Kuhn, 2014).

The same caution must prevail in explaining the outcome of the subsequent legislative elections. French legislative elections are increasingly interpreted as a confirmation of the preceding presidential election (Dupoirier & Sauger, 2010).[6] The data concerning the voting dynamics for the National Assembly in 2012 reveals a complex political landscape. The PS managed to get an absolute majority with 280 MPs in the National Assembly. But given the circumstances – the financial crisis, the loss of support for Sarkozy and Hollande's success – the PS did not increase its vote as dramatically as might

Table 10.2 French presidential election result, 2012 (%)

	1st round	2nd round
François Hollande (PS – Socialist Party)	28.6	51.6
Nicolas Sarkozy (UMP – Popular Majority)	27.2	48.4
Marine Le Pen (FN – National Front)	17.9	
Jean-Luc Mélenchon (FdG – Left Front)	11.1	
François Bayrou (MoDem – Democratic Movement)	9.1	
Eva Joly (EELV – Greens)	2.3	
Nicolas Dupont-Aignan (DLR – France Arise)	1.8	
Philippe Poutou (NPA – New Anti-Capitalist)	1.1	
Nathalie Arthaud (LO – Workers' Struggle)	0.6	
Jacques Cheminade (S&P – Solidarity & Progress)	0.2	
Turnout	79.5	80.4

Source: Ministère de l'Intérieur (various)

have been expected. If compared with the 2007 legislative elections, the PS only obtained 29.4% of the vote, an increase of less than 5% (Table 10.3). The gap between the PS and the UMP was quite narrow, with only 2.3 percentage points separating them. Ultimately, even if the PS could count on a vast majority in the National Assembly, its limited electoral success and its internal divisiveness did not guarantee a peaceful parliamentary life nor an easy government. The party was not in good shape, and the set of ambitious policies proposed by Hollande during the election campaign were quickly downsized to meet the financial demands required by the EU.

Nor could the wider left claim that the 2012 outcome was a great success. The election ended ambiguously for them. The Greens gained seats and votes, thus consolidating their presence in the National Assembly. The Left Front slightly increased its vote but lost almost half of its small number of parliamentary seats. This was particularly disappointing, since the Left Front's Jean-Luc Mélenchon had obtained over 11% of the votes in the presidential election.[7] Hewlett (2012) argues that the Left Front's weak result in the legislative election could be interpreted in the light of the bipolar logic of French electoral competition. In particular, the 2007 shock, when the left failed to pass the first round of the presidential election, could have played a role by inducing left-wing voters to concentrate their support on Hollande. Vasilopoulos et al. (2015) also argued that despite the effort to offer a manifesto against EU and austerity measures, Mélenchon's party was not able to mobilise those society sectors hurt the most by the economic crisis. Instead, these votes went to the National Front, which gained considerable success among workers and unemployed.

Table 10.3 French parliamentary election result, 10–17 June 2012

	1st round (% votes)	2nd round (% votes)	seats
PS – Socialist Party	29.4	40.9	280
UMP – Popular Majority	27.1	38.0	194
EELV – Greens	5.5	3.6	17
NC – New Centre	2.2	2.5	12
PRG – Radical Party of the Left	1.7	2.3	12
FdG – Left Front	6.9	1.1	10
FN – National Front	13.6	3.7	2
AC – Centrist Alliance	0.6	0.5	2
MoDem – Democratic Movement	1.8	0.5	2
Other right	3.5	1.8	15
Other left	3.4	3.1	22
Others	3.3	0.7	3

Source: Ministère de l'Intérieur (various)

In other words, the left won the 2012 electoral competition, but without fully convincing French voters. In a time of crisis, citizens tend to look for strong and clear solutions, and the PS represented an alternative to Sarkozy and the UMP. But it was not enough to respond to the dissatisfaction of citizens. Very soon it was clear that the reality of governing a country would prevent Hollande and the PS from delivering on many of their campaign promises. The fragility of the left even after its apparent victory in the presidential and legislative elections of 2012 was confirmed by opinion polls describing a very sudden decline in support for Hollande and the PS. Their proposals for increasing the tax on wealthy citizens as well as the promises about age retirement failed quite soon, increasing the perceived dissatisfaction of French citizens. This is yet another illustration of the 'sheer unsolvable equation' of executive politics in France: presidential elections are won by bold promises and expectations, but the bolder the pledges, the less likely they are to be implemented. As pointed out by Grossman and Sauger (2014), the context of austerity has heightened this paradox but not altered its nature. Long before the end of Hollande's *quinquennat* (five-year term of office), he had become deeply unpopular and was 'France's least-loved president' (*France24*, 2016), and he decided not to seek re-election, becoming the first incumbent Fifth Republic president to do so.

The PS sought to overcome its weakness on the eve of the presidential elections of 2017 by staging a broad left primary election, but with seven candidates standing in the primary, this only succeeded in exacerbating

Table 10.4 French presidential election, 2017 (%)

	1st round	2nd round
Emmanuel Macron (EM – En Marche!)	24.0	66.1
Marine Le Pen (FN – National Front)	21.3	33.9
François Fillon (LR – The Republicans)	20.0	
Jean-Luc Mélenchon (LFI – La France Insoumise)	19.6	
Benoît Hamon (PS – Socialist Party)	6.4	
Nicolas Dupont-Aignan (DLR – France Arise)	4.7	
Jean Lassalle (R – Résistons)	1.2	
Philippe Poutou (NPA – New Anti-Capitalist)	1.1	
François Asselineau (UPR – Popular Union)	0.9	
Nathalie Arthaud (LO – Workers' Struggle)	0.6	
Jacques Cheminade (S&P – Solidarity & Progress)	0.2	
Turnout	77.8	74.6

Source: Ministère de l'Intérieur (various)

tensions.[8] The left-winger Benoît Hamon defeated the centrist Manuel Valls in the run-off. Meanwhile, a number of left-wing parties refused to take part in the primary.[9] This was to be expected from radical left groups, where Jean-Luc Mélenchon ran on behalf of the new La France Insoumise (LFI – France unbowed) movement. More surprising was the candidacy of one of the ministers in Hollande's government, Emmanuel Macron. He left the PS to form his own En Marche! movement, standing on a centrist platform of economic liberalism and social progressivism. All of this highlighted the continuing ideological divisions on the French left.

The outcome of the first round of the presidential election was extremely close, with four candidates coming within 5% of each other at the top of the poll (see Table 10.4). The deep schisms on the left were evident, with Macron narrowly topping the poll, while Mélenchon also performed very strongly. However, the PS vote collapsed, with Hamon suffering a serious defeat. Macron's opponent in the second round was Marine Le Pen, the second time that a candidate of the extreme right Front National (FN) had reached the presidential run-off. And once again, this led to a broad anti-FN consensus, with both Hamon and the defeated Republican candidate François Fillon backing Macron. However, while Mélenchon made clear his opposition to Le Pen, he refused to endorse Macron. In the second round, Macron won comfortably, though Le Pen secured over a third of votes cast. The outcome presented Macron with a dilemma – how much of the vote is in favour of his policies, and how much is against the FN? In particular, the relatively low turnout in the second round signalled public disengagement from the political process.

Table 10.5 French legislative election, 2017

	1st round (% votes)	2nd round (% votes)	seats
REM – La République en Marche	28.2	43.1	308
MoDem – Democratic Movement	4.1	6.1	42
LR – The Republicans	15.8	22.2	112
UDI – Union of Democrats & Independents	3.0	3.0	18
Other centre right	2.8	1.7	6
PS – Socialist Party	7.4	5.7	30
PRG – Radical Party of the Left	0.5	0.4	3
Other centre left	1.6	1.5	12
LFI – La France Insoumise	11.0	4.9	17
PCF – French Communist Party	2.7	1.2	10
FN – National Front	13.2	8.8	8
Others	9.7	1.7	11
Turnout	48.7	42.6	

Source: Ministère de l'Intérieur (various)

Following the presidential elections, legislative elections were held. Macron's movement, now reformulated as La République En Marche!, contested them on a joint platform with the Democratic Movement. Between them, they won a third of the vote in the first round, but almost half the vote and over 60% of the seats in the second round. The result was bad for the left. It was a further clear disaster for the Socialist Party, which with its centre left allies saw its vote collapse and lost 286 seats. The radical left fared little better. La France Insoumise polled respectably in the first round, but well below Mélenchon's vote in the presidential election, and could only convert that into 17 seats. Of course, the Front National were similarly disadvantaged by the French electoral system, but notably they took five seats from the Socialists in the industrially depressed Nord-Pas de Calais region, indicating the extent to which the FN ate into the traditional left-wing vote.

However, once more the turnout levels were very low. All in all, France, just as other western countries, experienced a crisis in the relationship between politics and its citizens. The economic crisis only emphasised this feeling of distrust and dissatisfaction,[10] offering to more extreme parties a window of opportunity to increase their electoral support. In France, the Front National was able to take advantage of this, becoming a real (and threatening) competitor for mainstream parties. The electoral performance also registered by the Left Front led by Mélenchon reinforces the idea that the economic crisis weakened the ability of mainstream parties to respond to citizens'

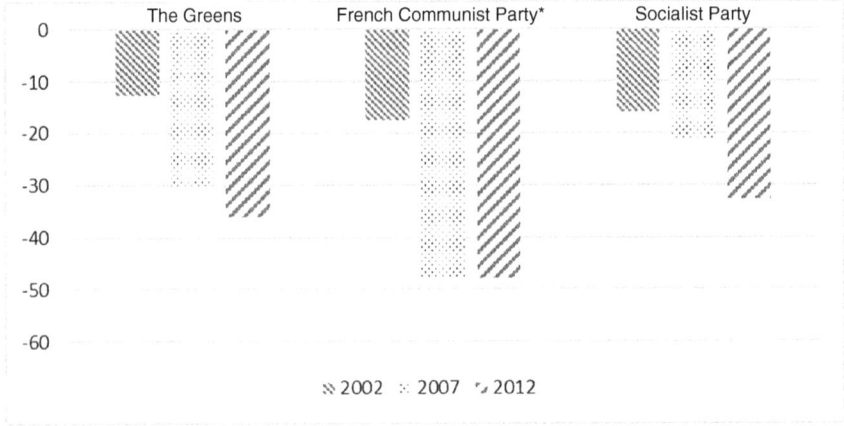

Figure 10.1 Left-right dimension of selected presidential election manifestos in France, 2002-2012
* Left Front in 2012
Composite left-right scale from +100 (farthest right) to -100 (farthest left)
Source: WZB (2018)

demands and dissatisfaction, leading voters to veer towards more extreme parties, which are also those more critical towards EU institutions.

The Great Recession as a catalyst of the European cleavage within the French left

The French left has been affected by profound changes in recent decades, especially since the end of the Mitterrand era. The PS, the PCF and the Greens all went through deep internal reorganisations, and ideological attitudes were challenged and reshaped. The left seems to be particularly divided, characterised by a heated dialectic that placed a more moderate social democratic tendency in opposition to a more radical one. This division was played out particularly in relation to the processes of European integration and the market economy. Party manifestos are useful indicators of the ideological divisions and changes that took place within political parties in the years of the crisis. In the light of the manifestos of the presidential elections since 1997 (Figure 10.1), there has been a common trend within the three parties towards a more left-wing approach. The shift is gradual in the PS; it is more sudden in the Left Front.

The two-dimensional left–right approach does not cover in a proper way the differences between French parties. One has to take into account also a third dimension: the EU dimension (Grunberg, 2014; Hanley, 2016). French politics has an ambiguous relationship with the EU integration project. It is characterised by a tension between enthusiasm for the concept in principle and a traditional caution regarding sovereignty. This crosses both left and right sides transversally, and according to Milner (2004) the EU represents a further political cleavage for French politics, creating thus a very divided and conflicted context. European integration emerged as a political issue in the late 1980s, especially within the left. The left was divided between a more Europhile attitude in the PS and Eurosceptic stances in the PCF. The EU was interpreted as a constraint on domestic public policy choices, undermining the government's capability to manage strategic policy issues, but also as a crucial opportunity to have a role on a broader level (Grossman, 2007; Cole & Drake, 2011).

This ambiguity deeply affected French politics, and became crucial for effectively assessing the impact of the economic crisis. The activism of the EU in addressing the financial crisis increased the visibility of the role played by EU institutions in domestic politics. EU pressure for regulating and orienting domestic policies in order to preserve austerity and balance for the internal market activated a revival of Euroscepticism in France, including among parties that had less negative approaches towards the EU traditionally. If one refers again to party manifestos (Figure 10.1), the general impression is that Euroscepticism had been declining in all three left-wing parties during the last 20 years, though there are huge differences between the PS and the two other parties. Free from government responsibility, the Left Front and the Greens could more easily promote policy proposals criticising integration, whereas the PS – also considering its role – could not put forward any real and hard criticism of the EU. The disagreements about the EU are the main fuel of divisiveness and conflict among the left-wing parties. But these differences are also extremely vivid within the PS, where the accommodating attitude of the Hollande government towards austerity measures perceived as a German *diktat* was very divisive.

To sum up, the 2012 French elections seemed on the surface to be a victory for the reformist French left with Hollande as President and an absolute majority for the PS in the National Assembly.[11] However, Hollande's attempt to push for growth policies as an alternative to austerity measures resulted in failure. The Stability and Growth Pact, imposing a public deficit limit of 3% of GDP, represented the main constraint for Hollande's policies. This in turn reinforced the increasing Euroscepticism in public opinion and strengthened criticism of the euro and the EU integration process by the extreme right National Front and by the Left Front. Similarly, globalisation limited the ability of the government to provide adequate policies on employment and the job market. Even if France enjoyed the potentialities offered by the globalised market economy, it was also challenged by an increasing outsourcing of jobs as well as by an acceleration of the decline of the manufacturing sector, which is particularly important for employing citizens with low education levels and employment skills.

The margins of manoeuvre were thus narrowed for Hollande, while parties such as the FN and the Left Front, traditionally against both EU and globalisation, found a field for developing support and consensus. The left was in crisis, characterised by internal conflict and competition. The antagonism between the PS and the radical left represented by Mélenchon's Left Front prevented any kind of strategic coordination between these two parties. The discord about the EU integration process represented an unresolved cleavage within the French left since the 2005 referendum; this hindered the possibility of reacting effectively to challenges coming from the right wing. The failure to implement policy oriented towards growth instead of austerity condemned the PS and the mainstream left to a limited role in 2017 presidential elections.

Europe played a central role in these elections, with the second round of the presidential election pitting the Eurosceptic Le Pen against the strongly pro-European Macron, and Macron's victory was enthusiastically welcomed by EU leaders. But the campaign showed once again the rift among the left. Macron undeniably promoted a pro-European vision, arguing that the EU was essential for peace and progress and that its strength was vital for France to prosper, though he also argued for 'a Europe that protects Europeans' (En Marche!, 2017). Jean-Luc Mélenchon's programme called for reform of the EU, while hinting at a 'plan B' of withdrawal if reform negotiations broke down, and he demanded an end to the 'ideological obsessions' dominating the EU – austerity and free trade – and instead a commitment to public investment (Mélenchon, 2016). Somewhere in between these two was the Socialist candidate, Benoît Hamon, who again suggested reform of the EU and opposition to unfettered free trade, but was more prepared to work within the EU for things like democratisation of governance of the Eurozone and a stronger social and green commitment (Hamon, 2017).

The impact of austerity politics on the French left

There are two dimensions that have to be taken into account to better assess the evolution and changes produced by the economic crisis in the French left. The first one is mainly domestic and concerns the political competition between old and new political actors. The economic crisis has revealed the weakness of neoliberalism and globalised financial market questioning the policy choices of several European governments. This entailed opening a window of opportunity for radical left parties, which at the beginning of the 2000s organised a significant mobilisation against globalisation. At that time, the criticism of globalisation was a symbolic issue, functioning to redefine the ideological horizon when the classical left and right coordinates were losing sense. The Great Recession, which has been interpreted as a failure of the globalised economy, offered a new momentum to this approach. It is therefore not surprising to find a renewed popularity for radical left parties along with the emergence of other new left-wing parties demanding stronger social policies and criticising austerity policies. Radical left-wing parties easily began to erode consensus from mainstream centre left parties. These different pressures produced centrifugal dynamics, which seriously weakened the Socialist Party.

The second dimension concerns the role of the EU in the management of the crisis and, consequently, the relationship that member states have woven with the European institutions. The Maastricht Treaty – along with amendments ratified in Amsterdam, Nice and Lisbon – established rigid constraints on national policy choices. This in turn has favoured the emergence (or strengthening where it was already present) of criticism towards the EU. The economic crisis has revealed the weaknesses of the European project bringing out a series of domestic interests often incompatible with each other in a common project. Inevitably, the need to comply with EU require-ments has reorganised the national policy agendas, redefining priorities and action strategies and above all changing the dynamics of responsiveness. The financial crisis thus revived the traumas of the 2005 referendum on the European Constitutional Treaty for the left, with parties competing with each other and with events proving deeply divisive for the PS.

The economic crisis emphasised feelings of anti-politics and dissatisfaction with politics, providing a fertile ground for populist and radical rhetoric. Mainstream parties, which were suffering already from a loss of consensus, were no longer recognised as adequate representatives, and in this situation the most radical parties – both left and right – took advantage. Without any government responsibility, they were able to contest and dispute the policy choices made by the government to comply with EU treaties. They were free to blame austerity policies and could gain support among citizens. The incapacity of the socialist government to propose a credible alternative half-way between full submission to EU-related constraints and the rejection of Europe now dominant on the far left managed to weaken the Socialist Party.

The ultimate consequence was very predictable. Benoît Hamon, the socialist candidate in the presidential election of 2017, was unable to find a space between the progressive and pro-European Macron and the EU-critical Mélenchon. Not only did Macron get elected as President but his new party received a majority of seats in the election to the National Assembly while the PS hit a historically low score at this election. The divisions of the left, which the financial crisis exacerbated, proved to be once more a poison for the left. While there is a strong urge among socialist politicians and voters to want to 'take a walk on the left side', the experience of the French left during the crisis shows that this is a difficult path to take. It runs next to several juggernauts: on one side, those of the markets and the European Union, and on the other side, the challenge of extreme right populism that is eating away at the left-wing vote.

Acknowledgements

The authors would like to thank Michael Holmes for his support and suggestions. Antonella Seddone received financial support from the Conseil Régional Hauts-de-France within the programme: *Mobilité entrante du Conseil Régional: Jeunes Chercheurs, Chercheurs Confirmés, chaires internationales*.

Notes

1 Including the Left Party and the Unitarian Left. There are also several extreme left Trotskyist parties outside the Left Front, which have had some sporadic electoral success but have never managed to elect an MP and have constantly refused to enter electoral cartels with other left-wing parties (De Waele & Seiler 2012).
2 A third grouping, Ensemble, has the status of partner organisation.
3 The Parti Radical de Gauche (PRG) is a centre left component of the French left to which we will not dedicate any specific attention here since it plays a minor role and is constantly allied to the PS.
4 This included the abolition of the death penalty, improved rights for workers, and political and institutional decentralisation.
5 Valery Giscard d'Estaing was elected with 50.8% in 1974.
6 Since 2002, elections to the National Assembly have been held immediately after the presidential elections.
7 Mélenchon was a former member of the Socialists who had left the PS in 2008.
8 Four were from the PS: Benoît Hamon (36% in the first round), Manuel Valls (31%), Arnaud Montebourg (18%) and Vincent Peillon (7%); there was one from the Ecologist Party (François de Rugy, 4%) and two from the centre left, Sylvia Pinel (2%) and Jean-Luc Bennahmias (1%). In the run-off, Hamon defeated Valls by 59%–41%.
9 These included EELV, who ran their own primary contest with Yannick Jadot winning the nomination. But he then agreed to stand down in support of Hamon's candidacy.

10 Data on turnout, for example, prove that the abstention rate was increasing since the 2007 legislative elections. Looking at the last three legislative elections one can see the sharp decline in turnout – from 64.4% in 2002 to 57.2% in 2012 in the first round; and from 60.3% in 2002 to 55.4% in 2012 in the second round.

11 As pointed out by Kuhn (2014), not even during Mitterrand's presidency was the left able to achieve such complete dominance of the representative French institutions.

Bibliography

Armingeon, K., C. Isler, L. Knöpfel, D. Weisstanner & S. Engler (2016) *Comparative Political Data Set 1960–2014*, Bern: Institute of Political Science, University of Bern.

Bachelot, C. (2011) 'Le Parti socialiste, la longue marche de la présidentialisation', in Bréchon, P. (ed.) *Les partis politiques français*, Paris, La documentation française, 103–128.

Bosco, A. & Verney, S. (eds) (2016) *Elections in hard times: southern Europe 2010–11*, London: Routledge.

Clift, B. (2005) *French socialism in a global era: the political economy of the new social democracy in France*, New York & London: Continuum.

Close, C. & Delwit, P. (2016) 'Green parties and elections', in E. Van Haute (ed.) *Green parties in Europe*, London: Routledge, 241–264.

Cole, A. (2012) 'The fast presidency? Nicolas Sarkozy and the political institutions of the fifth republic', *Contemporary French and Francophone Studies*, 16 (3): 311–321.

Cole, A. & Drake, H. (2000) 'The Europeanization of the French polity: continuity, change and adaptation', *Journal of European Public Policy*, 7 (1): 26–43.

Daley, A. (ed.) (2014) *The Mitterrand era: policy alternatives and political mobilization in France*, Basingstoke: Palgrave.

Damiani, M. & De Luca, M. (2016) 'From the Communist Party to the Front de gauche: the French radical left from 1989 to 2014', *Communist and Post-Communist Studies*, 49 (4): 313–321.

De Giorgi, E. & Moury, C. (2015) 'Conclusions: Great Recession, great cooperation?' *The Journal of Legislative Studies*, 21(1): 115–120.

De Waele, J. M. & Seiler, D. L. (eds) (2012) *Les partis de la gauche anticapitaliste en Europe*, Paris, Economica.

Ducange, J. N. (2015) 'The radical left in France', *Socialism and Democracy*, 29 (3): 62–70.

Dupoirier, E. & Sauger, N. (2010) 'Four rounds in a row: the impact of presidential election outcomes on legislative elections in France', *French Politics*, 8 (1): 21–41.

En Marche! (2017) 'Le programme d'Emmanuel Macron'. https://en-marche.fr/emmanuel-macron/le-programme/europe (accessed 1 July 2017).

France24 (2016) 'Opinion poll finds France's Hollande would lose big in presidential election', www.france24.com/en/20160907-france-hollande-would-lose-2017-presidential-election-poll-finds (accessed 1 July 2017).

Gerstlé, J. & François, A. (2011) 'Médiatisation de l'économie et fabrication de la popularité du président français (2007–2010)', *Revue Française de Science Politique*, 61 (2) : 249–281.

Grossman, E. (2007) 'France and the EU: from opportunity to constraint', *Journal of European Public Policy*, 14 (7): 983–991.

Grossman, E. & Sauger, N. (2014) 'Un président normal'? Presidential (in-) action and unpopularity in the wake of the great recession', *French Politics*, 12 (2): 86–103.

Grunberg, G. (2014) 'Le Socialisme français en crise', *Modern & Contemporary France*, 22 (4) : 459–471.

Hamon, B. (2017) 'Mon projet pour faire battre le coeur de la France'. www.benoithamon2017.fr/thematique/europe/#europe (accessed 1 July 2017).

Hanley, D. (2016) 'From 'la petite Europe vaticane' to the Club Med: the French Socialist Party and the challenges of European integration', *Modern & Contemporary France*, 1–17 (dx.doi.org/10.1080/09639489.2016.1256872).

Hernández, E. & Kriesi, H. (2015) 'The electoral consequences of the financial and economic crisis in Europe', *European Journal of Political Research*, 55 (2): 203–224.

Hewlett, N. (2012) 'Voting in the shadow of the crisis. the French presidential and parliamentary elections of 2012', *Modern & Contemporary France*, 20 (4): 403–420.

Hübscher, E. & Sattler, T. (2017) 'Fiscal consolidation under electoral risk', *European Journal of Political Research*, 56 (1): 151–168.

Kriesi, H., & Pappas, T. S. (eds) (2015) *European populism in the shadow of the great recession*, Colchester: ECPR Press.

Kuhn, R. (2014) 'Mister unpopular: François Hollande and the exercise of presidential leadership, 2012–14', *Modern & Contemporary France*, 22 (4): 435–457.

Kuhn, R. & Murray, R. (2013) 'France's left turn: mapping the 2012 elections', *Parliamentary Affairs*, 66 (1): 1–16.

Lewis-Beck, M. S. & Nadeau, R. (2000) 'French electoral institutions and the economic vote', *Electoral Studies*, 19 (2–3): 171–182.

Lewis-Beck M. S. & Stegmaier, M. (2007) 'Economic models of voting', in R. Dalton & H. D. Klingemann (eds) *The Oxford handbook of political behaviour*, Oxford: Oxford University Press, 518–527.

Marthaler, S. (2012) 'The yes–no dichotomy of the French left', in M. Holmes & K. Roder (eds) *The left and the European Constitution: from Laeken to Lisbon*, Manchester: Manchester University Press, 35–54.

Mélenchon, J. L. (2016) 'L'avenir en commun'. https://avenirencommun.fr/avenir-en-commun/ (accessed 1 July 2017).

Milner, S. (2004) 'For an alternative Europe: Euroscepticism and the French left since the Maastricht treaty', *European Studies: A Journal of European Culture, History and Politics*, 20 (1) : 59–81.

Ministère de l'Intérieur (various) 'Les résultats: élections'. www.interieur.gouv.fr/
Elections/Les-resultats/ (accessed 1 July 2017).

Moffitt, B. (2015) 'How to perform crisis: a model for understanding the key role of crisis in contemporary populism', *Government and Opposition*, 50 (2): 189–217.

Morlino, L. & Raniolo, F. (2017) *The impact of the economic crisis on South European democracies*, London: Palgrave Macmillan.

Moss, B. H. (1998) 'French left Euroscepticism and the myth of social Europe', *Modern & Contemporary France*, 6 (4): 535–538.

Moury, C. & De Giorgi, E. (2015) 'Introduction: conflict and consensus in parliament during the economic crisis', *The Journal of Legislative Studies*, 21 (1): 1–13.

Nadeau R., Bélanger, E., Lewis-Beck, M., Cautrès, B. & Foucault, M. (2012) *Les élections présidentielles : le vote des Français de Mitterrand à Sarkozy*, Paris: Presses de Sciences-Po.

Price-Thomas, G. (2016) 'Green party ideology today', in E. Van Haute (ed.) *Green Parties in Europe*, London: Routledge, 280–297.

Repaire, S. (2016) 'La création des verts: une intégration idéologique de l'écologie politique?', *Revue Française d'Histoire des Idées Politiques*, 44: 93–125.

Rozenberg, O. (2016) 'France in quest of a European narrative', *Les Cahiers européens de Sciences Po*, no. 4/2016.

Sainteny, G. (2000) *L'introuvable écologisme français?*, Paris: Presses Universitaires de France.

Serricchio, F., Tsakatika, M. & Quaglia, L. (2013) 'Euroscepticism and the global financial crisis', *Journal of Common Market Studies*, 51 (1): 51–64.

Talving, L. (2017) 'The electoral consequences of austerity: economic policy voting in Europe in times of crisis', *West European Politics*, 40 (3): 560–583.

Turgeon, M., Bélanger, E. & Nadeau, R. (2015), 'French popularity functions: different measures, different determinants?', *French Politics*, 13 (3): 266–286.

Vasilopoulos, P., Beaudonnet, L. & Cautrès, B. (2015) 'A red letter day: investigating the renaissance of the French far left in the 2012 presidential election', *French Politics*, 13 (2): 121–140.

Villalba, B. (2016) 'From the Greens to Europe Ecology–The Greens', in E. Van Haute (ed.) *Green Parties in Europe*, London: Routledge, 92–111.

WZB (2018) *The manifesto project*. Berlin: Social Science Research Centre. https://manifesto-project.wzb.eu/ (accessed 17 March 2019).

11

In the shadow of Merkel: the German left and the crisis

Knut Roder

Introduction

Germany's approach to tackling the financial and Eurozone crises was central to the entire issue. However, analyses have tended to focus almost entirely on the policy choices taken by Angela Merkel's centre right Christian Democratic Party. Surprisingly little attention has been given to the policy positions developed and adopted by Germany's political parties on the centre left, even though their policies have been those of a junior coalition partner and are potentially those of a future governing party. On the wider left, the question of whether there was a realistic opportunity for Germany's parties on the left to develop an alternative policy approach to the crisis has rarely been assessed.

This chapter evaluates the responses of Germany's parties on the left to the crisis. There are three parties worth examining when analysing the German left and the crisis. The Social Democratic Party of Germany (Sozialdemokratische Partei Deutschlands, SPD) is a member of the S&D Group in the EP and of PES. The Greens (Bündnis 90/Die Grünen) are members of the European Green Party and the Greens-EFA group. Die Linke is a member of GUE-NGL and of the Party of the European Left (Roder, 2012: 95).[1]

The chapter looks at three phases and analyses the left's role towards the crisis through the CDU/CSU-SPD (2005–2009); CDU/CSU-FDP (2009–2013), and CDU/CSU-SPD (2013–2017) coalition government periods. The 2013 election is particularly significant, and this chapter focuses on it. The result in 2013 made a left coalition possible, but instead, the SPD chose to go into a grand coalition with the right. The chapter concludes by evaluating the prospects for the left, particularly in relation to their cooperation and to challenging the dominance of the CDU/CSU.

The story of the German responses to the crisis goes back to the introduction of the euro. There were early doubts about the continuing competitiveness

Table 11.1 German general election results (in % of vote) and government coalitions, 2005–2017

	CDU/CSU	FDP	AfD	SPD	Greens	Linke	combined left	Coalition
2005	35.2	9.8	-	**34.2**	**8.1**	**8.7**	**51.0**	CDU/CSU & SPD
2009	33.8	14.6	-	**23.0**	**10.7**	**11.9**	**45.6**	CDU/CSU & FDP
2013	41.5	4.8	4.7	**25.7**	**8.4**	**8.6**	**42.7**	CDU/CSU & SPD
2017	32.9	10.7	12.6	**20.5**	**8.9**	**9.2**	**38.6**	CDU/CSU & SPD

Source: author's elaboration
Notes: Left parties in bold; Die Linke = PDS in 2004; electoral alliance between PDS, Linkspartei and WSAG in 2005

Table 11.2 European Parliament election results in Germany (in % of vote and seats), 2004–2019

	CDU/CSU	FDP	AfD	SPD	Greens	Linke	combined left
2004	44.5%	6.1%	-	**21.5%**	**11.9%**	**6.1%**	**39.5**
	(49)	(7)		**(23)**	**(13)**	**(7)**	**(43)**
2009	37.8%	11.0%	-	**20.8%**	**12.1%**	**7.5%**	**40.4**
	(42)	(12)		**(23)**	**(14)**	**(8)**	**(45)**
2014[a]	35.4%	3.4%	7.0%	**27.3%**	**10.7%**	**7.4%**	**45.4**
	(34)	(3)	(7)	**(27)**	**(11)**	**(7)**	**(45)**
2019	29.8%	5.4%	11.0%	**15.8%**	**20.5%**	**5.5%**	**41.8%**
	(29)	(5)	(11)	**(16)**	**(21)**	**(5)**	**(42)**

Source: author's elaboration
Notes: Left parties in bold; 'Die Linke' = PDS in 2004; electoral alliance between PDS, Linkspartei and WSAG in 2005.
[a] The abolition of the 5% threshold allowed more parties to win seats in 2014 and 2019. The overall number of seats allocated to German MEPs to the EP was reduced from 99 to 96.

of the economy, so German industry undertook huge efforts to boost productivity and to restructure. In 2003, SPD Chancellor Gerhard Schröder brought in a series of labour market reforms, known as Agenda 2010. These were 'harsh' and 'socially costly' due to dramatically increasing job insecurity and depressing incomes[2] (Pisani-Ferry, 2014: 48–9). They also created the idea that Germany's apparent export trade success was preceded by painful domestic structural reform and prolonged wage moderation that took place in the early years of the Eurozone, and this was overseen by an SPD/Green coalition (Dyson, 2015: 54). This fed into the German public's perception of the sovereign debt crisis and the euro crisis.

The reforms are important for at least four reasons. First, the reform package was commonly interpreted as decisively improving German economic competitiveness well before the euro crisis, enabling the country to outcompete the rest of Europe (Zimmermann, 2014: 326). Second, there is a widespread belief that this German success was due to painful reforms that paid off economically (Möller, 2013). While these two points are contested, they appear to hold substantial public traction. Third, the fact that it was an SPD/Green coalition that drove the reform agenda had a devastating electoral effect on the SPD (Tagesschau, 2013b) by alienating large numbers of the party's supporters (Niedermayer, 2015: 13). This is evident in general elections (see Table 11.1), European elections (see Table 11.2) and state elections. Finally, there was substantial criticism over the policies of the SPD/Green coalition in regard to its approach towards deregulating financial markets (Bundestag, 2008). This, in turn, became a key component for the successful establishment of Die Linke as a third nationwide party to the left of the SPD and Greens that challenged them over their policies in government.

The crisis starts: the SPD sharing responsibility

When the crisis began, the SPD was the junior partner in a CDU/CSU-led government. Initial German debates about how to respond to the crisis mirrored the European Commission's ideas of national rescue packages and a European stimulus plan. The German government brought in two stimulus packages, in October 2008 and March 2009 (*The Economist*, 2009). However, the SPD Minister of Finance, Peer Steinbrück, dismissed the use of generous spending packages by other European governments to soften the impact of the crisis as 'crass Keynesianism' (Hawley, 2012). He stressed instead a preference for largely unspecified far-reaching financial market and banking reforms.

In October 2008, a package of measures (Finanzmarktstabilisierungsgesetz) was introduced. It was intended to stabilise the financial market, and included bailout guarantees for banks, but also some funds to stimulate the economy. Peter Struck of the SPD stated that it was 'internationally embedded' but also 'explicitly served German needs', and he praised Chancellor Merkel for having 'rejected a French initiative' (Bundestag, 2008: 19657–61). Both the Greens and Die Linke welcomed the package but criticised the lack of proposals to re-regulate financial markets, and both voted against it. Renate Künast of the Greens spoke against what she saw as a 'blank cheque' for

German banks (Bundestag, 2008: 19663–68), while Gregor Gysi of Die Linke expressed dissatisfaction with the focus on national solutions over a European-level response (Bundestag, 2008: 19663–66).

The first full package of stimulus measures (Konjunkturpaket 1) was approved in parliament in December 2008. It provided €23 billion and anticipated €31 billion of additional economic activity (Bundesfinanzministerium, 2009). Both the Greens and Die Linke rejected this package, arguing it was insufficient and criticised the fact that it lacked proposals to change the financial market rules (Wolter, 2008).

By January 2009, the deteriorating situation forced the government to initiate a larger stimulus programme financed by borrowing €50 billion. This consisted of tax cuts, additional infrastructure spending and short-time work benefits (Bundesfinanzministerium, 2009). The SPD claimed credit for the inclusion of health insurance payroll tax cuts as well as the creation of a highly popular €2,500 payment to car owners for trading in old cars (FAZ, 2009). *The Economist* commented, 'we're all "crass" Keynesians now' (*The Economist*, 2009) as a sarcastic reminder of Steinbrück's earlier comment. However, the German government did stress the need for the adoption of national as well as European-wide constitutional commitments to rule out deficit spending in the medium term – what was to become the Fiscal Compact.[3]

Die Linke rejected this second package on the same grounds as the first. Oskar Lafontaine of Die Linke criticised the package as 'too small and socially unbalanced' (Bundestag, 2009: 21969–71).[4] However, in contrast to their rejection of the first package, the Greens abstained this time (see Table 11.3). Its representative, Jürgen Trittin, described the government's policies as 'working too slowly, being too timid and lacking focus' (Bundestag, 2009: 21971–73). The lack of a common left policy position on the crisis was excruciatingly clear, as each party on the left voted differently, with the SPD in government in favour of the package, the Greens abstaining and Die Linke rejecting it. The substantial disagreements indicated that few commonalities and little policy cooperation between the three parties could be expected for the foreseeable future. The 2009 election programmes of the three parties reflected those differences.

The crisis continues: responsible opposition?

In the general election of September 2009 the SPD suffered its worst electoral performance since 1949. The SPD lost votes to all competitors, but mostly to its rivals on the left – Die Linke picked up 1.1 million votes from previous SPD supporters, the Greens 0.87 million (Tagesschau, 2009). Both Die Linke

Table 11.3 Bundestag 'roll-call' voting patterns by the SPD, Die Linke and Greens on key votes dealing with euro/financial crisis, 2008–2016

Date	Issue	SPD Yes/No/Abst.	Die Linke Yes/No/Abst.	Greens Yes/No/Abst.	Overall Bundestag vote Yes / No
19.08.2015	Gewährung eines 86 Mrd. Euro Kreditpakets für Griechenland 3	**171** / 4 / 0 **Y**	0 / **45** / 7 **N**	**52** / 1 / 8 **Y**	454 / 113
17.07.2015	Stabilitätshilfe zugunsten Griechenlands	**175** /4 / 0 **Y**	0 / **53** / 2 **N**	23 /2 /**33 A**	439 / 119
27.02.2015	Finanzhilfen für Griechenland 2	**178** / 0 / 0 **Y**	41 / 3 / 10 **Y**	**60** / 0 / 0 **Y**	541 / 32
18.04.2013	Finanzhilfen für Zypern (ESM)	**122**/10/10 **Y**	0 / **72** / 0 **N**	**62** / 0 / 1 **Y**	487 / 101
30.11.2012	Finanzhilfen für Griechenland 1	111/11/9 **Y**	0 / **67** / 0 **N**	**65** / 0 / 1 **Y**	473 / 100
19.07.2012	Bankenhilfe für Spanien (EFSF)	118/14/2 **Y**	0 / **60** / 0 **N**	**54** / 1 / 10 **Y**	473 / 97
29.06.2012	Dauerhafter Euro-Rettungsschirm ESM	**128**/8/4 **Y**	0 / **71** / 0 **N**	**65** / 1/ 0 **Y**	493 / 106
29.06.2012	Fiskalpakt	**138**/ 1 / 4 **Y**	0 / **71** / 0 **N**	**65** / 1/ 0 **Y**	504 / 97
27.02.2012	Zweites Rettungspaket für Griechenland	**129**/7 / 1 **Y**	0 / **66** / 0 **N**	**85** / 4 / 1 **Y**	496 / 90
29.09.2011	Euro-Stabilisierungsfonds EFSF	**141**/ 1 / 1 **Y**	0 / **70** / 0 **N**	**67** / 1 / 0 **Y**	523 / 85
21.05.2010	Euro-Rettungsschirm	0 / 1 / **128 N**	0 / **76** / 0 **N**	0 / 0 / **63 N**	319 / 73
07.05.2010	Notkredit für Griechenland	4 / 0 / **134 N**	0 / **67** / 0 **N**	**61** / 0 / 5 **Y**	391 / 72
20.03.2009	Stabilisierung des Finanzmarktes (Finanzmarktstabilisierungsergänzungsgesetz)	**191** / 1 / 0 **Y**	0 / **47** / 0 **N**	0 / 0 / **43 A**	379 / 107
17.10.2008	Maßnahmenpakets zur Stabilisierung des Finanzmarktes (Finanzmarktstabilisierun gsgesetz)	**207** / 0 / 0 **Y**	0 / **50** / 0 **N**	0 / **48** / 0 **N**	476 / 99

Source: author's elaboration – (Bundestag, 2016) Plenum, Namentliche Abstimmungen
Note: A majority of 'No' votes or abstentions (failing to support government) designated as 'No'.

(11.8%) and the Greens (10.7%) achieved their best general election results ever. Here, in particular, the SPD's handling of the crisis had appeared blurred and lacking in distinctiveness, while the Greens and Die Linke as the sole left-wing parties in opposition were able to successfully articulate an alternative, gaining a kind of 'crisis bonus' (Korte, 2010: 14, 22). The SPD clearly failed to define itself as a centre left policy alternative to the CDU/CSU's policies. In contrast, Merkel's CDU/CSU experienced only a slight decline (-1.4%), and the free market Freie Demokratische Partei (FDP) had an exceptionally strong performance (14.6%, up from 9.8%). This led to a new centre right CDU/CSU-FDP government.

During this period, optimism about recovery began to fade and the collapse of the Greek economy and risk of contagion across the Eurozone added an even greater sense of urgency to dealing with the crisis. The three parties of the German left were all in opposition during this crucial phase, and adding to the left's dilemma was the sense that German public opinion appeared to support the centre right's policy of fiscal stability. Government policies were based on an idea that Germans had only agreed to the EMU on the premise that the arrangements contained a 'no bailout' clause, the prohibition of monetary financing of public deficits, and the obligation to avoid excessive public deficits, with the Stability and Growth Pact supposedly guaranteeing the maintenance of all of this (Pisani-Ferry, 2014: 54).

This period also witnessed separate actions filed in Germany's constitutional court that challenged the government's crisis management. While all three parties on the left were involved, each party prioritised different aspects and joined different actions. Again, this illustrates the absence of a common left approach.

The first judgment was declared the day after the Bundestag had voted in favour of the second Greek bailout package. The case had been brought by two SPD MPs, Peter Danckert and Swen Schulz. Their action argued that the Bundestag had not been allowed to properly scrutinise decisions that could lead to Germany committing vast sums of money to rescue the euro.[5] On 19 June 2012, the constitutional court ruled in favour of their case. While the government had passed a new law to allow the use of a very small special Bundestag committee of nine MPs, the court ruled that an amendment to German basic law was necessary to legitimise such wide-ranging decisions. The second case was a complaint filed by the parliamentary party of the Greens against the government for its failure to inform the Bundestag as early as possible about the negotiations of EU-related treaties (Zeit-Online, 2012a). Again, the court found in favour of the complainants.

A third case was brought by single members of the governing FDP and CSU and the entire parliamentary party group of Die Linke (DW, 2014). They claimed that the ESM was unconstitutional and ran counter to legal commitments made to Germany at the start of EMU. The Constitutional Court decided that the EU's permanent bailout fund was compatible with Germany's Basic Law and that parliament had sufficient powers to control national liabilities. However, the ruling contained measures designed to strengthen the future role of parliament in this process (DW, 2014).

Overall, all three cases succeeded in raising crucial questions about the ESM and eventually led to the recognition by the Constitutional Court that the Bundestag's role required strengthening, in particular in the face of new intergovernmental approaches to EU integration. While the three parties on the left challenged the government over the constitutional legality of its handling of the crisis, the SPD, Greens and Die Linke did not attempt to develop a common rallying point to oppose the government's handling of the crisis. They did not explore the possibility of any centre left or socialist alternative to the solutions advocated by the CDU/CSU-led government.

Programmatic alternatives in the 2013 election

The years preceding the 2013 election can be viewed as the height of the euro crisis. Therefore, the left's programmatic choices on the crisis can be analysed through the manifestos for the 2013 general election.

The SPD's 120-page-strong 'das Wir entscheidet' manifesto[6] dealt with the crisis on around ten pages. The party avoided making the euro crisis a key campaign issue over which to attack the Merkel government. Since it had mostly supported Merkel's approach towards the euro crisis in the Bundestag, this was at least consistent. The party did not aim to formulate concrete alternatives to Merkel's policy direction of balanced budgets and austerity. Instead, the SPD used its manifesto to emphasise its status as the 'party of social justice' in an attempt to win back voters that had abandoned the party in 2009 by stressing social justice as the party's core competency (Spier & von Alemann, 2015: 57).

The SPD emphasised the need for a 're-foundation of a social market economy' that would replace the 'neoliberal ideology of conservatives' and end 'the period of market radicalism' (SPD, 2013: 14). However, the manifesto avoided criticising the government's anti-debt and pro-austerity logic. Instead, it demanded the 'reduction of public debt as an indispensable precondition' for development (SPD, 2013: 26). Macroeconomic causes of the crisis received only a brief mention, with the party seemingly not wanting to propose alternative policy instruments to tackle the crisis, such as an expansionary budgetary policy. In fact, the SPD appeared to accept the existing EMU debt reduction mechanisms, such as wage adjustment, tax increases and budget cuts.

The SPD advocated more generally the need to 'tame financial market capitalism' (SPD, 2013: 13–16). It pledged to 're-regulate financial markets' and 're-establish a social market economy' (SPD, 2013: 14–18), and it argued that 'Europe should play a key role in creating market rules that tame financial markets' (SPD, 2013: 13). The problem with many of these pledges was that they lacked detail. They also ignored the fact that key financial markets are based in other parts of the world where a German government would have little credible ability to do much about re-regulation. For that reason, pledges should have stressed more strongly the determination to attempt to influence multilateral institutions such as the G20 to re-regulate such markets. The SPD did call, however, for the creation of a European-level Financial Transaction Tax (SPD, 2013: 15) and demanded stricter capital requirements for banks; but avoided concrete figures.

The lack of detail in the programme was interpreted as exposing the party's lack of determination to engage with the deeper causes of the crisis and challenge the banking industry (Münchau, 2013c). Overall, consistent with the SPD's voting record over the previous four years, the SPD offered few ideas on how to deal with the crisis that were new or different from those of the sitting government. It could be argued that, as a result, the SPD offered insufficient incentives to the electorate to switch allegiances to the SPD based on the party's policy proposals for dealing with the crisis (Münchau, 2013c).

In contrast, the Greens' voluminous 337-page manifesto dealt on a third of its pages with matters more or less strongly related to the financial and euro crisis and its fallout. Predictably, the party prioritised environmental policies and was somewhat less focused on the narrowly economic aspects of the crisis. Instead, it linked them strongly to wider environmental themes. A substantial amount dealt with social justice and policies centred around redistribution of wealth (mainly through taxation) that were aimed at challenging the SPD and Die Linke in this policy area (Niedermayer, 2015: 17).

The Green Party offered a substantial review of the causes of the crisis. The party stressed that the crisis should not only be blamed on irresponsible budgetary policies of southern European countries, but also on harmful capital movements due to economic imbalances within the Eurozone (Grünen, 2013: 56). They blamed 'economic imbalances within the European Union equally on the budget deficits as well as trade surpluses' (Grünen, 2013: 55). In addition, the programme directly criticised the Merkel government for 'hiding the truth about bailout programmes and stabilisation mechanisms', arguing they had benefited German banks and insurers rather than being a 'display of generosity' (Grünen, 2013: 55). The manifesto was also highly critical of the government's policy of austerity, which the Greens held responsible for having deepened the economic crisis and weakened social cohesion within the EU (Grünen, 2013: 55).

However, the solutions appeared less clear-cut. The Greens called for a 'common European economic policy' that would focus more on the 'cohesive development' of its member states' economies. One suggestion to increase overall economic activity within the Eurozone was to increase domestic demand levels in countries with a trade surplus, such as Germany (Grünen, 2013:56). There were also wider demands to tackle tax evasion and tax competition between member states. Furthermore, the party argued that the 'financial and climate crisis' were part of the same systemic problem and would have to be tackled together (Grünen, 2013: 46).

There are some inconsistencies in the programme. For example, the Greens pledged the establishment of common euro bonds as the party's long-term goal (Grünen, 2013: 56), but suggested that countries caught by the sovereign debt crisis should pay off their debts in full instead of partly writing them off. This would still force them to adopt restrictive austerity measures, which the Greens had appeared to reject (Münchau, 2013b). Overall, while the sheer volume of the programme reflected deep discussion in the party, at the same time it did not offer comprehensive clear-cut solutions to the crisis. Overall, the Green manifesto sat slightly uneasily with their positions in the preceding Bundestag. Their manifesto embraced a far more critical approach towards the government's policies and understanding of the crisis than had been communicated by the party's voting patterns over the previous four years, when they had offered substantial support to the Merkel government's initiatives, bailouts and creation of the ESM as well as the Fiscal Compact.

Another policy angle was apparent in Die Linke's 100-page manifesto. Its title was '100% Social', and large parts of its manifesto focused on social justice. The party linked this to the unjust burden sharing of the costs that arose from the crisis (Niedermayer, 2015: 17). It came out most strongly in linking the crisis to a more general critique of capitalism as a system that was 'producing systemic economic imbalances'' (Münchau, 2013a). The manifesto accused the Merkel-led government of 'confusing cause with effect' when it 'reinterpreted the financial crisis into a sovereign debt crisis' (Die Linke, 2013: 46). Die Linke blamed instead 'a triad of redistribution of wealth to the top, deregulation and privatisation' for the crisis (Die Linke, 2013: 46).

The party accused the Merkel government of diverting attention from the real causes, which it described as the unsustainable high sovereign debt levels in crisis countries, needing bailouts in a system that was ultimately rigged to benefit German banks (Die Linke, 2013: 46, 47). Consistent with this, the party advocated radical measures by calling, for example, for a new 75% income tax for top earners, a one-off European tax on the wealthy;

the nationalisation of large private banks; legislation to tackle tax evasion; and short-term direct help from the ECB to finance the deficits of struggling member states (Die Linke, 2013: 48). It is markedly the most Eurosceptic of all three left parties' programmes, calling for the 're-foundation of the European Union' and abandonment of the EU's 'neoliberal orientation' (Die Linke, 2013: 49). But importantly, the manifesto also stressed that although Die Linke felt that the 'current setup contains huge errors', it did 'not to want an end to the euro' (Die Linke, 2013: 49).

Some observers criticised Die Linke's manifesto on similar grounds to the SPD in terms of falling short of recognising sufficiently the need for increased international policy coordination instead of focusing excessively on domestic measures aimed at redistributing wealth on the national level (Münchau, 2013a). The manifesto was consistent with the party's voting record in the Bundestag from the previous four years of parliamentary rejection of government initiatives, including the refusal to support the ESM and the Fiscal Compact.

The three parties on the left failed to benefit from the crisis in the 2013 election (see Table 11.1). The SPD increased its vote by less than 3%, and recorded their second worst performance since 1949, while the Greens and Die Linke both lost votes. However, since the SPD went into government and since Die Linke won more votes than the Greens, Die Linke became the largest opposition party in the Bundestag. Chancellor Angela Merkel remained popular, with 84% of the electorate stating their belief that Merkel's policies had improved the wellbeing of the country; 58% of the electorate felt that the CDU had been competent in managing the euro crisis, and only 20% thought the SPD had shown competence (Tagesschau, 2013a). The government party's strategists had been right to 'emphasise how well Germany had fared throughout the financial and euro crisis under Merkel's leadership' (Tagesschau, 2013a).

Indeed, from the outset of the crisis, public opinion polls in Germany indicated a high degree of approval for Merkel's centre right governments, which continued to be widely perceived as looking after Germany's interests (Kinkel, 2012). In addition, Germany's economy appeared to have performed solidly in recent years, delivering low unemployment figures and even generating a national budget surplus (OECD, 2016). Furthermore, from past experience we know that when a majority of the electorate feels it is not directly affected by an economic crisis, voting on economic issues becomes far less pronounced, meaning that party political competition and electoral performances are likely to be determined by other issue areas than, as in this case, the crisis (Belanger & Meguid, 2008: 477–491).

With the Merkel government's policies on the crisis being widely perceived as a success story by the German public, political parties on the left struggled to exploit government policy failures on the crisis. This positive perception was strengthened by the fact that the parties on the left failed to cooperate and agree a common alternative that might have challenged the government more effectively. A final factor possibly contributing to the left's inability to exploit the crisis electorally was Merkel's apparent strategy of 'asymmetric demobilisation', whereby sharp conflicts over (crisis) policy choices were deliberately defused in addition to purposely dull campaigning, thus creating a sense of security among voters that seemed to persuade 'competitor' voters not to bother voting (Wahl.de, 2013).

An opening to new political options

The 2013 general election led to another change of coalition. The FDP failed to return MPs to the Bundestag, and another grand coalition was formed between the CDU/CSU and the SPD. This left the Greens and Die Linke as the sole opposition parties in the Bundestag again. The election saw a slight recovery of the SPD vote (by 2.7% to 25.7%), but the Greens and Die Linke were unable to sustain their previous strong showing, with the Greens declining to 8.4%, and Die Linke to 8.6%. Two parties just failed to reach the required 5% threshold to qualify for any seats – the FDP with 4.8% and the new Eurosceptic Alternative für Deutschland with 4.7%.

Numerically, the parties on the left had a majority of seats, though their combined total of 320 would have been only a tiny Bundestag majority. Due to the previous lack of common political ground, on the handling of the crisis and other issues, no such left majority coalition emerged (Lederer & Miemiec, 2016: 98). This was consistent with the SPD's pre-election pledge, ruling out any possibility of entering an agreement with Die Linke to establish a so-called Red-Red-Green (R2G) coalition. This left the SPD with only one strategic choice, namely to be the junior partner in a CDU/CSU-led coalition (Zeit-Online, 2012b).

Two months after the election, the SPD decided to abandon its rejection on principle of cooperation with Die Linke (FR, 2013). Discussions began about an R2G option with members of the SPD, Die Linke and the Greens (Gathmann et al., 2016b; Neuerer, 2016; Zeit-Online, 2016).[7] By late 2016, two R2G coalition governments had been formed successfully at Länder level, in Thuringia and Berlin. However, the presence of the SPD in a grand coalition prevented the further development of a distinctively left narrative among the three parties in response to the crisis.

It was only towards the end of the government's legislative period and the run-up to the 2017 election that possible grounds for left cooperation were developed further. This was partly because of a 'bounce' in opinion poll support for the SPD after Martin Schulz became their Chancellor-candidate, which made an R2G government seem feasible for a short while. An attempt to intensify the R2G discussions took place in the run-up to the 2017 election, but failed when it became increasingly evident that the SPD, Greens and Die Linke would not have an electoral majority. Indeed, the combined vote for Germany's parties on the left declined from over 50% in 2005 to under 40% in 2017 (see Table 11.1), so that the possibility of a left majority, even in the medium term, 'may have been running out' (Lederer & Miemiec, 2016: 104).

For a short period in the summer of 2015, public attention was on the crisis when Minister of Finance Wolfgang Schäuble made a much-publicised suggestion that a 'Grexit' could be an alternative to a third Greek bailout (FAZ, 2015). But otherwise, the 2013–2017 grand coalition focused less on the economic crisis. In fact, only three Bundestag roll-call votes relating to the crisis were held during that coalition period, and these were on technical questions concerning Spanish, Cypriot and Greek bailout packages (see Table 11.3). This was due in part to the rapid recovery of the country's export-led economy. But the government was also increasingly preoccupied with the challenge of the so-called refugee crisis (FAZ, 2016). Public opinion showed a steady decline in fears over issues such as unemployment, the economic situation and the financial crisis, giving way to issues such as terrorism and the influx of large numbers of refugees (ZDF, 2016). This was reflected in party programmes for the 2017 general election. Programmatic pledges on the crisis and issues of EU and EMU reform were far less evident.

However, in the immediate aftermath of the 2017 election, the issue of EU integration came back to the top of the political agenda. This was partly due to a 'Macron effect', after the election of the strongly pro-integration President in France, and there were also renewed concerns over the sustainability of EMU. It is also because the 2017 election produced a dramatic change in German party politics (see Table 11.1). The two coalition partners lost heavily. The SPD lost over 5% of its vote and recorded its worst result since the creation of the Federal Republic, while the CDU/CSU dropped almost 9%. The Greens and Die Linke won small increases, but the big winners were the FDP and the Eurosceptic Alternative für Deutschland.

The outcome proved inconclusive, and coalition formation dragged on for an unprecedented six months. Initially, a 'Jamaica coalition' between the CDU/CSU, FDP and the Greens seemed the most likely option, and the Greens held successful preliminary talks with the right.[8] This broke down unexpectedly when the FDP pulled out of negotiations (Handelsblatt, 2017).

The SPD had contested the election on a commitment not to return to a grand coalition, and the steep electoral losses at first strengthened their resolve not to go back into government with the CDU/CSU. Their hesitancy and Merkel's lack of alternative coalition partners placed the SPD in an exceptionally strong position. The SPD eventually agreed to talks with the CDU/CSU, but needed to prove to its own membership that the party would make a decisive difference to German government policy this time. Five months after talking about 'renewal in opposition', the SPD leadership was once again seeking the approval of its party members to enter yet another CDU/CSU-led grand coalition. A new 'Groko', or grand coalition, emerged in March 2018.

One of the key arguments put forward by the leadership was the claim that the party had so successfully negotiated the new coalition agreement that it could now 'ensure a fundamental shift in German government policy on Europe. Namely, to abandon Wolfgang Schäuble-style policies of austerity, and by responding positively towards French President Emmanuel Macron's proposed EU reform agenda' (SPD, 2018a: 31).[9] In other words, the SPD leadership justified the need for entering another grand coalition as a way to ensure Eurozone reform, end the austerity agenda, and enhance the creation of a more 'social and democratic' Europe (SPD, 2018b). The SPD position was interpreted as being 'even more avidly pro-EU', with the party determined to 'renew the Franco-German duopoly' and to improve the sustainability of the Eurozone by initiating 'faster movement on European fiscal integration, and seek to edge towards a combined Eurozone budget' (McElvoy, 2018).

The SPD's vote on a national level has declined sharply over the past ten years, and the party's decision to prop up a Merkel-led grand coalition once again does not bode well for any rapid recovery at the polls. Such recovery, however, would be a major precondition for the emergence of a left majority at the polls. Some leading members of Die Linke have declared the 'death of Red-Red-Green as an option' (taz, 2018) and proposed instead the foundation of an all-encompassing cross-party left-wing electoral movement as 'the only realistic path' to enable the three traditional parties on the left to successfully challenge the right and generate a left majority in the process (Hagen & Teevs, 2018). But grave questions remain over Die Linke's cohesion and its ability to commit to any cooperation with the SPD and Greens on the national level (Roder, 2017). In addition, any possible future prospect for a left-wing majority may well be undermined by the apparent strategic repositioning of the Greens, following their serious involvement in coalition negotiations with the right after the 2017 general election.

Conclusion

The analysis of the policy positions of the SPD, Greens and Die Linke offers some positive evidence of programmatic commonalities among the parties on the left, based on their desire to revise the German policy approach to the crisis. There are numerous policies the parties agree upon. They accept the need for some kind of re-foundation of the social market model with general agreement over the need to readjust the role of markets and reinforce government interventionism. Similarly, all three parties are sensitive towards addressing the general ills of social exclusion and stress the need to reform the EU by deepening the Union's social, political and economic dimensions. All three also advocate the re-regulation of financial markets, including the introduction of policies to better tackle tax evasion and implementation of a financial transaction tax, while also appealing for more effective tools to achieve greater redistribution of wealth and social cohesion on the national as well as European level.

Throughout the three periods analysed in this chapter, Germany's parties on the left were strongly divided over the causes of the crisis as well as the policy choices available to best respond to it. In case of the SPD, this was due to the fact that the party had been a junior partner in Merkel-led governments for most of the period, sharing responsibility for the German government's policy choices. And when in opposition (2009–2013), the SPD was not only run by much of the same leadership personnel, but for that reason also had to appear consistent in policy choices, which clearly limited the extent to which the party could openly disavow the policies of the Merkel government.

As for the other two parties on the left and in opposition, the Greens adopted a policy strategy similar to that of the SPD, meaning that criticism was often matched by a highly pragmatic policy approach that was mostly supportive of the government's initiatives. In contrast, Die Linke mostly rejected the policy choices taken by the three Merkel administrations, and voted consistently against the government's legislative proposals put forward in the Bundestag (see Table 11.3).

On a final note, it appears that in all those years since the crisis broke, the various CDU/CSU-led government coalitions never felt threatened by parties on the left over the crisis to the same extent as they were by the emergence of the populist right Alternative für Deutschland over immigration. This is even more remarkable if one bears in mind that the euro crisis is far from over. The failings of the EMU structure will continue to expose the Eurozone's unsustainability in its current form, requiring major political, economic and institutional reform (see Flassbeck, 2012; Pryce, 2012; March, 2013; Streeck, 2013; Hickel & Koenig, 2014; Stiglitz, 2016). For this reason, the parties on left will continue to find themselves faced with the challenge of developing a more common policy approach to enhance their influence and step more successfully out of the shadow of Merkel and her former finance minister Wolfgang Schäuble. It remains to be seen if the moves towards cooperation by the SPD, Die Linke and the Greens in recent years can be the first steps in laying down the necessary groundwork for a policy rapprochement process.

Similarly, it remains to be seen if a German government led by parties on the left would be able to abandon what has been widely viewed as an 'inactive' waiting game approach (Guérot, 2018: 5) by successive Merkel-led governments, and instead agree an alternative strategy of active endorsement of new EU-level instruments and institutional arrangements (Hacker & Koch, 2016: 34) that advocate a stronger 'community spirit' (Laïdi, 2018) in order to tackle the Eurozone's systemic problems and prevent a further crisis in a socially more sustainable manner. A precondition for this, however, would be a new left-of-centre electoral majority. This appears to be more unlikely than ever after the 2019 European elections, where the SPD's share of vote declined further (see Table 11.2). Intriguingly, politicians like Die Linke's Oscar Lafontaine have suggested the merger of his party and the SPD as a possible response to 'revive Germany's social democracy' (FAZ, 2019). It remains to be seen if this could yet be another option for Germany's left to step out of the shadow of the continuing domination of German politics by the centre-right.

Notes

1 The party Die Linke will be referred to by its German name throughout the chapter to avoid confusion with the term 'left' as used to describe the position of parties within the wider political spectrum.
2 Incomes rose by 18% between 1998 and 2008, representing an actual loss of purchasing power for many wage earners in the country (Pisani-Ferry, 2014: 48–9).
3 The key parliamentary debate on the second package took place in January 2009 with a final vote on 20 March 2009 (Amend, 2009).
4 Co-chair of Die Linke's parliamentary party, and previously finance minister in the SPD-led government in 1998–99.
5 Specifically, Danckert and Schulz challenged the government's use of a very small 'special committee' of nine MPs, with the vast majority of the Bundestag not consulted on such an important decision (Focus-Online, 2012).
6 It translates rather awkwardly as: 'It's the "We" that counts'.
7 These common forums included 'denkwerk demokratie', the 'Oslo-Gruppe', 'Denkfabrik', and the 'Institut Solidarische Moderne' (Gathmann, 2016a).
8 So called because the colours of the parties – black for the CDU/CSU, yellow for the FDP and of course green – match those of the Jamaican flag.
9 Macron had set out ambitious plans for a 'profound transformation' of the EU including deeper political integration as well as initiatives to provide the Eurozone with a finance minister, budget and parliament (*The Guardian*, 2017).

Bibliography

Amend, A. (2009) 'Das Finanzmarktstabilisierungsergänzungsgesetz oder der Bedeutungsverlust des Insolvenzrechts', *Zeitschrift für Wirtschaftsrecht*, ZIP online. www.zip-online.de/heft-13–2009/zip-2009–589-das-finanzmarktstab ilisierungsergaenzungsgesetz-oder-der-bedeutungsverlust-des-insolvenzrechts/ (accessed 17 October 2016).

Belanger, E. & Meguid, B. M. (2008) 'Issue salience, issue ownership, and issue-based vote choice', *Electoral Studies*, 27: 477–491.

Bundesfinanzministerium (2009) 'Informationen zum Konjunkturpaket vom Januar 2009', 30 January. www.bundesfinanzministerium.de/Content/DE/Monatsberichte/2009/01/Artikel/uebersichten_und_termine/UT0-Konjunkturpaket/Konjunkturpaket.html (accessed 27 August 2016).

Bundestag (2008) 'Plenarprotokoll 16/184, 16. Wahlperiode – 184. Sitzung', Berlin: Bundestag, 17 October. http://dip21.bundestag.de/dip21/btp/16/16184.pdf (accessed 20 August 2016).

Bundestag (2009) '16. Wahlperiode, 203. Sitzung', Berlin: Bundestag, 30 January. http://dipbt.bundestag.de/dip21/btp/16/16203.pdf#P.21969 (accessed 28 August 2016).

Bundestag (2016) 'Abstimmungen 16, 17 & 18 Wahlperiode'. www.bundestag.de/bundestag/plenum/abstimmung/grafik (accessed 5 August 2016).

Die Linke (2013) *100% Sozial: Wahlprogramm zur Bundestagswahl 2013*, Berlin: Die Linke.

DW (2014) 'Germany's top court upholds legality of ESM rescue fund', *Deutsche Welle*, 18 March. www.dw.com/en/germanys-top-court-upholds-legality-of-esm-rescue-fund/a-17503069 (accessed 16 August 2016).

Dyson, K. (2015) 'Germany, the euro crisis, and risk management: Europe's reluctant and vulnerable hegemonic power', in G. D'Ottavio & T. Saalfeld (eds), *Germany after the 2013 elections: Breaking the mould of post-unification politics?* Farnham: Routledge, 49–66.

The Economist (2009) 'How very stimulating: somewhat belatedly, Germany goes for a €50 billion fiscal stimulus', 15 January. www.economist.com/node/12947570 (accessed 27 August 2016).

FAZ (2009) 'Finanzkrise: SPD will Konjunktur mit € 40 Milliarden ankurbel', *Frankfurter Allgemeine Zeitung*, 5 January. www.faz.net/aktuell/politik/finanzkrise-spd-will-konjunktur-mit-40-milliarden-euro-ankurbeln-1752656.html (accessed 27 August 2016).

FAZ (2015) 'Schäuble soll Athen zum Euro-Austritt geraten haben', *Frankfurter Allgemeine Zeitung*, 4 January. www.faz.net/aktuell/wirtschaft/eurokrise/griechenland/euro-krise-schaeuble-soll-athen-zum-euro-austritt-geraten-haben-13352302.html (accessed 22 August 2016).

FAZ (2016) 'Werner Mussler: Europäische Solidarität?' *Frankfurter Allgemeine Zeitung*, 17 February. www.faz.net/aktuell/wirtschaft/wirtschaftspolitik/europaeische-solidaritaet-in-zeiten-der-euro-und-fluechtlingskrise-14073957.html (accessed 22 August 2016).

FAZ (2019) 'Neuanfang für Sozialdemokratie: Lafontaine hält Fusion von SPD und Linken für notwendig', Frankfurt: Frankfurter Allgemeine Zeitung, 12 June.

https://www.faz.net/aktuell/politik/inland/neuanfang-fuer-sozialdemokratie-lafontaine-fuer-fusion-von-spd-und-linken-16232415.html (accessed 12 June 2019).

Flassbeck, H. (2012) *Zehn Mythen der Krise*, Berlin: Suhrkamp.

Focus-Online (2012) 'Urteil zu Beteiligungsrechten des Bundestags: Wer darf die Milliarden für Griechenland freigeben?' 27 February. www.focus.de/finanzen/news/staatsverschuldung/bundesverfassungsgericht-karlsruhe-will-ueber-euro-sondergremium-urteilen_aid_718385.html (accessed 16 August 2016).

FR (2013) 'Koalition mit Linkspartei: SPD sieht rot-rot grün künftig als Option', Frankfurter Rundschau Online, 12 November. www.fr-online.de/bundestagswahl—hintergrund/koalition-mit-linkspartei-spd-sieht-rot-rot-gruen-kuenftig-als-option,23998104,25011212.html (accessed 26 August 2016).

Gathmann, F. (2016a) 'Großes Treffen von SPD, Linken und Grünen: Bisschen schnuppern, bisschen stänkern', *Spiegel-Online*, 16 October. www.spiegel.de/politik/deutschland/grosses-rot-rot-gruen-treffen-r2g-in-berlin-a-1116976.html (accessed 16 October 2016).

Gathmann, F., Hagen, K. & Meiritz, A. (2016b) 'Linksbündnis: So realistisch ist Rot-Rot-Grün', *Spiegel-Online*, 14 July. www.spiegel.de/politik/deutschland/rot-rot-gruen-auf-bundesebene-codename-r2g-a-1102664.html (accessed 26 August 2016).

Grünen (2013) *Zeit für den Grünen Wandel: Teilhaben. Einmischen. Zukunft schaffen – Bundeswahlprogramm 2013*, Berlin: Bündnis 90/Die Grünen.

The Guardian (2017) 'Macron lays out vision for 'profound' changes in post-Brexit EU', 26 September. www.theguardian.com/world/2017/sep/26/profound-transformation-macron-lays-out-vision-for-post-brexit-eu (accessed 1 March 2018).

Guérot, U. (2018) 'Macron en marche: Tauziehen um Europa', *Blätter für deutsche und internationale Politik*, 4 (18): 5–8.

Hacker, B. & Koch, C. M. (2016) *Was wird aus der Eurozone: Eine Landkarte der Interessenkonflikte zur Reform der Währungsunion*, Institut für Makroökonomie und Konjunkturforschung, No. 52, November, Düsseldorf: Hans-Böckler-Stiftung. www.boeckler.de/pdf/p_imk_study_52_2016.pdf (accessed 25 March 2018).

Hagen, K. & Teevs, C. (2018) 'Wagenknecht und Lafontaine: #fairLand als Motto für linke Sammlungsbewegung', *Spiegel-Online*, 17 May. www.spiegel.de/politik/deutschland/linke-sammlungsbewegung-koennte-fairland-heissen-a-1208340.html (accessed 23 May 2018).

Handelsblatt (2017) 'Jamaika-Verhandlungen: Grüne und FDP drücken aufs Tempo', 7 November. www.handelsblatt.com/politik/deutschland/jamaika-verhandlungen-gruene-und-fdp-druecken-aufs-tempo/20553424.html?ticket=ST-3942842-WZOgGpaJCNhhS6mLm5Y7-ap2 (accessed 30 May 2018).

Hawley, C. (2012) 'Does Peer Steinbrück have the stuff to be Chancellor?' *Spiegel-Online*, 28 September. www.spiegel.de/international/germany/spd-candidate-steinbrueck-faces-uphill-battle-in-campaign-versus-merkel-a-858608.html (accessed 17 September 2016).

Hickel, R. & Koenig, J.-G. (2014) *Euro stabilisieren EU demokratisieren: Aus den Krisen lernen*, Bremen: Kellner Verlag.

Kinkel, L. (2012) 'Umfragehoch für die Union: Zehn Gründe, warum Merkel so beliebt ist', *Stern-Online*, 5 September. www.stern.de/politik/deutschland/

stern-politikerranking-merkels-ansehen-erreicht-hoechsten-wert-seit-wiederwahl-1889398.html (accessed 23 November 2012).

Korte, K.-R. (ed.) (2010) *Die Bundestagswahl 2009: Analysen der Wahl-, Parteien-, Kommunikations- und Regierungsforschung*, Wiesbaden: VS Verlag.

Laïdi, Z. (2018) 'The German rules trap', *Project Syndicate*, 24 May. www.project-syndicate.org/commentary/germany-rules-fetish-blocking-european-reform-by-zaki-laidi-2018-05 (accessed 29 May 2018).

Lederer, K. & Miemiec, O. (2016) 'Was kommt nach dem Protest?', *Blätter für deutsche und internationale Politik*, 10: 2016.

March, D. (2013) *Europe's deadlock: how the euro crisis could be solved – and why it won't happen*, Yale: Yale University Press.

McElvoy, A. (2018) 'Germany's coalition deal safeguards the Merkel/Macron vision of Europe', *The Guardian*, 5 March. www.theguardian.com/commentisfree/2018/mar/04/germany-coalition-merkel-macron-europe-eu (accessed 5 March 2018).

Möller, J. (2013) 'Mythen der Arbeit: Die Agenda 2010 hat gar keine neuen Jobs geschaffen', *Spiegel-Online*, 1 May. www.spiegel.de/karriere/berufsleben/hat-die-agenda-2010-neue-jobs-geschaffen-a-897492.html (accessed 27 August 2016).

Münchau, W. (2013a) 'Rot-Rot-Grün ist die beste Lösung für Europa', *Spiegel-Online*, 28 August. www.spiegel.de/wirtschaft/soziales/wolfgang-muenchau-ueber-das-wahlprogramm-der-linken-a-919067.html (accessed 28 August 2013).

Münchau, W. (2013b) 'Wenn Politiker vom Stammtisch aufstehen', *Spiegel-Online*, 21 August. www.spiegel.de/wirtschaft/soziales/gruenen-wahlprogramm-praezise-analyse-und-weniger-praezise-forderungen-a-917728.html (accessed 21 August 2013).

Münchau, W. (2013c) 'Die SPD kämpft die falsche Schlacht', *Spiegel-Online*, 13 July. www.spiegel.de/wirtschaft/soziales/spd-wolfgang-muenchau-ueber-das-wahlprogramm-der-spd-a-914027.html (accessed 13 August 2013).

Neuerer, D. (2016) 'Operation "R2G": Rot-Rot-Grün ist längst kein Schreckgespenst mehr', *Handelsblatt*, 20 June. www.handelsblatt.com/politik/deutschland/operation-r2g-rot-rot-gruen-ist-laengst-kein-schreckgespenst-mehr/13759228.html (accessed 26 August 2016).

Niedermayer, O. (2015) *Die Parteien nach der Bundestagwahl 2013*, Berlin: Springer VS.

OECD (2016) *Germany – economic forecast summary*, Paris: OECD. www.oecd.org/economy/germany-economic-forecast-summary.html (accessed 25 August 2016).

Pisani-Ferry, J. (2014) *The euro crisis and its aftermath*, Oxford: Oxford University Press.

Pryce, V. (2012) *Greekonomics: the euro crisis and why politicians don't get it*, London: Birkbeck Publishing.

Roder, K. (2012) 'The German left from Laeken to Lisbon', in Michael Holmes & Knut Roder, *The left and the European Constitution*, Manchester: Manchester University Press, 95–117.

Roder, K. (2017) 'The missing Linke? Restraint and realignment in the German left, 2005–2017', *Revista Española de Ciencia Política – Ciencia Política y de la Administración*, 45: 43–65.

SPD (2013) *Das Wir entscheidet: Das Regierungsprogramm 2013–2017*, Berlin: SPD.

SPD (2018a) *Eine neue Zeit braucht eine neue Politik: Protokoll des Ausserordentlichen Bundesparteitages der SPD*, SPD: Bonn, 21 January.

SPD (2018b) *Begleitsschreiben der Parteispitze zum Mitgliedervotum*, SPD: Berlin, 8 February.

Spier, T. & von Alemann, U. (2015) 'In ruhigerem Fahrwasser, aber ohne Land in Sicht? Die SPD nach der Bundestagswahl 2013', in O. Niedermayer (ed.) *Die Parteien nach der Bundestagwahl 2013*, Berlin: Springer VS, 49–70.

Stiglitz, J. (2016) *The Euro: and its threat to the future of Europe*, London: Allen Lane.

Streeck, W. (2013) *Gekaufte Zeit: Die vertagte Krise des demokratischen Kapitalismus*, Berlin: Suhrkamp.

Tagesschau (2009) 'Analysen Wählerwanderung: Bundestagswahl 2009'. https://wahl.tagesschau.de/wahlen/2009-09-27-BT-DE/analyse-wanderung.shtml (accessed 26 August 2016).

Tagesschau (2013a) 'Gut für unser Land: Bundestagswahl 2013'. http://wahl.tagesschau.de/wahlen/2013-09-22-BT-DE/index.shtml (accessed 21 September 2016).

Tagesschau (2013b) 'Zehn Jahre 'Agenda 2010': Eine Reform mit Wirkungen und Nebenwirkungen', *Tagesschau*, 7 April. www.tagesschau.de/inland/agendazwanzigzehn-hintergrund100~_origin-166337e9–42e1–40c1–913f-fa447ff74064.html (accessed 27 August 2016).

taz (2018) 'In der heutigen Welt kann es keine offenenen Grenzen für all geben', *Die Tageszeitung*, 7 March.

Wahl.de (2013) 'Die symmetrische Demobilisierung – frustriertes und gelangweiltes Ausblenden aus dem Wahlkampf', appstretto & civey, 24 July. www.wahl.de/aktuell/2013/07/24/symmetrische-demobilisierung-wahlkampf-btw13/ (accessed 3 September 2016).

Wolter, P. (2008) 'Interview mit Gesine Lötzsch: Das ist mehr als politische Blindheit', *Junge Welt-Online*, 14 October. www.linksfraktion.de/im-wortlaut/das-mehr-politische-blindheit/ (accessed 27 August 2016).

ZDF (Forschungsgruppe Wahlen) (2016) 'Wichtige Probleme in Deutschland seit 01/2001'. www.forschungsgruppe.de/Umfragen/Politbarometer/Langzeitentwicklung_-_Themen_im_Ueberblick/Politik_II/ (accessed 28 August 2016).

Zeit-Online (2012a) 'Verfassungsgericht stärkt Bundestag bei Euro-Hilfen', 19 June. www.zeit.de/politik/deutschland/2012-06/urteil-verfassungsgericht-esm-bundestag (accessed 16 August 2016).

Zeit-Online (2012b) 'Gabriel schließt Koalition mit Linkspartei für 2013 aus', 25 January. www.zeit.de/politik/deutschland/2012-01/spd-gabriel-linke (accessed 26 August 2016).

Zeit-Online (2016) 'Bundestagswahl 2017: Historisches Fenster für Rot-Rot-Grün', 29 June. www.zeit.de/politik/deutschland/2016-06/bundestagswahl-2017-gregor-gysi-koalition-rot-rot-gruen (accessed 26 August 2016).

Zimmermann, H. (2014) 'A grand coalition for the euro: the second Merkel cabinet, the euro crisis and the elections of 2013', *German Politics*, 23 (4): 322–336.

12

Between Scylla and Charybdis: Europe, nationalism and left politics

Andy Storey

> Struggles for the welfare state and popular rule are becoming struggles against Europe. (Mason, 2017)

> Having the same currency as the most advanced countries has a tremendous power over people's imagination. (Kouvelakis, 2016: 45)

> [Is] it really… possible to promote a progressive nationalism without legitimizing the chauvinistic nationalism of the right-wing populists? (Attac Norway, 2018)

Introduction

How does the radical left in Europe approach the issue of European governance? The leaderships of almost all social democratic parties have long since embraced an overall commitment to European integration (Bailey, 2005), while being sometimes critical of particular aspects of it, but the same is not true of left-wing *voters* nor of the parties (the ones here defined as radical) to the left of social democracy.[1] How then have these latter voters and parties responded to growing – if often diffuse and volatile – popular criticism of the 'European project'? And how might they respond in the future?

This chapter seeks to answer these questions by, first, locating left-wing criticism of European integration within a historical context – there is a particular tradition of left 'Euroscepticism' that is distinct from that of the right. While still partly nationalist in orientation, this left tradition is not necessarily opposed to European integration provided it delivers greater economic justice and equality – the problem with the *current* pattern of integration is that it tends to do precisely the opposite. Can that pattern be reversed? The chapter briefly discusses some proposals for reversal or reform (shared in some cases by people from both the radical and social democratic left), but highlights the difficulties faced in trying to implement any such programme of left-wing reform at the European level.

Responding to those difficulties, a current of (mainly) radical left opinion argues that left-wing economic objectives can only be achieved by countries opting for a 'left exit' (Lexit) from the European Union and/or the Eurozone. Such a Lexit might be mobilised around an inclusionary nationalism (itself part of a long-established left tradition) that counterposes itself to the xenophobic positions of the Eurosceptic right. The chapter outlines this Lexit argument and also its own challenges, which are rooted in the balance of power across Europe and within countries, and also within the minds of left-wing voters (including radical left ones) themselves. Many of even the staunchest left-wing critics are loath to break from the EU and/or the Eurozone – because they fear the economic costs of doing so might be high; because they remain attached to aspects of EU integration (or at least what that integration is associated with); and because they fear that the disintegration of the EU might add further fuel to far right fires already burning across the continent.

Opposition to (forms of) EU integration on the part of the left

Euroscepticism is clearly not the sole preserve of the political right, though the left-wing variant can be argued to be rather more nuanced than its right-wing counterpart. Based on survey data from across the EU collected between 2008 and 2014, van Elsas et al. (2016) note that left-wing opposition to the EU tends to take the form of rejecting the current policies and practices of the EU rather than rejecting the idea of European integration in principle (the latter tends to be the case with right-wing opponents, as is discussed further below).

This left-wing rejection is rooted in egalitarian attitudes and is associated with a preference for redistributive economic policies. Survey respondents identifying as left-wing were found to be, on average, *more* dissatisfied with the current form of the EU than were right-wing respondents. The van Elsas et al. study found that left-wing citizens were by no means immune from cultural chauvinism (see also Steenvoorden & Harteveld, 2017), but what distinguished those on the left (whether radical or social democratic) from their right-wing counterparts was the extent to which it was their socio-economic egalitarian impulses that drove their opposition to the EU.[2] (As will be discussed in the conclusion to this chapter, what many left-wingers *like* about the EU are its *non*-economic dimensions.)

Identifying as left-wing does not necessarily mean that one will *vote* for a party of the left: for example, radical left views are relatively strong in Bulgaria and Slovenia, yet in both countries electoral support for radical left parties is weak (Visser et al., 2014: 554–555).[3] However, Ramiro (2016), using cross-European data from 1989 to 2009, found that people who believed EU membership to be negative for their country were, on balance, more likely than others to vote for a party of the radical left, i.e. to adopt *more* left-wing positions.

This, historically, is an unsurprising finding: Gomez et al. (2015: 10), in their study of party manifestos, found that negative attitudes to the EU (and its predecessors) have long constituted a very prominent distinguishing characteristic of radical left parties. More significantly, March and Rommerskirchen (2015) found that expressions of Euroscepticism have tended to impact *positively* on the electoral performance of such parties.[4]

Interestingly, this last finding was largely based on pre-crisis data. Beaudonnet and Gomez (2017: 2–3), looking at the European Parliament elections of 2009 and 2014, found that Eurosceptic and generally dissatisfied voters became much more likely to vote for radical left parties over that five-year period: 'during the economic crisis, the radical left has been particularly successful, and increasingly so, in reaching out to a heterogeneous group of voters including not only left-wing Eurosceptics but also fundamentally pro-EU voters who were disappointed by the economic consequences of the crisis' (Beaudonnet & Gomez, 2017: 2). The number of European Parliament seats held by radical left parties rose by almost 50% – from 35 to 52 – between 2009 and 2014 (Beaudonnet & Gomez, 2017: 1).[5]

The national question

Note that Ramiro's finding (above) referred to people's views of how EU membership impacted on their *country*. That, in turn, begs the question of the relationship between left-wing sentiment, nationalism and attitudes to the EU. While potentially more supportive (in theory) of EU integration than their right-wing counterparts, left-wingers have not, for the most part, abandoned (or moved beyond) nationalism – it is, rather, that they define nationalism in different terms from those on the right. (However, left-wing leaders and activists may still be uneasy about couching their appeals in national(ist) terms, a point returned to in the concluding sections of this chapter.)

Halikiopoulou et al. (2012) emphasise the left-wing tradition of 'civic nationalism', through which the national interest is identified with the interests of the popular classes, whose economic interests are seen as threatened by both national and foreign elites.[6] Radical left-wingers, in particular, tend to 'perceive the EU as a vehicle for elite and great power domination at the expense of the popular classes' (Halikiopoulou et al., 2012: 512; see also Charalambous, 2011; van Elsas & van der Brug, 2015).

Some right-wing Eurosceptic parties, such as France's National Front, have been able to tap into these same currents by calls for trade protectionism, for exit from the Euro and/or for opposition to 'financial elites', but their policies tend to remain predominantly pro-business – as evident in an emphasis on tax cuts and increased supports for the corporate sector (Morini, 2017: 3). Right-wing Eurosceptic parties in Scandinavia also position themselves as defenders of the welfare state – but largely from the claimed 'threat' of immigration rather than from economic liberalisation (Anderson, 2017).

More broadly, right-wing Euroscepticism tends to extend beyond economic matters, to be rooted in ethno-nationalism based on the EU's claimed role in the erosion of national independence *per se* and of the nation's putative cultural 'values'. This is typically based on a yearning for what Tokatlian (2016) terms a 'regressive arcadia', a mythical past of national greatness unsullied by immigration or cultural diversity (Steenvoorden & Harteveld, 2017).

This helps explain why right-wing opposition to the EU tends to be more 'existential' in nature – insofar as European political integration (as distinct from the economic liberalisation of the Single Market programme) is seen to dilute cultural specificities and national independence, it is, for the right, to be opposed *tout court*. Economic ('bread and butter') issues loom much larger, as wellsprings of anti-EU sentiment, for left Eurosceptics than for those on the right (Spierings & Zaslove, 2017; see also Lachat, 2017).

The threat that the EU is seen as posing to the economic interests of the popular classes (which is the principal basis of left-wing opposition) could, in theory at least, be neutralised by reforming the EU in such a way as to advance egalitarian and redistributive goals, including through more democratic political governance of the liberalised Single Market (van Elsas et al., 2016; see also below). This, of course, has long been the stated objective of the 'mainstream' social democratic left, i.e. 'to replicate the national social democratic mode at the European level' (Escalona & Vieira, 2014: 23).[7] It is precisely that long-standing question of reform – and its feasibility (or not) – that lies at the heart of left debates around European integration and, specifically, the future of the euro.

Reform proposals, and their discontents

The former Greek Finance Minister under the ostensibly radical left government of SYRIZA, Yanis Varoufakis, has set up a movement called Democracy in Europe.[8] Its central call is for democratisation of the EU, arguing that no national government can implement progressive policies so long as it remains straitjacketed by the undemocratic, neoliberal structures and policies of the EU.

Varoufakis's proposed solution is not for countries to exit the Eurozone or the EU (see below) but, rather, to radically reform European integration into a much more progressive political and economic governance framework (Navarro, 2016), thus sidestepping (or superseding) the dilemma SYRIZA faced between Eurozone membership and austerity (discussed further below). Varoufakis is, therefore, to some extent in the tradition of left Euroscepticism, and not just that of the radical left, that identifies the problem as the *current* nature of European integration rather than the principle of integration itself (see above; and van Elsas et al., 2016).

Varoufakis's demands include full transparency in EU decision-making (livestreaming of EU Council meetings, publication of ECB governing council minutes) and the convening of an 'Assembly of Citizens' to deliberate upon, and ultimately rework, EU governance (Patomaki, 2017: 8). These calls are (in part) echoed by some on the social democratic (rather than radical) left such as Martin Schulz of the German Social Democratic Party and Jürgen Habermas, who want to tackle the 'democratic deficit' by, among other measures, greatly increasing the powers of the European Parliament (Wahl, 2017: 2).

But Varoufakis and the social democrats are faced with a very practical problem, and it is one that has long bedevilled the stated social democratic approach to Europe: how are the pro-democracy reforms they envisage to be brought about, and by whom? The answer (implicitly) afforded to those last questions by Wolfgang Streeck[9] (and many others) is that such reforms simply *cannot* feasibly be brought about because there is no capacity or agency at the European level to make them happen (see also Fassina, 2016). Streeck (2014: 217) asks:

> can what would amount to nothing less than a revolution be achieved through reform, within a framework of institutional continuity? Who would sit at the convention that would have to break with the present and embark on a new and better future, if not the interminable Giscards, van Rompuys, Barrosos, Junkers *e tuttti quanti*?

Where, Streeck demands, is 'a market-correcting European-democratic politics' (Streeck, 2014: 218) going to come from when the current democracy-curtailing, neoliberal tenets are enshrined in the legal DNA of the EU itself (Scharpf, 2013; Storey, 2014), underpinned by the powers of the ECB and Commission and buttressed by the rulings of the European Court of Justice. These, furthermore, could only be changed by the agreement[10] of all member country governments, a prospect described by Peter Wahl as a 'utopian project' (2017: 4).

Varoufakis and his allies (e.g. Galbraith, 2017) make the point that massively increased public investment through, for example, the European Investment Bank, could be facilitated without treaty change, as could debt restructuring and other Keynesian-style measures. The question is whether any such policies – so radically at odds with the current ones – are likely to be contemplated under the existing power structures and political dispensation (Patomaki, 2017: 8). Macron's election in France in 2017 raised hopes in some quarters of some such shift but his proposals in this regard represent no fundamental break with the neoliberal model and, in any event, are unlikely to be implemented given the scale of opposition on the part of other governments (de la Baume, 2017; Fazi, 2017). This has proven to be the case even with the SPD re-entering coalition government in Germany (Karnitschnig, 2017).

In the absence of such changes (at least on anything like the scale necessary) at the overarching European level, national governing parties such as SYRIZA (discussed further below) even seeking to mildly challenge the EU's neoliberal economic governance regime will inevitably be faced with responses like that of the then German Finance Minister Wolfgang Schäuble when he said, 'elections change nothing … [t]here are rules'; or that of European Commission President Jean-Claude Juncker when he said, 'there can be no democratic choice against the European treaties' (cited in Hewitt, 2015).

A counter-argument from Varoufakis and his allies (see Varoufakis, 2016) is that while formal treaty change may indeed be utopian, defying the treaties, or not implementing them fully, is not. They point to the re-imposition of border controls by several member states in 2016, which was clearly contrary to commitments under the Schengen agreement, and also the failure to impose deficit fines on Spain and Portugal despite their breach of Fiscal Treaty rules (Watkins, 2016a: 27). An alliance between social democrats and radical left parties in Portugal has been able to at least mitigate austerity by, in part, creative interpretation of the EU fiscal rules (Gois, 2017; Louca, 2017). Thus, for those on this side of the debate, an alternative governance model can perhaps be constructed in Europe by selective non-compliance – what Varoufakis (2016) terms 'wilful disobedience'[11] – on the part of like-minded governments with the existing treaties and rules rather than by their revocation or renegotiation (Wahl, 2017).

Exit stage left?

However, critics of such strategies argue that creative non-compliance/ defiance is ultimately doomed to failure. The EU is by no means the strict, rules-bound body it is often presented as by both its admirers and critics alike – supposedly rigid rules are indeed routinely breached, such as to facilitate the post-crisis bailout of the banks (Storey, 2017). But Lee Jones (2016) has a point when he accuses Varoufakis of engaging in 'fantasy politics', mistaking the willingness of governments to breach EU rules in the interests of capital and other powerful interests with their willingness to countenance substantial 'wilful disobedience' of the rules on the part of those suffering austerity. The rules were broken or bent to ensure the banks were bailed out, but not Greece. The question is *who* gets to break the rules and whose interests are thereby served. Ryner and Cafruny (2017: 224) charge both Varoufakis and Habermas with 'a rather fanciful overestimation of the transnational capacities of post-conventional civil society organisations' to reform Europe by these or other methods.

Also critical of Varoufakis, French economist Frederic Lordon (2015: 1) bluntly states that 'The Euro radically precludes any possibility of progressive policies'.[12] Note that Lordon is here narrowing the debate to the question of Eurozone membership, rather than the rules governing the EU as a whole. The reason for this is that he, like Varoufakis, largely bases his argument on the experience of the SYRIZA-led government in Greece in its attempts to negotiate with the EU (and other creditor institutions) in 2015. But he draws very different conclusions to Varoufakis from that experience and one of them concerns the centrality of the euro for the way in which events unfolded. Ironically, Varoufakis's own account of his experiences as a minister in Greece – carefully documenting the implacable hostility of EU actors and institutions to even the most modest of SYRIZA's reform proposals – seems to lend support to his critics' case (Varoufakis, 2017).

For Lordon, the central dilemma (or weakness, depending on how one views it) of the SYRIZA position was that they wished to renegotiate the austerity strategy being imposed on Greece by the 'troika' (the EU Commission, the ECB and the IMF; with the EU Council standing behind them) while at the same time remaining a member of the Eurozone. Thus, despite being granted an overwhelming popular mandate against austerity in a July 2015 referendum, SYRIZA responded to a threat from the German Finance Minister that Greece would be expelled from the Eurozone (and to the ECB's shutting down of liquidity to Greek banks)[13] by largely conceding to creditor demands (Heilig, 2016: 15–6).[14]

This chastening experience led many to draw the conclusion that 'the promise of a break with austerity *within* the Eurozone had come to seem ever more likely a contradiction in terms' (Miley, 2017: 268, emphasis added). Crucially, such pressure and subversion could again be deployed against other dissident debtor countries regardless of how creatively they sought to reinterpret EU rules or flout some of the treaty provisions (see above), a point elaborated upon by Streeck (2016: 162):

> Today the ECB can at its discretion withhold liquidity from the banking systems of states that refuse to follow its precepts as to their public finances, the size and composition of their public sectors, and even the structure of their wage setting systems. States and governments that do not 'reform' themselves in line with capitalist rectitude, and thereby fail to earn the confidence of international *haute finance*, can be punished in a broad variety of ways – while states that carry out institutional reforms as promoted by the Bank can be rewarded, even by the ECB printing fresh money for them, in violation or circumvention of EMU treaties.

Acknowledging the weight of pressures such as these, Costas Lapavitsas (2015), writing before the Greek referendum, was clear: 'lenders have used the framework of the Eurozone to create a liquidity and funding shortage that has crippled the Greek side'. As a representative of SYRIZA's Left Platform, Lapavitsas instead urged the government to exit the Eurozone in order to 'free the country from the trap of the common currency'. But to the SYRIZA leadership, this proved an unthinkable (or at least unacceptable) option, with the party's (post-Varoufakis) Finance Minister hyperbolically stating that Greece leaving the Euro would see a return to the conditions of the 1930s (Kouvelakis, 2016: 46; see also Nikolakakis, 2016).

The commitment of radical left leaders to continued membership of the Eurozone is not confined to Greece. Podemos parliamentarian Manolo Monero describes the EU as 'a major obstacle to any political, social, or economic change that challenges the neoliberal model' (Monero, 2017), but the leader of that party,[15] Pablo Iglesias, has stated:

> We do not like the way the euro has been built ... but we think that the euro is now impossible to do without. Certainly, we have to improve the way that the single currency is managed, and we think that there should be democratic control of this, but we are not partisans of leaving the euro ... Even if we don't like the way the ECB works, we accept [that Spain should remain] in the Eurozone. (cited in Lordon, 2015: 6).[16]

While the prospects of Podemos participating in government in Spain now appear to have receded, this makes clear that any future government there with radical left participation would be unlikely to countenance a voluntary rupture with the single currency (Heilig, 2016: 26; Kouvelakis, 2016: 69; Ramiro & Gomez, 2017). This is generally true of other radical left leaderships also, though there is no absolute consensus on the issue across different parties, with both memberships and leaderships divided (March, 2012: 335–6). Of 'radical' parties currently with some substantive influence over state power, only Italy's Five Star movement (and by no means is this unambiguously a party of the left) has sometimes called for a referendum on Italy exiting the Eurozone (Watkins, 2016a: 28; Watkins, 2016b: 20; Caruso, 2017; Conti, 2017: 536; Broder, 2018).

Nationalism *redux*?

In his response to Habermas (and, implicitly, to Varoufakis) Streeck (see above) makes the point that the most important channels of oppositional politics in Europe – voting, striking and otherwise protesting – 'remain firmly anchored at the national level' (Streeck, 2014: 219). Of course, there have been examples of cross-European strikes and protests against EU directives and other proposals (Turnbull, 2007; Storey, 2014; Dierckx, 2015) but the overwhelming site of political struggle in Europe remains determinedly national. This national focus can be a serious challenge for the left: for example, when workers' rights are attacked at the supranational level through European Court of Justice rulings and other measures, a nationally based response on the part of the trade unions is obviously problematic (Horn, 2012; Dribbusch, 2015; Dufresne, 2015; Erne, 2015).

And yet, might this also be an *opportunity* for the left? If one accepts the arguments of Lordon, Lapavitsas and others that exit from the Eurozone at least (and perhaps from the EU as a whole) is a *sine qua non* for the implementation of more progressive politics, then the mobilisation for such an exit must, almost by definition, be primarily national.[17] And this is where, one could argue, the left's tradition of civic or inclusionary nationalism as the basis of its Euroscepticism (see above) could be seen as a potentially important resource.

Indeed, some (e.g. Ali, 2016) claim that the failure of the left to articulate an inclusive national programme that explicitly challenges EU neoliberalism (and here the argument is being extended back again from the specificities of Eurozone membership to the broader question of how the EU as a whole operates) has surrendered the political field to right-wing Euroscepticism. It is the National Front in France (albeit somewhat stymied in 2017) and the United Kingdom Independence Party (in terms of Brexit, if not, ultimately, their own electoral fortunes) in the UK that have been best able to make political capital in their countries from a rising tide of hostility to the EU.

Tariq Ali (2016), among others, argues that Labour leader Jeremy Corbyn's failure in 2016 to campaign for Brexit in the UK on left-wing grounds proved a mistake (see also Watkins, 2016a: 18–19): he was, it is claimed, trying to keep his largely Europhile parliamentary Labour party united but ended up with them turning on him anyway, while the UK right was left to frame the Brexit debate in largely ethno-nationalist, exclusionary terms, especially vis-à-vis immigration.[18] That debate rumbles on with some in the British Labour Party urging the leadership to seek to overturn Brexit, while others on the left argue that it provides an opportunity to implement progressive policies free of the shackles of neoliberal Europe (Woolfson, 2017; Shaft, 2018).

Lordon (2015: 8) makes a similar point to that of Ali: 'In a sort of unconscious self-realisation syndrome, the Europeanist left seems to be devoting all its efforts to making sure that only the far-Right exit door is left open'. Likewise, Kagarlitsky (2017: 6) argues that by standing alongside EU elites in defence of the existing model of integration, the left (of whatever hue) is more or less guaranteeing that popular mobilisation against the EU can *only* be led by right-wing nationalists.

These points are valid and important – but they do not settle the debate. While Callinicos (2017: 12) is surely correct to argue that 'Progressive alternatives are unlikely to gain traction unless the existing EU is broken up', a problem is that these are not the *only* alternatives that may gain traction in such a scenario. There is no guarantee that the left joining more vigorously in the anti-EU battle would not result in victory still being claimed by a right that might remain the numerically stronger and more dominant force on the Eurosceptic side (see below). It is precisely that prospect which has caused left-wing Norwegian activists to ask whether 'it really is possible to promote a progressive nationalism without legitimizing the chauvinistic nationalism of the right-wing populists' (Attac Norway, 2018).

The left's dilemma: the enduring appeal of the euro and of an 'idea of Europe'[19]

Implicit or explicit in the arguments of Ali, Lordon and others is that there is a favourable historical conjuncture for those on the radical left who are highly critical of an increasingly authoritarian and neoliberal EU. An inclusionary nationalism, seeking to pit the bulk of a country's population against the diktats of the supranational state and its local elite allies, would seem to provide potentially fertile ground for a radical (civic nationalist) left movement to not only build its own programme for progressive reform, but also to undercut the forces of right-wing ethno-nationalism that currently tend to dominate anti-EU discourses and campaigns. It might also allow them to undercut social democratic rivals who largely remain committed to that increasingly authoritarian and (in many, but not all, senses) unpopular EU.

And yet there are also very severe impediments to such a project, as reflected in the fact, discussed earlier, that prominent radical left leaderships (such as those of SYRIZA and Podemos) have proven loath to fully embrace it. One such impediment is the fear of EU fracturing being accompanied by further right-wing advances at the national level, as already discussed and which will be returned to below. But there is also the impediment of the EU remaining very popular in some respects.

The quote at the start of this chapter from Kouvelakis (2016: 45) refers to the grip that Eurozone membership, especially, continues to exert on the popular imaginations of people in countries including Greece, Spain and Portugal. The same writer adverts to the way in which that membership has come to be seen, by many in those countries, as a badge of 'modernity', of democracy (a bulwark against the return of a relatively recently experienced authoritarianism), of membership of the 'West' more generally. As Mason puts it (2017), 'where coups and dictatorships are still living memory … "Europe" still has a powerful appeal as the embodiment of liberal democracy and the rule of law'. Himself a member (like Lapavitsas) of SYRIZA's Left Platform, Kouvelakis concedes that 'those of us who'd been in favour of exiting the euro since the start of the crisis tended to underestimate' this popular appeal (Kouvelakis, 2016: 46).

Popular support for the euro and the EU is extraordinarily high in most countries and it can be argued that many (perhaps even most) Greek people, in particular, wanted continued Eurozone membership even at the price of their continued oppression at the hands of the troika.[20] Certainly the retreat of the SYRIZA leadership did not occur in a vacuum. According to Eurobarometer survey data collected in May 2015, 69% of Greeks supported membership of the single currency, with only 29% against.[21] (The equivalent figures at that time for the Eurozone as a whole were 69–25, for Italy 59–30, for Portugal 62–31, for Spain 61–31, and for Ireland 70–14.)[22]

A poll taken in Greece in June 2015 (i.e. closer to the July referendum date) found that some 56% of Greeks wanted to stay in the Eurozone even if it meant the continuation of severe austerity measures (Chrysopoulos, 2015). One can interpret (at a stretch) the 5 July referendum result as an implicit popular acceptance of the need for a rupture with the Eurozone (Lordon, 2015: 8) but, if so, it was a position adopted with great reluctance and trepidation.

Conclusion

There is a tradition of left-wing Euroscepticism that has garnered increased support in recent years as dissatisfaction with the EU and its handling of the European economic crisis has grown. Those who register such support are not necessarily opposed to European integration in principle, they are opposed to the particular form that integration has taken. This does not make them 'post-national' – rather they tend to espouse an inclusionary, civic nationalism that is potentially compatible with a more democratic and socially progressive EU governance model.

Proposals for such a reformed governance model have been put forward (including by some on the radical left) but they face severe practical constraints given the institutionalised (often constitutionalised) nature of the neoliberal EU framework. It is not clear how (if at all) the recommended reforms could be brought about, leading others on the radical left to call for a 'left exit', with membership of the Eurozone seen as especially prohibitive to the implementation of anti-austerity, egalitarian economic policies. On the face of it, this might seem to offer an opportunity for radical left parties to mobilise their (inclusionary, civic) nationalist constituency (potentially a growing one) behind a project for the restoration of national, egalitarian democracy against the straitjacket of EU (especially Eurozone) neoliberalism.

Yet the straitjacket holds a formidable appeal, or at least the thought of being without it kindles significant fears. As Watkins (2016a: 23) laments, 'for years now, fear that systemic change would only bring more misery has kept Europe's voters pinned to a widely detested socio-economic status quo – most recently, Greek qualms about leaving the euro for a new drachma' (see also Ronzoni, 2015: 7). Those fears are solidly founded: a left-wing national government attempting to exit the Eurozone would certainly face economic sabotage, including capital flight and ECB choking off of liquidity – the required counter-measures of bank nationalisation and capital controls might not ward off significant economic damage and hardship in the short term at least (Heine & Sablowski, 2016: 25).

However, this desire to maintain the status quo is also related to non-economic factors, including the identification of the euro (and EU membership more generally) with modernity, liberalism and western identity. Added to this mix is popular attachment on the left to not just the euro but also privileges such as free movement (for most EU citizens) across EU borders and somewhat progressive EU regulations in areas such as environmental standards[23] and (however limited) EU measures against corporate tax avoidance (Cerioni, 2016; Cobham, 2017; European Network on Debt and Development, 2017; Kalaitzake, 2017).[24] It is perhaps precisely because right-wing voters tend to be hostile to many of these wider measures and initiatives – seeing free movement (for others), environmental regulation and taxation as threats – that it was possible for the right to build support for exiting the EU as a whole, as a predominantly right-wing movement was able to do in the UK (and which Le Pen has pushed for in the case of France).

But the right has another significant advantage in these debates – it is unapologetic about its nationalism, about operating in the realm of 'emotions, identity and fears' (March, 2016). By contrast, many left-wingers may have a certain unease with couching appeals in national (identity) terms, perhaps seeing such discourse as obscurantist and diversionary from the 'real' politics of class, even as a retreat from the politics of reason.[25] Desai (2013: 17) goes so far as to accuse some left commentators of having 'a dangerous disdain for the national'.

Jean-Luc Mélenchon's La France Insoumise (France Unbowed) campaign for the French presidency in 2017 was a rare example of a radical left party overtly positioning itself, to some extent at least, in nationalist terms. But it would be difficult to see a left-wing party go so far as to label itself along the lines of right-wing formations such as True Finns (Finland) or United Patriots (Bulgaria). Podemos, as a case in point, has found it hard to negotiate a political space for itself amidst the force fields of Spain's competing nationalisms (Tamames, 2017).[26]

In countries like Germany especially (Straub, 2017), but in many others also where xenophobia and racism are potent forces, some suspicion of nationalism is understandable – and it is the reactionary form of nationalism that has usually taken the lead in Eurosceptic movements. The left must ask itself: will disintegrative and potentially inward-orientated tendencies that might be enhanced by national 'exits' (even if they were to be in part driven by the left) do more, in the end, to boost the right than the left? Especially as it is the already most marginalised and vulnerable in society – migrants and refugees in particular – who bear the brunt of a rising right tide.

At the same time, the question of migrants and refugees also highlights much of what the left opposes about the *current* EU governance regime, not least cynical deals with Turkey and Libya that deny many asylum seekers the ability to access Europe at all (Human Rights Watch, 2016) coupled with a set of wider policing actions in the Mediterranean that have contributed to the deaths of thousands (Amnesty International, 2017). Of course, the only problem right-wing Euroscepticism has with all of that is that the anti-migrant measures are not, to their minds, harsh enough.

The radical left finds itself, in a sense, caught between the Scylla of authoritarian EU neoliberalism (including the violation of the rights of non-Europeans) and the Charybdis of right-wing nationalist reaction that could make things even worse. Navigating a path through these treacherous straits represents a very formidable challenge indeed. The results of the 2019 European elections indicate that the radical Left has, for the most part, performed poorly in electoral terms, suggesting that this challenge has, to date, not been risen to, and that shipwreck remains as likely an outcome as reaching safer shores.

Notes

1 On the definition of radical left parties, see Fagerholm (2017: 3).
2 March (2017) also notes the emphasis placed on socio-economic issues by the radical left, in this case in the British context.
3 Though the United Left Coalition did make a breakthrough in Slovenia in elections in 2014, winning 6% of the vote (Kirn, 2014).
4 This trend has been heightened by the tendency on the part of 'mainstream' social democratic parties to move towards largely uncritical support for EU integration and/or globalisation more generally (O'Connell, 2017), thus clearing a space for radical left parties to fill.
5 I do not here go into the debate about European Parliament elections being 'second order' ones, though that may clearly be relevant to these outcomes (Schmitt & Teperoglou, 2015). Note also that this does not mean that right-wing parties cannot gain from a worsening economic situation – the National Front in France, for one, has been able to do so (Morini, 2017).
6 There is a parallel here with the idea of 'inclusionary populism', as coined by Stavrakakis and Katsambekis (2014: 138) to describe the pre-2015 discourse of SYRIZA in Greece.
7 My thanks to Stephen O'Connell for drawing my attention to this quote.
8 https://diem25.org/ (accessed 1 March 2019).
9 He was actually replying specifically to criticism from Jürgen Habermas at the time.
10 Albeit not necessarily unanimous, some countries might abstain.
11 What Varoufakis elsewhere describes as 'constructive, responsible, realistic disobedience' in the specific context of Greece: www.yanisvaroufakis.eu/2018/02/12/support-constructive-responsible-realistic-disobedience-in-greece-support-diem25s-new-political-party-in-greece/ (accessed 1 March 2019).
12 For a repository of such views, see http://lexit-network.org/ (accessed 1 March 2019).
13 Likewise, during the 2013 Cypriot 'bailout' negotiations, the ECB told the Cypriot government that liquidity support to banks in Cyprus would be stopped unless reform conditionalities – including many that had nothing to do with monetary policy, and therefore were well outside the legal mandate of the ECB – were accepted (Flassbeck & Lapavitsas, 2013: 37); see also Kreuder-Sonnen, 2017: 16–18.
14 In an illustration that national differences may often override radical left solidarities, opinion polls indicate that 53% of Die Linke (Germany's radical left party) supporters backed the position of the German government at this time (Lordon, 2015: 4).
15 I here sidestep the debate as to whether Podemos *is* a radical left party, or a party of the left at all, by noting that this is simply how the vast majority of Spanish people see it (Miley, 2017: 271; see also Vidal, 2017).
16 A 2016 Pew Research Center survey found that only 32% of Spaniards identifying with Podemos took a favourable view of the EU (Pew Research Center, 2016), but there is a difference between criticism of the EU as it is currently

organised/constituted and support for an exit from it, especially exit from the Eurozone.

17 Of course a number of countries could choose to leave the Eurozone on a coordinated and negotiated basis, or the whole edifice could even be dismantled by all its members, but the political momentum for such an outcome is still likely to be generated by national movements campaigning for greater policy freedom at the national level. The same is probably true for any half-way house scenario, such as the conversion of the euro into a 'common clearing currency' while individual countries (re)introduced separate currencies for fiscal purposes (e.g. Amato et al., 2016).

18 Corbyn was dealing with the reality that those identifying themselves as left-wing in the UK overwhelmingly (69%) held a favourable view of the EU (Pew Research Center, 2016). Labour is an unusual hybrid in terms of our current discussion – it is a largely social democratic party led by, essentially, the radical left.

19 With a nod to De Gaulle's conception of France – Fenby (2010).

20 Doubtless many also believed that exiting the Eurozone would have caused even greater misery than the status quo.

21 http://data.europa.eu/euodp/en/data/dataset/S2099_83_3_STD83_ENG (accessed 1 March 2019).

22 http://data.europa.eu/euodp/en/data/dataset/S2099_83_3_STD83_ENG; these broadly positive attitudes towards membership of the Eurozone have been maintained: http://ec.europa.eu/commfrontoffice/publicopinion/index.cfm/ Survey/getSurveyDetail/instruments/STANDARD/surveyKy/2143 (accessed 1 March 2019), with the partial exception of Italy (Delcker, 2018).

23 Though the EU's environmental policies are much less impressive than its rhetoric – see, for example, Levidow (2013) and Vlachou and Pantelias (2016).

24 As Lexit from the Eurozone cannot but require a rupture with the EU treaties, wider concerns about overall EU membership – and its apparent advantages when it comes to issues such as the environment and taxation – inevitably come into play when leaving the Eurozone is discussed (Heine & Sablowski, 2016: 26).

25 A relevant example comes from Ryner and Cafruny (2017: 227) who, at the end of a book that is highly critical of the current form of EU governance, nonetheless refer to the 'ominous rise of nationalism in Europe'.

26 Relatedly, on the challenges facing the left in Greece and Macedonia in the face of nationalist mobilisations, see Lefteast (2018).

Bibliography

Ali, T. (2016) 'Panic in the house: Brexit as revolt against the political establishment'. www.counterpunch.org/2016/06/24/panic-in-the-house-brexit-as-revolt-against-the-political-establishment/ (accessed 15 July 2017).

Amato, M., Fantacci, L., Papadimitriou, D. B. & Zezza, G. (2016) 'Going forward from B to A? Proposals for the Eurozone crisis', Levy Economics Institute Working Paper 866. www.levyinstitute.org/pubs/wp_866.pdf (accessed 15 July 2017).

Amnesty International (2017) 'EU refugee crisis: Human rights violations and migrant deaths are being ignored'. www.amnesty.ie/eu-refugee-crisis-human-rights-violations-migrant-deaths-ignored/ (accessed 15 July 2017).

Anderson, P. (2017) 'Why the system will still win', *Le Monde Diplomatique*, March (English edition).

Attac Norway (working group on Europe) (2018) 'The EU debate in Norway: left positions and recent developments'. https://lexit-network.org/the-eu-debate-in-norway-left-positions-and-recent-developments (accessed 1 March 2019).

Bailey, D. J. (2005) 'Obfuscation through integration: Legitimating 'new' Social Democracy in the European Union', *Journal of Common Market Studies*, 43 (1): 13–35.

Beaudonnet, L. & Gomez, R. (2017) 'Red Europe versus no Europe? The impact of attitudes towards the EU and the economic crisis on radical-left voting', *West European Politics*, 40 (2): 316–335.

Broder, D. (2018) 'Italy's terrible alternatives', *Jacobin*. www.jacobinmag.com/2018/01/italian-election-berlusconi-five-star-movement (accessed 15 February 2018).

Callinicos, A. (2017) 'Britain and Europe on the geopolitical roller-coaster', *Competition and Change*, 21 (3): 185–198.

Caruso, L. (2017) 'Digital capitalism and the end of politics: the case of the Italian Five Star Movement', *Politics and Society*, 45 (4): 585–609.

Cerioni, L. (2016) 'The quest for a new corporate taxation model and for an effective fight against international tax avoidance within the EU', *Intertax*, 44 (6/7): 463–480.

Charalambous, G. (2011) 'All the shades of red: Examining the radical left's Euroscepticism', *Contemporary Politics*, 17 (3): 299–320.

Chrysopoulos, P. (2015) 'Poll: 7 in 10 Greeks want the euro at any cost', *Greek Reporter*, 16 June. https://greece.greekreporter.com/2015/06/16/poll-7-in-10-greeks-want-the-euro-at-any-cost/ (accessed 1 March 2019).

Cobham, A. (2017) 'Blacklisting the EU: paradise lost?', for the tax justice network. www.taxjustice.net/2017/11/27/blacklisting-the-eu-paradise-lost/ (accessed 15 February 2018).

Conti, N. (2017) 'The Italian political elites and Europe: Big moves, small change?', *International Political Science Review*, 38 (5): 534–548.

de la Baume, M. (2017) 'Dutch Prime Minister says more EU integration "not the answer"', *politico.eu*. www.politico.eu/article/mark-rutte-eu-integration-not-the-answer/ (accessed 15 February 2018).

Delcker, J. (2018) 'Italy most adrift from EU, study finds', *Politico*. www.politico.eu/article/italy-most-adrift-from-eu-study-finds/ (accessed 1 March 2019).

Desai, R. (2013) *Geopolitical economy: after US hegemony, globalization and empire*. London: Pluto Press.

Dierckx, S. (2015) 'European Unions and the repoliticization of transnational capital: Labor's stance regarding the Financial Transaction Tax (FTT), the Transatlantic Trade and Investment Partnership (TTIP), and the Comprehensive Economic and Trade Agreement (CETA)', *Labor History*, 56 (3): 327–344.

Dribbusch, R. (2015) 'Where is the European general strike? Understanding the challenges of trans-European trade union action against austerity', *Transfer*, 21 (2): 171–185.

Dufresne, A. (2015) 'The trade union response to the European economic governance regime: transnational mobilization and wage coordination', *Transfer*, 21 (2): 229–242.

Erne, R. (2015) 'A supranational regime that nationalizes social conflict: explaining European trade unions' difficulties in politicizing European economic governance', *Labor History*, 56 (3): 345–368.

Escalona, F. & Vieira, M. (2014) '"It does not happen here either": why Social Democrats fail in the context of the great economic crisis', in D. J. Bailey, J.-M. De Waele, F. Escalona & M. Vieira (eds) *European Social Democracy During the Global Economic Crisis*, Manchester: Manchester University Press, 19–41.

European Network on Debt and Development (2017) 'Tax games: the race to the bottom. Europe's role in supporting an unjust global tax system'. www.debtireland.org/download/pdf/taxgamestheracetothebottom_final.pdf (accessed 15 February 2018).

Fagerholm, A. (2017) 'What is left for the radical left? A comparative examination of the policies of radical left parties in western Europe before and after 1989', *Journal of Contemporary European Studies*, 25 (1): 16–40.

Fassina, S. (2016) 'Saving the EU from the euro, the most extreme neoliberal trap', *Social Europe*. www.socialeurope.eu/2016/09/saving-eu-euro-extreme-neo-liberal-trap/ (accessed 15 February 2018).

Fazi, T. (2017) 'The reforms that Europe doesn't need', *Green European Journal*. www.greeneuropeanjournal.eu/the-reforms-that-europe-doesnt-need/ (accessed 15 February 2018).

Fenby, J. (2010) *The General: Charles de Gaulle and the France He Saved*, London: Simon and Schuster.

Flassbeck, H. & Lapavitsas, C. (2013) 'The systemic crisis of the euro: true causes and effective therapies', *STUDIEN*, Rosa Luxemburg Foundation. www.rosalux.de/publikation/id/6773/the-systemic-crisis-of-the-euro-true-causes-and-effective-therapies/ (accessed 15 July 2017).

Galbraith, J. (2017) 'Europe and the world after Brexit', *Globalizations*, 14 (1): 164–167.

Gois, B. (2017) 'How to go beyond the Portuguese 'contraption' government?'. www.esquerda.net/en/artigo/how-go-beyond-portuguese-contraption-government/48534 (accessed 15 February 2018).

Gomez, R., Morales, L. & Ramiro, L. (2015) 'Varieties of radicalism: examining the diversity of radical left parties and voters in western Europe', *West European Politics*, 39 (2): 351–379.

Halikiopoulou, D., Kyriaki, N. & Vasilopoulou, S. (2012) 'The paradox of nationalism: the common denominator of radical right and radical left Euroscepticism', *European Journal of Political Research*, 51 (4): 504–539.

Heilig, D. (2016) *Mapping the European left: socialist parties in the EU*, New York: Rosa Luxembourg Stiftung. www.rosalux-nyc.org/wp-content/files_mf/theleftineurope_eng.pdf (accessed 15 July 2017).

Heine, F. & Sablowski, T. (2016) *Monetary union unravelling? Trade and capital relations, causes of the crisis and development perspectives of the euro area*, New York: Rosa Luxemburg Stiftung. www.rosalux.de/fileadmin/rls_uploads/pdfs/sonst_publikationen/Analysen26_European_Monetary_Union_Web__2_.pdf (accessed 15 July 2017).

Hewitt, G. (2015) 'Greece: the dangerous game'. www.bbc.com/news/world-europe-31082656 (accessed 15 July 2017).

Horn, L. (2012) 'Anatomy of a "critical friendship": organized labour and the European state formation', *Globalizations*, 9 (4): 577–592.

Human Rights Watch (2016) 'EU policies put refugees at risk: an agenda to restore protection'. www.hrw.org/news/2016/11/23/eu-policies-put-refugees-risk (accessed 15 July 2017).

Jones, L. (2016) 'Yanis Varoufakis's fantasy politics', *Jacobin*. www.jacobinmag.com/2016/09/yanis-varoufakis-eu-syriza-diem25-europe-brexit/ (accessed 15 July 2017).

Kagarlitsky, R. (2017) 'Brexit and the future of the left', *Globalizations*, 14 (1): 110–117.

Kalaitzake, M. (2017) 'Death by a thousand cuts? Financial political power and the case of the European financial transaction tax', *New Political Economy*, 22 (6): 709–726.

Karnitschnig, M. (2017) 'The Germans are coming', *politico.eu*. www.politico.eu/article/the-germans-are-coming-united-states-of-europe-martin-schulz/ (accessed 15 February 2018).

Kirn, G. (2014) 'A ground breaking result: Slovenia's United Left coalition gets 6 seats in parliament'. www.criticatac.ro/lefteast/historic-victory-united-left-slovenia-6-seats/ (accessed 15 July 2017).

Kouvelakis, S. (2016) 'SYRIZA's rise and fall', *New Left Review*, 97: 45–70.

Kreuder-Sonnen, C. (2017) 'Political secrecy in Europe: crisis management and crisis exploitation', *West European Politics*, 41 (4): 958–980.

Lachat, R. (2017) 'Which way from left to right? On the relation between voters' issue preferences and left–right orientation in west European democracies', *International Political Science Review*, 39 (4): 419–435.

Lapavitsas, C. (2015) 'Greece is being blackmailed: exiting the euro is the way out', *The Guardian*, 25 June. www.theguardian.com/commentisfree/2015/jun/25/greece-blackmailed-eurozone-troika-syriza-common-currency (accessed 15 July 2017).

Lefteast (2018) 'The left in Greece & Macedonia: we can write new pages of common struggle!'. www.criticatac.ro/lefteast/the-left-in-greece-macedonia-we-can-write-new-pages-of-common-struggle/ (accessed 1 March 2019).

Levidow, L. (2013) 'EU criteria for sustainable biofuels: accounting for carbon, depoliticising plunder', *Geoforum*, 44 (1): 211–223.

Lordon, F. (2015) 'The left and the Euro: liquidate, rebuild'. www.versobooks.com/blogs/2150-the-left-and-the-euro-liquidate-rebuild (accessed 15 July 2017).

Louca, F. (2017) 'An agenda for Europe: the struggle for the solution of the debt and the euro', 22 December. www.cadtm.org/An-Agenda-for-Europe-The-struggle (accessed 15 February 2018).

March, L. (2012) 'Problems and perspectives of contemporary radical left parties: chasing a lost world or still a world to win?', *International Critical Thought*, 2 (3): 314–39.

March, L. (2016) '2016: The ebbing of Europe's radical left tide?', *European Futures*, 7 November. www.europeanfutures.ed.ac.uk/article-4395 (accessed 15 July 2017).

March, L. (2017) 'Left and right populism compared: the British case', *The British Journal of Politics and International Relations*, 19 (2): 282–303.

March, L. & Rommerskirchen, C. (2015) 'Out of left field? Explaining the variable electoral success of European radical left parties', *Party Politics*, 21 (1): 40–53.

Mason, J. W. (2017) 'A cautious case for economic nationalism', *Dissent*, Spring. www.dissentmagazine.org/article/cautious-case-economic-nationalism-global-capitalism (accessed 15 February 2018).

Miley, T. J. (2017) 'Austerity politics and constitutional crisis in Spain', *European Politics and Society*, 18 (2): 263–283.

Monero, M. (2017) 'What's next for Podemos?', *Jacobin*, 4 May. www.jacobinmag.com/2017/05/podemos-spain-congress-vistalegre-psoe-ciudananos (accessed 15 July 2017).

Morini, M. (2017) 'Front National and Lega Nord: two stories of the same Euro-scepticism', *European Politics and Society*, 19 (1): 1–19.

Navarro, V. (2016) 'Is the nation state and its welfare state dead? A critique of Varoufakis'. www.counterpunch.org/2016/08/26/is-the-nation-state-and-its-welfare-state-dead-a-critique-of-varoufakis/ (accessed 15 July 2017).

Nikolakakis, N. (2016) 'SYRIZA's stance vis-à-vis the European Union following the financial crisis: the persistence of left Europeanism and the role of the European Left Party', *European Politics and Society*, 18 (2): 1–20.

O'Connell, S. (2017) 'How globalisation weakens the left: an empirical analysis', Undergraduate thesis, School of Politics and International Relations, University College Dublin.

Patomaki, H. (2017) 'Will the EU disintegrate? What does the likely possibility of disintegration tell about the future of the world?', *Globalizations*, 14 (1): 168–177.

Pew Research Center (2016) 'Euroskepticism beyond Brexit'. www.pewglobal.org/2016/06/07/euroskepticism-beyond-brexit/ (accessed 15 July 2017).

Ramiro, L. (2016) 'Support for radical left parties in western Europe: social background, ideology and political orientations', *European Political Science Review*, 8 (1): 1–23.

Ramiro, L. & Gomez, R. (2017) 'Radical-left populism during the great recession: *Podemos* and its competition with the established radical left', *Political Studies*, 65 (1): 108–126.

Ronzoni, M. (2015) 'How social democrats may become reluctant radicals: Thomas Piketty's *Capital* and Wolfgang Streeck's *Buying Time*', *European Journal of Political Theory*, 17 (1): 118–127.

Ryner, M. & Cafruny, A. (2017) *The European Union and global capitalism: origins, development, crisis*, London: Palgrave Macmillan.

Scharpf, F. W. (2013) 'Monetary union, fiscal crisis and the disabling of democratic accountability', in A. Schafer & W. Streeck (eds) *Politics in the age of austerity*, London: Polity Press, 108–142.

Schmitt, H. & Teperoglou, E. (2015) 'The 2014 European Parliament elections in southern Europe: second-order or critical elections?', *South European Society and Politics*, 20 (3): 287–309.

Shaft, J. (2018) 'Yanis Varoufakis's argument that there is a 'Marxist' case for staying in the EU isn't as simple as it seems', *The Independent*, 1 February. www.independent.co.uk/voices/yanis-varoufakis-s-marxist-argument-staying-eu-tony-blair-a8189151.html (accessed 15 February 2018).

Spierings, N. & Zaslove, A. (2017) 'Gender, populist attitudes, and voting: explaining the gender gap in voting for populist radical right and populist radical left parties', *West European Politics*, 40 (4): 821–847.

Stavrakakis, S. & Katsambekis, G. (2014) 'Left-wing populism in the European periphery: the case of SYRIZA', *Journal of Political Ideologies*, 19 (2): 119–142.

Steenvoorden, E. & Harteveld, E. (2017) 'The appeal of nostalgia: the influence of societal pessimism on support for populist radical right parties', *West European Politics*, 41 (1): 28–52.

Storey, A. (2014) 'Chronicle of a European crisis foretold: Building neoliberalism from above and options for resistance from below', in L. Fioramonti (ed.) *Civil society and world regions: how citizens are reshaping regional governance in times of crisis*, Lanham, MD: Lexington Books, 33–48.

Storey, A. (2017) 'The myths of ordoliberalism', Working Paper 17–02, ERC Project 'European Unions', University College Dublin. www.erc-europeanunions.eu/working-papers/ (accessed 15 February 2018).

Straub, H. (2017) 'Comparatively rich and reactionary: Germany between 'welcome Culture' and re-established racism', *Critical Sociology*, 43 (1): 3–10.

Streeck, W. (2014) 'Small-state nostalgia? The currency union, Germany and Europe: a reply to Jürgen Habermas', *Constellations*, 21 (2): 213–221.

Streeck, W. (2016) *How will capitalism end? Essays on a failing system*, London: Verso.

Tamames, J. (2017) 'The roots of Spanish rage', *Jacobin*. www.jacobinmag.com/2017/11/the-roots-of-spains-rage (accessed 15 February 2018).

Tokatlian, J. G. (2016) 'What Brexit and ISIL have in common'. http://fpif.org/brexit-isil-common/ (accessed 15 June 2017).

Turnbull, P. (2007) 'Dockers versus the directives: battling port policy on the European waterfront', in K. Bronfenbrenner (ed.) *Global unions: challenging transnational capital through cross-border campaigns*, New York: ILR Press, 117–136.

van Elsas, E. J., Hakhverdian, A. & van der Brug, W. (2016) 'United against a common foe? The nature and origins of Euroscepticism among left-wing and right-wing citizens', *West European Politics*, 39 (6): 1181–1204.

van Elsas, E. & van der Brug, W. (2015) 'The changing relationship between left–right ideology and Euroscepticism, 1973–2010', *European Union Politics*, 16 (2): 194–215.

Varoufakis, Y. (2016) 'Joining forces! In reply to Stefano Fassina'. https://yanisvaroufakis.eu/2016/09/14/joining-forces-in-reply-to-stefano-fassina/ (15 June 2017).

Varoufakis, Y. (2017) *Adults in the room: my battles with Europe's deep establishment*, London: Bodley Head.

Vidal, G. (2017) 'Challenging business as usual? The rise of new parties in Spain in times of crisis', *West European Politics*, 41 (2): 261–286.

Visser, M., Lubbers, M., Kraaykamp, G. & Jespers, E. (2014) 'Support for radical left ideologies in Europe', *European Journal of Political Research*, 53 (3): 541–558.

Vlachou, A. & Pantelias, G. (2016) 'The EU's Emissions Trading System, Part 2: a political economy critique', *Capitalism Nature Socialism*, 28 (3): 108–127.

Wahl, P. (2017) 'Between Eurotopia and nationalism: a third way for the future of the EU', *Globalizations*, 14 (1): 157–163.

Watkins, S. (2016a) 'Casting off?', *New Left Review*, 100: 5–33.

Watkins, S. (2016b) 'Oppositions', *New Left Review*, 98: 5–30.

Woolfson, C. (2017) 'The politics of Brexit: European free movement of labour and labour standards', TheMES: Themes on Migration and Ethnic Studies, occasional paper 45, Linkoping University. www.isv.liu.se/remeso (15 February 2018).

13

Alter-Europeanism? The left and European integration after the crisis

Michael Holmes and Knut Roder

A confluence of crises in a difficult decade

A crisis is a time of intense difficulty or danger, usually associated with a clear choice between alternatives. It involves three features: an event that occurs at a specific moment in time, a serious challenge to established norms, and the opportunity for a transformative moment. The economic crisis that erupted in 2008 proved to be a 'dangerous opportunity' for left-wing parties, whether social democrats, the green left, or the radical left. Initially, it seemed to offer new political and economic opportunities for the left.

The first of these is the economic crisis itself. The events that began in 2008 certainly fit the criteria outlined above: there was a clear trigger moment – the autumn of 2008, when several banks collapsed and others needed rescue; there was a clear systemic challenge – to economies, to societies, to polities; and there was the possibility of economic, social and political transformation. As explained in Chapter 1, the economic crisis itself includes at least four elements. The banking collapse of 2008 led to a sovereign debt crisis after governments intervened to try to prop up their banking systems. This in turn contributed to the very specific Eurozone crisis that developed due to the constraints of EMU, and these three financial and economic factors in turn caused a widespread social and political crisis.

The second overarching crisis is that of European integration. One analysis identified at least 13 different areas where the EU integration process has been challenged by 'separate though related crises' that are 'multi-faceted in their sources, characteristics, and consequences' (Dinan et al., 2017: xx). Apart from the economic recession and the attendant Eurozone crisis, the EU has also had to respond to crises in areas such as migration policy and foreign policy. Indeed, these contributed to an overall legitimacy crisis of the Union, particularly towards the end of this 'difficult decade' when Britain voted to leave the EU and parties on the right within various EU member states were electorally successful on anti-EU integration platforms.

The third crisis is that of the left. The idea that 'social democracy is in crisis' is widespread (Keating & McCrone, 2015: 1; see also Callaghan et al., 2009; Hickson, 2016). In a wider left context, Sassoon argues that left-wing parties face an 'agonising dilemma' (1997: 12) between defending welfare gains and responding to globalisation. This crisis is evident both in an ongoing electoral decline and a search for a new programmatic vision. This predates the economic crisis, with Anderson identifying in the 1990s 'a wider moral crisis in the identity of the major organizations of the West European left' (1994: 2). But the economic crisis certainly impacted on the left, with former British Labour Party minister Peter Hain asking bluntly, 'why have social democratic parties been in abject retreat?' (2016: v).

One common explanatory factor could be globalisation. Mitchell and Fazi argue that the decline of the left is not just electoral, it reflects a change of core values within society. For them, 'the extreme right have been more effective than left-wing or progressive forces at tapping into the legitimate grievances of the masses – disenfranchised, marginalised, impoverished and dispossessed by the 40-year long neoliberal class war waged from above' (Mitchell & Fazi, 2017: 3). The right has been better able to 'provide a (more or less) coherent response to the widespread – and growing – yearning for greater territorial or national sovereignty, increasingly seen as the only way, in the absence of effective supranational mechanisms of representation, to regain some degree of collective control over politics and society, and in particular over the flows of capital, trade and people that constitute the essence of neoliberal globalisation' (Mitchell & Fazi, 2017: 3).

This book has analysed the confluence of these three crises, and has sought to explain how the economic crisis and the European crisis contributed to the crisis of the left. The analyses have touched on the political challenge of globalisation in Europe and the rise of the right. This concluding chapter argues that the conventional interpretations of the relationship between the left and European integration have been altered by the crises. We start by summarising the existing interpretations of the left and integration, before setting out the argument that the crises created an opportunity for a new left perspective on the European Union, which we term 'alter-Europeanism'. We then analyse the main obstacles baulking the achievement of any new form of programme for the European left in the context of the current form of European integration.

Judging from the case studies in this book, the European left remains broadly supportive of EU integration and is reluctant to embrace Euroscepticism fully. Arguments for any form of 'Lexit' (Guinan & Hanna, 2017) – withdrawal from the EU specifically to pursue a left-wing agenda – are an exception. However, extensive debates have emerged over the direction of the European Union, indicating that there are limits to the Europeanisation of the left. The economic crisis has significantly altered the relationship of the left and Europe.

Interpreting the left and European integration

The analysis of the impact of European integration on political parties has generally revolved around two dimensions. The first dimension focuses on the impact on individual parties, with arguments ranging from Euroscepticism to ones saying that parties are becoming more pro-European. The second dimension is more about the impact on party systems than on individual parties, and debates whether or not a single European polity is developing. Both of these dimensions have an impact on parties of the left.

The Eurosceptic line of argument stresses that the left has always been wary of the market principles that underpin European integration. Many social democratic parties were cautious about integration at the outset, as Newman (1983) and Featherstone (1988) point out. Indeed, some were downright hostile to it, notably the British Labour Party and Greece's PASOK, which did not warm to the idea until the 1990s at the earliest. And this tendency was even more pronounced among green left parties and radical left parties. Bomberg comments that 'the EU represents much that greens instinctively oppose' (1998: 3), while March notes that among radical left parties, 'opposition to the "really existing" EU has proven a consolidating factor' (2012: 202). Their view often reflects disappointment at the perceived failure of the EU to deliver on its promise of a 'social Europe' (Attac, 2017: 80).

The alternative perspective to Euroscepticism emphasises the Europeanisation of the left. Ladrech (2002) and Poguntke et al. (2007) argue that the Europeanisation of political parties involves a subtle pressure on parties to adapt policies, strategies and structures to enable them to deal more effectively with the EU. This does not necessarily imply pressure towards a more pro-European position, but in the case of social democratic parties there is plenty of evidence of such a shift (see *inter alia* Featherstone, 1988; Ladrech & Marlière, 1999; Lightfoot, 2005). Even among the green left and radical left, there are suggestions that some see the EU as essentially a flawed but progressive project. Bomberg notes that 'for many green actors, participation in the EU is attractive if not imperative' (1998: 3), while March accepts that several radical left parties 'are increasingly integrationist' (2012: 203).

In overall terms, the Europeanisation thesis works especially effectively in explaining the position of the social democratic left. From the very outset of the integration process there has been an apparently inexorable move among members of this party family to a more pro-EU stance. It is evident too among green left parties, although here the centripetal force has been less strong. The Europeanisation of the left is least evident among radical left parties, but even here the pattern had been visible, as we argued in our previous analysis (Holmes & Roder, 2012; see also Holmes & Lightfoot, 2016). This is at least partly because of a strong rhetorical commitment to internationalism that exists on the left. Left-wing parties of all types are very supportive of the principle of international cooperation, and that creates a prima facie case for them to support European integration.

The relationship between left-wing parties and integration was changed by the economic crisis. The seemingly inexorable drift towards Europeanisation was halted and in some cases reversed. But this does not necessarily mean that the left became more Eurosceptic. Instead, the crisis highlighted the vulnerability of individual states in the face of global financial forces. So while left parties could see many reasons to leaven their enthusiasm for the EU, they were also sharply aware that some form of European integration could be a valuable safeguard for social rights and freedoms.

Finally, we return briefly to the second dimension of the impact of integration on party systems. Some analysts argue that the EU represents an evolving party political system, different from national systems and still underdeveloped, but nonetheless distinctly a party political system (see for example Hix & Lord, 1997). Others contend that the EU has not fundamentally changed party system structures, and that 'party systems appear to remain relatively impervious to the direct impact of Europeanization' (Mair, 2000: 47). No single EU polity has developed, and instead party politics in the EU remains steadfastly national in its orientation.

In this conclusion, we will argue that the crisis constituted an EU-wide political shock, though the responses to it are still not wholly Europeanised. But rather than having 28 separate national reactions, the analyses in this book suggest the emergence of regional political systems within the larger EU. And while Mair's argument does have validity, the crisis led left groups in the European Parliament to call for an alternative form of certain aspects of the Europeanisation process – most notably relating to EMU and the single currency. GUE/NGL published a series of 'economic discussion documents on the future of the Eurozone' (Clancy, 2017), the social democrats suggested the 'completion and rebalancing of economic and monetary union as a democratic call out of the crisis' (Socialists & Democrats, 2015) and the Greens called for agreed roadmaps to 'put the EMU on a sustainable footing' (Greens-EFA, 2016).

Impact of the crisis

The economic crisis is a strange case of simultaneous left harmony and left disunity. When the banking crisis first erupted, there was a clear and consistent analysis shared across the left. They argued that the essential cause of the crisis was a failure of the private sector. The banks had become too greedy and too focused on short-term profit maximisation rather than long-term development. In addition, there was also recognition of a degree of governmental culpability, for allowing too much deregulation and failing to keep the banks in check. This was not a rejection of the role of governments in general, rather it was seen as governments having become too complicit in right-wing policies.

This view was by no means out of line with mainstream analysis of the crisis. For example, the Levin-Coburn report (US Senate, 2011) concluded that the crisis was the result of failures of both the market and the regulatory system, which had allowed the emergence of very high-risk and complex financial products. In similar vein, the commission established under Barack Obama's presidency highlighted excessively risky borrowing and investments in the financial services sector, excessive deregulation, and a 'systemic breakdown in accountability and ethics' (FCIC, 2011).

However, the common left analysis led to two different interpretations about how to respond. The social democratic approach was that the economic system had been allowed to get out of control, but it could be reined in. What was needed was a return to greater regulation and supervision, greater management of the economy, and a shift away from a corporate culture of excess towards one of long-term sustainability. Essentially, the system had been allowed to run loose; it needed tighter control, but there was nothing fundamentally wrong with the system. In contrast, radical left parties put forward a much more succinct interpretation. Rather than see it as an aberration, the crisis was better understood as evidence of a systemic failure of capitalism, and rather than trying to repair the system the aim should be to replace a broken model.

However, when it came to practical policy responses to the crisis the ideological distinctions on the left were reduced. The social democrats, the green left and the radical left all argued for greater regulation of the financial services sector. They also advocated that the response to the economic recession should involve investment rather than austerity. Indeed, the chapter by Cláudia Toriz Ramos highlights how opposition to austerity was the strongest binding agent when the social democrats, the radical left, the communists and the greens were putting together a framework for government in Portugal. Tapio Raunio's chapter shows a similar case in Finland when the radical left went into government there.

The problem was how to achieve these things. The first barrier to overcome was to get into government, but across Europe, right-wing parties dominated both before and after the onset of the crisis. Indeed, as we noted in Chapter 1, several analyses have pointed out that economic depressions generally tend to favour the right more than the left (Gamble, 2009: 109–110). Nor were social democratic parties in a strong position to challenge the economic orthodoxy being propounded by the right, since they had only relatively recently embraced those policy programmes themselves. Even though those policies were now being questioned, it was hard for social democratic parties to convince voters that their re-conversion was sincere.

This was also because when social democratic parties did have a chance of getting into government after the onset of the crisis, it was often as a junior partner in a coalition with the right. That meant the social democrats were implementing austerity and cuts, not reversing them. This is evident in Ireland, where the Labour Party came to power in 2011 on promises of renegotiating the strict bailout constraints, only to accept them once in office. The same could be said of the SPD in Germany, which accepted restrictive policies as part of its grand coalition agreement with the CDU-CSU. And while the radical left only rarely tasted government in this period, it could even be applied to SYRIZA in Greece and AKEL in Cyprus, which came to power promising to challenge the diktats of Brussels, only to end up acceding to those demands.

The implication would seem to be that EU constraints made it extremely hard for left parties to pursue any different policy programme when in government. There are some suggestions that the *geringonça* government succeeded in steering Portugal away from stringent austerity, but apart from that, most have accepted – and rather meekly, at that – the parameters set down by the EU and the ECB.

Thus, one overall feature is the collapse of the traditional social democratic vote in several countries. It is particularly noticeable in some of the bailout countries. In Greece, Spain and Ireland (and in Italy, which did not actually receive a bailout but which went through a very similar socio-economic and political crisis), the main social democratic parties suffered significant losses. But it is evident elsewhere too. The traditional social democratic parties suffered bad reversals in France and in the Netherlands, while in Germany and Austria, a steady decline has persisted. In eastern Europe, the social democratic left suffered badly in Poland, Hungary and the Czech Republic. Some even refer to social democratic parties becoming 'pasokified', in other words 'reduced to parliamentary insignificance, or at least largely removed from the ability to achieve electoral majorities on the national level' (Mitchell & Fazi, 2017: 2).

In some cases, the vote has gone to the radical left, suggesting that left-wing voters have become disillusioned with the compromises of government. Again, this is especially noticeable in some of the bailout countries, with the rise of SYRIZA in Greece, of Podemos in Spain, of Sinn Féin and other smaller parties in Ireland, and of the contribution to an alternative government on the part of radical left parties in Portugal. But the radical left is not widespread. In 12 EU member states, there was no radical left party in parliament at any time during the crisis. They are a particularly rare creature in eastern European countries.

In overall terms, the economic crisis highlighted the persistent absence of a single European polity. However, the analyses in this book indicate that the crisis had an immense impact on the EU member states' party political systems. There was no single consistent pattern across the EU, due to different historical contexts and national circumstances. But there is evidence of a three-way split in the European Union. The crisis contributed to the development of what could be termed 'regional political systems' in the EU. Our analysis suggests the emergence of three such 'regional systems'. We can refer to them using geographical labels, though this is perhaps slightly misleading.

There is a group composed predominantly of southern European states, though there is a case to be made for Ireland to be seen as an 'honorary' southern state. These have often been referred to as the 'PIGS' (Dainotto, 2007: 2) and are characterised by historical under-development compared to other EU states, with some rapid growth prior to the crisis, but with particularly sharp crises that resulted in bailouts and severe austerity programmes. The second group is one made up of northern European states characterised by more developed economies and generally by creditor status in the debt crisis. The third group is that of eastern European member states, which have gone through a recent post-communist economic and political transformation.

If there is a positive 'left effect' of the crisis, it is in the 'southern' region. All of these countries were marked by extensive public protest against austerity. This translated into party politics in slightly different ways, but generally, social democratic parties did badly, either straight away or after a period in government. It also meant the rise of radical left parties in some of these countries, particularly in Greece, Spain and Ireland, but also to some degree in Portugal. The picture in Italy is less clear. A traditionally strong radical left was marginalised during the crisis, but a new populist party emerged, the Five Star Movement, which mixed some left-wing policies with a more conventional right-wing agenda.

The 'northern' group includes many traditional social democratic strong-holds, such as Germany, the Netherlands and the Nordic states. Here, the impact of the economic crisis was more about limiting austerity rather than opposing it, and there was little evidence of any sense of European solidarity with struggling states. Attitudes to Greece were a litmus test of this, and as Ehl notes laconically, 'helping Greece is a synonym for trouble' (2015). Social democratic parties at best held static, and at worst suffered serious defeats, as in Germany and the Netherlands in 2017. The green left and radical left also did not benefit significantly in any of these countries. There were occasional successes, such as the surge to the Green Left in the Netherlands in 2017, but also setbacks, such as for the Austrian Greens that same year.

Finally, the European left is weakest in the 'eastern' group of states. Indeed, the chapter on Latvia by Karlis Bukovskis and Ilvija Bruge highlights how the term 'left' remains electorally toxic. The analysis in this volume has not looked extensively at these states, partly because few of them have adopted the euro (one of our selection criteria) and partly because the left was already weak in these states before the crisis. Green parties in these states tend to be right- rather than left-leaning, while radical left parties are hardly evident at all in eastern Europe. Social democrats were more prominent, but even here several well-established parties suffered bad defeats during the years of the economic crisis. Notably, the Hungarian MSZP collapsed from over 43% of the vote in 2006 to less than 12% in 2018, the Czech ČSSD went from over 32% in 2006 to 7.3% in 2017, and left parties failed to win any seats in the 2015 election in Poland. These results are not specifically to do with the crisis, but they do link to a growing mood of Euroscepticism in many of these countries.

In overall terms, the crisis created a political opening, but the left was unable to seize that opportunity in Europe. Social democratic parties continued their slow decline, and in some cases, this was accelerated. Green left and radical left parties had pockets of success, but generally remained marginal to politics in most EU countries. The dominant reason for the failure of the left lies in their approach to the European Union itself, and as we argue in the next section, this remains a major stumbling block for the development of a coherent alternative to current notions of European integration.

Alter-Europeanism

While the European Union could not be accused of triggering the initial financial crash, it was a central player in the evolution of the crisis in Europe, particularly with the sovereign debt crisis. This brought to the fore the relationship of the left with the EU. The left responded to the developing crisis with mounting criticism, although this varied in intensity both according to party ideology and to national setting. But very few left parties actually moved towards a Eurosceptic position. Instead, the speeches and statements and comments across the left are replete with calls for 'another Europe', a 'different Europe', a 'better Europe'. Adopting the idea of *alter-mondialisme* from the French left,[1] there is a clear commitment to the idea of alter-Europeanism.

Alter-Europeanism implies both support for European integration and a commitment to changing the path of integration in a more progressive, leftist direction. The core analysis of alter-Europeanism is that the EU is here to stay but that it must be reformed. Indeed, the analysis argues that the crisis was caused by globalisation, and that the EU is the only possible bulwark against that globalisation. The individual states are simply too small to be able to deal with the might of global capital on their own, and they need the collective strength of the Union to respond effectively.

However, there is also an acceptance that the EU as presently constituted is flawed, in two main ways. First, there is general acceptance on the left that the EU suffers from a democratic deficit, and that it needs institutional reform to make it more open and accountable. Second, there is broad agreement that the EU is biased towards business interests at the expense of the broader public. For some, this involves a demand for a return to a European social model; for others, it means a more trenchant critique of a neoliberal Europe. Overall, the crisis has strengthened the idea that there needs to be a distinct left vision of a new policy direction for European integration and a more democratic institutional architecture for the EU.

The problem is that the commitment to alter-Europeanism lacks any real substance. There is no agreed agenda, no agreed platform, and this goes right across the spectrum of the left. Even before the economic crisis, Unger stated 'the left is missing an alternative' (Unger, 2005: 12). More recent arguments suggest that 'despite a crisis of neoliberalism, no clear and viable social democratic alternative appears to have (thus far) been forthcoming' (Bailey et al., 2014: 2), and that 'the failure of the centre left to set the political agenda in the wake of the 2008 financial crisis was notable' (Bickerton, 2018). Similar analyses exist further to the left. Gabriele Zimmer, chair of GUE/NGL, accepts that 'left-wing progressive forces have faced a complete absence of a common vision for Europe' (2018), while March notes that 'attitudes to the EU are still too divided for a clear vision of "another Europe" to evolve' among the radical left (2012: 203).

Why is there no consensus? The first problem lies in the nature of the political system of the EU. The power structure in the Union reflects deeply embedded policies and practices that are very difficult to alter. There is a 'treaty fatigue', with governments having little appetite for the long negotiations required to amend existing treaties or introduce new ones. The various agreements reached by EU governments during the crisis, such as the Fiscal Compact Treaty, were inter-governmental ones that sidelined even the weak supervisory procedures at the EU level. Furthermore, the EU political system acts against the development of alternative programmes. It has no space for a 'loyal opposition': if you are in government, you have a say; if you are not, you have virtually no voice. Even the EP is muted because its dominant approach is to aim for a pro-integration consensus.

The second problem lies in the often fractious relationships on the left. The parties of the left are political competitors, and the European Union has become a means of differentiating themselves from each other. This competition inevitably makes it harder to find common ground. While there might be broad agreement about the need to reform the EU, it comes from quite distinct standpoints and leads to different approaches. There is no shared left vision of what integration should be about. This is reflected in Gabriele Zimmer's appeal that 'instead of tearing ourselves apart over the degree to which the EU is a neoliberal project, something we mostly agree on, we should ask ourselves if we have a vision of what our Europe should look like' (Zimmer, 2018).

This does not just apply to relations between different left-wing parties, it is also evident within parties. Within the social democratic family, there are increasing calls for parties to realise not just the importance of cooperating and developing common programmes and campaigns, but that they should reform their cross-national communication structure by using the PES to enhance the ability to solve problems and take common policy decisions (Nehmitz, 2017). But judging from the case study contributions to this project, the long-term political process of the left debating, never mind agreeing, on a future vision of the EU integration process that distinguishes itself significantly from the direction of previous decades has only started and, lessons learned, needs to become far more coordinated and potent.

In fairness, to link ideas into an attractive and coherent programme of societal change is a difficult task. It is not made any easier in a political context where majorities are difficult to achieve, while EU treaties and other international agreements rule out any radical action, and where the threats of severe market and banking responses deter the implementation of radically different policy agendas. Understandably, most of the electorate were reluctant to risk economic meltdown and political instability, even in the depths of the crisis.

But this creates a third problem. Parties of the left are not the only ones reacting to the EU and the pressures of globalisation, and other parties found it easier to commandeer the terrain. The centre right was best placed to promote an agenda emphasising stability and a return to an assumed 'normal', while the populist right could exploit people's fears when faced with economic hardship. Their mantra of what former German Green leader Joschka Fischer calls 'neo-nationalism' (Fischer, 2018) includes a very strong dose of Euroscepticism.

However, our analysis here does not suggest that the left across Europe has moved to a similar Eurosceptic position. The experience of a decade of crisis and the EU's response has undoubtedly made the parties on the European left more critical of significant aspects of the integration process. This corresponds to what Leruth, Startin and Underwood have described as the 'embedding' and 'mainstreaming' of Euroscepticism (2017: 4), and indeed the term 'critical Europeanism' is used in their work (Bourne & Chatzopoulou, 2017). But left parties have clearly not followed the 'hard' Eurosceptic stance of 'outright and unqualified opposition' to the process of European integration (Taggart, 1998: 336). Instead, they have expressed 'soft' Euroscepticism, a 'contingent or qualified opposition' (Taggart 1998: 335) rather than outright rejection.

A number of significant new left-wing analyses emerged during the crisis. These include Thomas Piketty's hugely influential re-analysis of capitalism (2014) and the critiques of inequality put forward by Joseph Stiglitz (2012) and Richard Wilkinson and Kate Pickett (2009). These fed into new analyses among left-wing parties, groups and activists, and indeed much of this discussion was characterised by attempts to find a broad common ground among 'diverse political traditions – green, radical left, liberal' (DiEM25, n.d.). Europe's left was searching for a common understanding of the crisis and an agreement on common policy priorities, characterised by a critical but constructive interpretation of European integration. Their aim was 'to repair the EU' (DiEM25, n.d.).

DiEM25, or the Democracy in Europe Movement 2025, was set up by a number of politicians and activists, including notably the economist and former Greek Finance Minister, Yanis Varoufakis. They argue that 'the EU will either be democratised or it will disintegrate' (DiEM25, n.d.) and their manifesto calls for a more democratic and decentralised EU and a new European constitution, based on what Varoufakis terms 'decentralised Europeanisation' (Varoufakis et al., 2013: 11–12). A similar initiative was Plan B in Europe, which consisted of two conferences held in 2015, one in Paris and one in Madrid. These called for 'a complete renegotiation of the European treaties' and the need for strong involvement of civil-society movements in developing an alternative left trajectory for EU integration (Plan B in Europe, 2015). Similarly, Thomas Fazi argues that 'the best hope for the citizens and workers of Europe lies in a radical reform of the EU and EMU, not in their rejection' (Fazi, 2014: 164).

From interregnum to an altered Europe

Gramsci made the well-known observation that a 'crisis consists precisely in the fact that the old is dying and the new cannot be born; in this interregnum a great variety of morbid symptoms appear' (Hoare & Sperber, 2016: 69). The economic crisis produced a moment of serious challenge and significant opportunity for left-wing political parties in Europe. But rather than seize the moment, the left has struggled to turn the crisis to its advantage. As Keating and McCrone note with reference to one branch of the left family, 'given that capitalism itself appears to be in crisis, and the hegemony of neoliberalism may be coming to an end, it seems strange that social democracy should fail to reap the benefit' (2015: 2). The same could equally be said of the green left and radical left.

This is because the two traditional approaches of the left to the EU both involve an awkward dilemma. The first option would be akin to renewed Europeanisation. The left should support the idea of the further deepening of the EU, by strengthening its economic governance structures. Elements of this can be seen in the proposals put forward by French President Emmanuel Macron in 2017, calling for a qualitative leap in integration (OuestFrance, 2017). Macron had, of course, come from a left of centre background, having been a minister in the previous Socialist Party administration of François Hollande, but had left the PS to form his own En Marche! movement. But these ideas run the risk of simply continuing to accede to a neoliberal European Union and accepting a swathe of policy restrictions. This might have been a necessary or even an acceptable compromise before the crisis, but since 2008 the economic and political discourse has shifted.

The second option would be for the left to go down the Eurosceptic path, by rejecting the EU as a tool for European integration and the Eurozone as impossible to reform and propose credible alternatives that promote a detailed credible alternative vision of a Lexit Europe. But as Chapter 12 by Storey in this volume has argued, there are obstacles to this. Furthermore, Zimmer warns of the danger of demanding a restart of the EU as this can easily be understood as breaking up EU integration processes. Zimmer argues that this 'would only play into the hands of right-wing nationalists as the vacuum created would lead to the disappearance of social and legal rights ultimately affecting most those weakest parts in society' (Zimmer, 2018). If you break the Humpty Dumpty Union, all the left's men would find it almost impossible to put it back together again in their preferred shape, particularly given the strength of the anti-international and anti-European forces on the right.

So we return to the third option of alter-Europeanism. This involves keeping the existing European Union but developing a comprehensive programme to alter it. The problem lies in the failure of the left to construct its own narrative for a new social, political and economic balance in Europe. For the social democratic left, they had been relatively recent converts to neoliberalism, which made it harder for them to undertake another sudden volte-face. The green left struggled to make their environmental agenda heard during the crisis, while the radical left were much more focused on a defensive agenda, trying to protect existing structures rather than promoting new goals or ideals.

In the meantime, the debate is moving on. The economic crisis is very far from finished. The political consequences are only beginning to be felt, and for many the social and economic damage to their lives is still a very real, daily experience. But as we write in 2019, the daily headlines have moved on, to issues of migration and Brexit and Trump and illiberalism. The left therefore needs not only a convincing new agenda for the EU, it needs to connect this effectively to broader issues.

An alter-Europe needs to put forward a programme for three things. First, it needs to present an argument for a reformed, democratic political structure for the EU, with greater democratic governance of the euro being a priority. Second, it needs to set a new policy agenda for the EU, including not just the Eurozone and other economic policies, but also a vision for all the EU's policies, including social policy, foreign policy and environmental policy. Third, it needs to present a strategy by which the left can gain power in order to implement these reforms.

The experience of the European left, across all three left party families, has been quite varied and ranges from electoral rise to collapse. In general, parties of both the radical left and the green left have remained stable or even increased their national shares of vote, though only by limited amounts in most cases. The occasional triumphs, such as that of the Dutch green left in 2017 and the exceptional success of newcomers such as Podemos and SYRIZA, should be noted in particular. But the radical left and green left remain confined to just a few countries, and in most of those they are no more than a marginal political presence.

Social democrats have had a tougher time. Several have suffered serious electoral defeats, notably in Greece, Spain, Ireland, Netherlands, Germany and France. They have held on to power in several countries, though this has been something of a poisoned chalice. When they attain governmental office, it is usually as a junior partner in a right-led coalition, meaning that they end up implementing austerity policies – and thus further alienating core supporters.

For the time being, it appears that most parties on the radical left, in line with parties from the more centre left green and social democratic parties, accept the need to work for a common left future vision of a reformed EMU and EU integration processes. Similarly, Busch et al. (2016: 82) argue not only that the left has a major role to play in reforming an EU and a Eurozone that has been marred by a decade of crisis, but go even further by arguing that this is inevitable, as 'the EU will only survive, if it adopts the best discourse for the future that allows progressive actors to push for a different model that is Europe based on solidarity' (Busch et al., 2016: 82).

The crisis is far from over. Economic growth is one thing, but the social damage from years of austerity is much more long lasting. And the political fallout is also still developing. The rise of populism and identity politics and the resurgence of the far right represent an ongoing challenge. As we write in 2019, the crisis is in the daily headlines less than before. But it is very far from being resolved or from having played itself out. The analysis in this book suggests that for the left, the transformations triggered by the crisis are only just starting to take effect.

Indeed, the 2019 European election results indicate the continuing problems for the left across Europe. There were some successes. It was a good election for the Greens, benefitting from the 'climate strikes' by school students that had started in 2018. Their vote increased by over 3% and they gained 22 seats to become the fourth largest group in the Parliament. In addition, the PSOE in Spain and the PvdA in the Netherlands both had successful elections. But the left in general saw its vote share continue to decline. The social democratic vote was down by 4.3%, and the group lost 32 seats, while GUE/NGL's vote was down by 1.9% with a loss of 14 seats (European Parliament, 2019).

There is a steadily emerging conversation about reform of the EU, encompassing both a rebalancing of the political architecture and a refocusing of the policy agenda. On the political aspect, the main aim is to enhance the democratic legitimacy of the EU; on the policy side, the ideas focus strongly on a rejection of austerity and neoliberalism, and on promoting reform of the EMU and strengthening the social dimension of the EU. However, one significant problem remains. These reform discussions remain strongly at the elite level. In terms of appealing to voters and electorates, the left is still struggling to find a way of selling a vision of another Europe. The left might be starting to generate new ideas, but it is not yet turning that into the hard currency of votes.

Notes

1 The term *alter-mondialiste* emerged in France as a positive alternative to the label 'anti-globalisation', which was often inaccurately applied to critics of globalisation. The contention was that these critics are not against greater global connections, they want stronger but better connections, in the sense of

being more just, more fair and more equal. Thus, *alter-mondialisme* implies changing the direction of globalisation rather than being against it (see Massiah & Massiah, 2010).

Bibilography

Anderson, P. (1994) 'Introduction', in P. Anderson & P. Camiller (eds) *Mapping the West European left*, London & New York: Verso, 1–22.

Attac – C. Mayrhuber (2017) 'Sozialpolitik', in *Entzauberte Union: Warum die EU nicht zu retten und ein Austritt keine Lösug ist*, Vienna: Mandelbaum Kritik und Utopie, 80–85.

Bailey, D. J., De Waele, J.-M, Escalona, F. & Vieira, M. (eds) (2014) *European Social Democracy During the Global Economic Crisis*, Manchester: Manchester University Press.

Bickerton, C. (2018) 'The European trap', *The New Statesman*, 27 April–3 May, 35–38.

Bomberg, E. (1998) *Green parties and politics in the European Union*, London & New York: Routledge.

Bourne, A. & Chatzopoulou, S. (2017) 'Euroscepticism and the crisis: "critical Europeanism" and anti-austerity protests', in B. Leruth, N. Startin & S. Usherwood (eds) *The Routledge handbook of Euroscepticism*, Abingdon: Routledge, 306–316.

Busch, K., Troost, A., Schwan, G., Bsirske, F., Bischoff, J. Schrooten, M. & Wolf, H. (2016) *Europa geht auch solidarisch: Streitschrift für eine andere Europäische Union*, Hamburg: VSA Verlag.

Callaghan, J., Fishman, N., Jackson, B. & McIvor, M. (eds) (2009) *In search of social democracy: responses to crisis and modernisation*, Manchester: Manchester University Press.

Clancy, E. (2017) *The future of the Eurozone*, an economic discussion document, commissioned by Matt Carthy MEP, Brussels: European United Left/Nordic Green Left (GUE/NGL). www.mattcarthy.ie/wp-content/uploads/The-future-of-the-Eurozone.pdf (accessed 1 March 2019).

Dainotto, Roberto M. (2007) *Europe (in theory)*, Durham, NC: Duke University Press.

DiEM25 (n.d.) 'What is DiEM25?'. https://diem25.org/what-is-diem25/ (accessed 12 July 2018).

Dinan, D., Nugent, N. & Paterson, W. E. (2017) *The European Union in crisis*, Basingstoke: Palgrave Macmillan.

Ehl, M. (2015) 'Not exactly friends of Greece', *Transitions Online*, 30 June. www.tol.org/client/article/24856-not-exactly-friends-of-greece.html?utm_source=TOL+mailing+list&utm_campaign=7dc428533a-TOL_newsletter_21_11_2014&utm_medium=email&utm_term=0_35d0a711b5-7dc428533a-298049902 (accessed 1 July 2015).

European Parliament (2019) European election results. Online at www.europarl.europa.eu/news/en/press-room/elections-press-kit/8/european-elections-results (accessed 13 June 2019).

Fazi, T. (2014) *The Battle for Europe: how an elite hijacked a continent and how we can take it back*, London: Pluto Press.

FCIC (2011) *The financial crisis inquiry report*, Washington: Financial Crisis Inquiry Commission.

Featherstone, K. (1988) *Socialist parties and European integration: a comparative history*, Manchester: Manchester University Press.

Fischer, J. (2018) *Der Abstieg des Westens: Europa in der neuen Weltordnung des 21*, Jahrhunderts, Cologne: Kiepenheuer & Witsch.

Gamble, A. (2009) *The spectre at the feast: capitalist crisis and the politics of recession*. Basingstoke: Red Globe Press.

Greens-EFA (2016) *Putting the Economic and Monetary Union on a sustainable footing: the Greens-EFA roadmap*. www.greens-efa.eu/files/doc/docs/f97c4d-f8e1f3d676e554c52f3ad6aeaf.pdf (accessed 17 March 2019).

Guinan, J. & Hanna, T. M. (2017) 'Lexit: the EU is a neoliberal project, so let's do something different when we leave it', *New Statesman*, 20 July. www.newstatesman.com/politics/brexit/2017/07/lexit-eu-neoliberal-project-so-lets-do-something-different-when-we-leave-it (accessed 1 May 2018).

Hain, P. (2016) 'Foreword: rediscovering confidence and soul', in K. Hickson (ed.) *Rebuilding social democracy: core principles for the centre left*, Bristol: Policy Press, v–xxi.

Hickson, K. (2016) *Rebuilding social democracy: core principles for the centre left*, Bristol: Policy Press.

Hix, S. & Lord, C. (1997) *Political parties in the European Union*, Basingstoke: Palgrave Macmillan.

Hoare, G. & Sperber, N. (2016) *An introduction to Antonio Gramsci: his life, work and legacy*, London: Bloomsbury.

Holmes, M. & Lightfoot, S. (2016) 'To EU or not to EU? The transnational radical left and the crisis', in L. March & D. Keith (eds) *Europe's radical left: from marginality to the mainstream?* London: Rowman & Littlefield, 333–351.

Holmes, M. & Roder, K. (eds) (2012) *The left and the European Constitution: from Laeken to Lisbon*. Manchester: Manchester University Press.

Keating, M. & McCrone, D. (2015) *The crisis of social democracy in Europe*, Edinburgh: Edinburgh University Press.

Ladrech, R. (2002) 'Europeanization and political parties: towards a framework for analysis', *Party Politics*, 8 (4): 389–403.

Ladrech, R. & Marlière, P. (eds) (1999) *Social democratic parties in the European Union: history, organization, policies*, Basingstoke: Palgrave Macmillan.

Leruth, B., Startin, N. & Usherwood, S. (eds) (2017) *The Routledge handbook of Euroscepticism*. Abingdon: Routledge.

Lightfoot, S. (2005) *Europeanizing social democracy? The rise of the Party of European Socialists*, London: Routledge.

Mair, P. (2000) 'The limited impact of Europe on national party systems', *West European Politics*, 23 (4): 27–51.

March, L. (2012) *Radical left parties in Europe*, London & New York: Routledge.

Massiah, G. & Massiah, E. (2010) *Une stratégie altermondialiste*, Paris: La Découverte.

Mitchell, W. & Fazi, T. (2017) *Reclaiming the state: a progressive vision of sovereignty for a post-neoliberal world*, London: Pluto Press.

Nehmitz, P. (2017) 'Elf Thesen zur Erneuerung der deutschen und europaeischen Sozialdemokratie', *Neue Gesellschaft / Frankfurter Hefte*, 12: 48–52.

Newman, M. (1983) *Socialism and European unity: the dilemma of the left in Britain and France*, London: Junction Books.

OuestFrance (2017) 'Sorbonne speech of Emmanuel Macron', full text, English version. http://international.blogs.ouest-france.fr/archive/2017/09/29/macron-sorbonne-verbatim-europe-18583.html (accessed 20 June 2018).

Piketty, T. (2014) *Capital in the twenty-first century*, Cambridge: Harvard University Press.

Plan B in Europe (2015) *A Plan B in Europe*. www.euro-planb.eu/?page_id=96&lang=en (accessed 17 March 2019).

Poguntke, T., Aylott, N., Carter, E., Ladrech, R. & Lowther, K. R. (eds) (2007) *The Europeanization of national political parties: power and organizational adaptation*, London: Routledge.

Sassoon, D. (ed.) (1997) *Looking left: European socialism after the Cold War*, London: IB Tauris.

Socialists & Democrats (2015) *Completing and rebalancing economic and monetary union: a democratic call*. www.socialistsanddemocrats.eu/position-papers/completing-and-rebalancing-economic-and-monetary-union-democratic-call (accessed 17 March 2019).

Stiglitz, J. (2012) *The price of inequality: how today's divided society endangers our future*, New York: W. W. Norton.

Taggart, P. (1998) 'A touchstone of dissent: Euroscepticism in contemporary Western European party systems', *European Journal of Political Research*, 33 (3): 363–388.

Unger, R. M. (2005) *What should the left propose?* London & New York: Verso.

US Senate (2011) *Wall Street and the financial crisis: anatomy of a financial collapse*, Washington: Senate Permanent Sub-Committee on Investigations.

Varoufakis, Y., Holland, S. & Galbraith, J. K. (2013) *A modest proposal for resolving the Eurozone crisis, Version 4.0*, July. https://varoufakis.files.wordpress.com/2013/07/a-modest-proposal-for-resolving-the-eurozone-crisis-version-4-0-final1.pdf (accessed 1 March 2019).

Wilkinson, R. & Pickett, K. (2009) *The spirit level: why equality is better for everyone*, London: Penguin.

Zimmer, G. (2018) 'Keine gemeinsame Vision von Europa', *Neues Deutschland*, 6 February, 3.

Index

CPSIA information can be obtained
at www.ICGtesting.com
Printed in the USA
LVHW080854190422
716614LV00004B/26